BROKEN
ALLIANCES

By the same authors

Shift: Inside Nissan's Historic Revival, Crown Business, 2004
(first published as *Citoyen du Monde,* Grasset, 2003)

BROKEN ALLIANCES

INSIDE THE RISE AND FALL OF A GLOBAL AUTOMOTIVE EMPIRE

CARLOS GHOSN AND PHILIPPE RIÈS

Translated from the French by Peter Starr

Tanooki
Press

A TANOOKI PRESS BOOK

Copyediting by Kris Ellingboe-Olson
Indexing by Linda Presto
Printed by Maple Press
Typeset using Caslon Pro by Hewer Text U.K. Ltd., Edinburgh

Library of Congress Cataloging-in-Publication Data
is on file with the Library of Congress.

ISBN: 978-1-954306-00-4

PRINTED IN THE UNITED STATES OF AMERICA

This book was originally published in France as *Le temps de la vérité* by Carlos Ghosn and Philippe Riès in 2020 by Bernard Grasset. © Éditions Grasset & Fasquelle, 2020.

First U.S. edition: © September 2021. Translated from the French by Peter Starr. All trademarks are the property of their respective companies.

Contents

To Adélia, whose illness took away
her role as primary reader half-way through,
and who left this world a poorer place without her.

Acknowledgments

It was in Tokyo in July 2019, that we decided to team up again—fifteen years after the publication of *Shift: Inside Nissan's Historic Revival* in 2004 (first published in France as *Citoyen du Monde* in 2003)—to oppose a global campaign of defamation that was being orchestrated at the time. Interviews took place in October, in the offices of lawyers or at the house in Azabu which was under strict and constant surveillance with visitors being recorded. The list of women and men who decided to help us is short. They appear in the following pages, sometimes under the cover of anonymity given the climate of intimidation created by those making the accusations. We would like to express our warmest thanks.

This book does not end the debate or the pursuit for the truth which will continue, notably here: www.carlosghosn.info

Introduction

"I have striven not to laugh at human actions not to weep at them nor to hate them but to understand them."
Baruch Spinoza, *Political Treatise*

To understand the "Carlos Ghosn affair" is to comprehend two major events in the history of the twentieth century. The first is the Moscow show trials that Joseph Stalin used to physically eliminate the Bolshevik old guard—the last of Lenin's companions. Carried out between 1936 and 1938, the trials strengthened his hold over the socialist motherland. The criminal undertaking culminated in Mexico City on August 20, 1940, when Leon Trotsky was assassinated with an icepick by Ramón Mercader, an agent of the Soviet People's Commissariat for Internal Affairs, known by its Russian abbreviation NKVD. As I wrote in the *Financial Times* in January 2019, the procedures and proceedings used by the bureaucrats of the Tokyo Public Prosecutors' Office against the head of the Renault-Nissan-Mitsubishi Alliance recall the methods of Andrey Vychinsky, the chief operator of the Stalinist judicial machine that crushed its opponents.

At the heart of the system was the confession, whose acquisition alone was enough to make credible accusations that veterans of the October revolution were spying for American or German imperialists. The accused was physically and psychologically coerced, indefinitely placed in solitary confinement and relentlessly interrogated without defenders. And if he had the impudence not to confess, his family could be targeted. The merciless purge of all elements considered too close to the accused was an indispensable complement. And, to convince a domestic and international audience, a vast campaign of character assassination could be carried out, fed by an endless series of leaks to a compliant and complacent media. All these traits and several more can be found in the "Carlos Ghosn affair."

To be sure, Carlos Ghosn was never threatened with summary execution, a bullet to the head in a Stalinist gulag on a glacial dawn. Quite simply, his existence would be extinguished in a Japanese prison, his reputation tarnished, his family life shattered and his marriage reduced to exchanges of letters. And at the end of an interminable trial, which probably would have lasted five years, he faced being sentenced for several years in a country whose conviction rate of 99.4 percent would have made Josef Stalin green with envy.

The other historical event is Pearl Harbor. On December 7, 1941, a carefully chosen Sunday, the naval forces of the Empire of Japan launched a surprise attack on the largest U.S. naval base in the Pacific with no declaration of war. Prepared in great secrecy for almost a year and approved by Emperor Hirohito on December 1, the bombing of Pearl Harbor came amid growing tensions between the two sides of the Pacific, although diplomatic relations had not been severed. The initial military success of the attack started a march towards the abyss for Japan and her people, concluding with an unconditional surrender on August 15, 1945, and a prolonged occupation.

Here, we could compare Nissan employees with Americans of Japanese ancestry in Hawaii after the attack on Pearl Harbor. These children of Japanese immigrants grew up in America, and most of them spoke only English. Despite being U.S. nationals, many were placed in concentration camps immediately after the attack. The Japanese 442 Battalion was formed with volunteers from the camps to fight on European fronts. It was later called the Purple Heart Battalion, because of the highest rates of deaths and injuries in U.S. military history. They fought not only on the front lines, but also against prejudice against Japanese immigrants in their home country. After the war, they received scholarships and took Hawaii's political and business world by storm. Among them was George Ariyoshi, the first state governor of Japanese ancestry, and Senator Daniel Inouye. Many others were elected, leading the political and cultural changes that became known as the Democratic Revolution in Hawaii. President Barack Obama grew up in that environment. But it is not only in wartime that people suffer from leadership failures. Just like more than ninety-nine percent of the accused end up with guilty verdicts in Japanese courts, more than ninety-nine percent of Nissan employees were victims of incompetent management and political collusion, and more than ninety-nine percent of Nissan employees understood and welcomed "Ghosn-style management." Nissan's revival made them proud and safe, and led a mismanaged company to an impressive recovery. Carlos Ghosn was the one who understood and released the power of Nissan, and respected its culture.

When he was arrested by agents of the Tokyo Public Prosecutors' Office at 4:30 p.m. on November 19, 2018, Carlos Ghosn was chairman of the Renault-Nissan-Mitsubishi Alliance. The tie-up between two Japanese and one French automaker was considered a rare if not exceptional venture between entities separated by geography, culture and social environments. By 2017, the Alliance was the world's largest automaker in terms of volume, surpassing both Volkswagen and Toyota.

The venture started almost 20 years earlier in March 1999, when Renault arrived to help Nissan, the country's second-biggest carmaker, which was then on the verge of bankruptcy. Over those two decades, there was no shortage of tensions. But never a crisis.

Prepared by an internal inquiry and conducted in great secrecy by Nissan executives since the spring of 2018, the arrest of Carlos Ghosn amounted to an act of war. With no declaration.

At no stage during the months of preparation did the small clique of plotters from the Nissan Old Guard find it necessary to inform Renault, the company's main shareholder with 43.4 percent of the capital. Curiously, this trampling on shareholder rights—while not uncommon in Japan—did not come to the attention of the business community or regulators in Japan or France.

Who decided to start this war? How was it prepared? Who authorized it? How was it carried out and with what degree of success? That's what this book establishes, taking into account the extent of our current knowledge, the force of reason and the firmness of convictions. The impact of Carlos Ghosn's removal on the Alliance can be seen in the numbers: the shares of all three companies have plummeted, whereas the combined value of the international auto sector recorded double-digit growth in 2019. Nissan and

Renault have seen massive departures of senior executives, purged for their allegiance to their former boss or discouraged by the deleterious atmosphere created by the affair. Jobs have been cut, factories closed, markets deserted and investments shelved.

The damage to Japan's image, sullied by the discovery of a totalitarian judicial system in a country reputed to be democratic, is not yet clear. After the Great Escape of Carlos Ghosn from Japan at the end of 2019, the trial of the builder of the Alliance has become the global trial of a judicial machine based on what Japanese lawyers and human rights defenders say is based on hostage justice. An industrial and political Pearl Harbor, in effect.

What did the United Nations Human Rights Council think about Carlos Ghosn's treatment by the Japanese justice system? During a five-day meeting in Geneva in August 2020, the council's Working Group on Arbitrary Detention adopted a legal opinion on the case. Released in November—almost eleven months after his escape to Lebanon—the 17-page document found that Carlos Ghosn's detention from November 19, 2018 to March 5, 2019 and from April 4 to 25, was indeed "arbitrary" as it contravened articles 9, 10 and 11 (1) of the Universal Declaration of Human Rights and articles 9, 10 (1) and 14 of the International Covenant on Civil and Political Rights.

"The Working Group requests the Government of Japan to take the steps necessary to remedy the situation of Mr. Ghosn without delay and to bring it into conformity with the relevant international norms, including those set out in the Universal Declaration of Human Rights and the International Covenant on Civil and Political Rights," the document said. "Taking into account all the circumstances of the case, the appropriate remedy would be to accord Mr. Ghosn an enforceable right to compensation and other reparations, in accordance with international law." The Working Group also urged the Japanese government to "ensure a full and independent investigation of the circumstances surrounding the arbitrary detention of Mr. Ghosn, and to take appropriate measures against those responsible for the violation of his rights."

The decapitation of the Renault-Nissan-Mitsubishi Alliance came at a critical time for the global automobile sector. Never had the 130-year-old industry faced so many challenges as the internal combustion engine made way for electric engines and passengers prepared for driverless vehicles. If personal cars are not driven out of the megalopolises and other large cities where half of humanity now lives, there is little doubt that the relationship between humans and motor vehicles will be profoundly changed. Navigating through the turbulent waters of this transition requires not only a firm hand at the helm on a well-marked course, but also the mobilization of vast human and financial resources.

Industry and Politics

The automobile industry is notably political—by its economic weight, its social dimension, its links between cities and country-side, and its massive presence in international trade. Even if the automakers themselves are usually privately owned companies, they are never far from the shadow of public authorities. Returning to Paris from Frankfurt, where he spent eight years as president of the European Central Bank, Jean-Claude Trichet noted that no political decision in Germany was ever taken without getting the opinion of the country's exporters, especially automakers. In the few countries with a significant auto industry, no government can ignore a sector that can amount to ten percent of gross domestic product if upstream and downstream activities are taken into account.

The freedom of movement has come at a heavy price for those who drive vehicles or who are in their path at the wrong place at the wrong time. And now we know the impact of transport in general, and driving in particular, on global warming.

The Renault-Nissan Alliance was a political paradox from the start. The French were hostile to open borders, reducing tariffs and the free movements of goods, services, capital and labor. The Japanese distrusted the system.

Most French people rejected "neo-liberal" globalization, according to public opinion polls and research (Pew Research Center, YouGov and the Organisation of Economic Cooperation and Development). This partly resulted from a persistent Marxist tradition, especially in the public education system, and a resulting lack of economic culture. But it also reflected psychology as seen in the typical pessimism of the French, and record consumption of anti-anxiety medications. There was also a political aspect since globalization is seen as undermining a strong protective central state that has overseen French destiny for centuries.

In Japan, globalization is not an object of hatred but distrust. Although Japan benefited more than any economy from opening up to international trade for more than 70 years, most Japanese seem to view the outside world with ambivalence. Those who travel abroad are a small minority and the recent opening of the country to mass tourism, especially from China, has provoked negative reactions. Knowledge of foreign languages is not progressing among young people, and many do not possess a passport. "The dream of Japan is that the rest of the world leaves us alone," said Toyoo Gyoten, from the small "internationalist" faction at the Ministry of Finance in the 1980s.

That's why it was all the more remarkable that the Japanese accepted with such equanimity that one of their industrial flagships should come under foreign control in 1999. It was not difficult to imagine the reaction of the French majority to Renault coming under the control of Nissan.

Nissan and Renault were not like other companies. For instance, Toyota was an empire built by a commercial family from Nagoya. Honda was a motorcycle manufacturer that entered the car industry only after clashing with the powerful Ministry of International Trade and Industry. Nissan, on the other hand, took off under government leadership and was the tool of the industrial strategy in Japanese-occupied Manchuria, whose young administrators included Nobosuke Kishi, the grandfather of Shinzo Abe, prime minister of Japan from December 2012 to September 2020.

Renault was nationalized after World War II and became a symbol of France's state-owned economic and social culture for half a century. Its headquarters in Billancourt near Paris were the "workers' fortress" and "social laboratory" under a joint management arrangement with the CGT, the trade union affiliated with the French Communist Party.

The French government privatized Renault in stages from 1995, but never completely cut the umbilical cord, retaining 15.01 percent of the shares and 22 percent of voting rights through the French Government Shareholding Agency, part of the Ministry of

Economy and Finance. But the government considered itself differ-ent—and acted differently—from other main shareholders. The crisis triggered by the arrest of Carlos Ghosn brought to light this behavior which had long been the source of friction within the Alliance.

In Japan, government influence on industrial groups does not have to hide behind the screen of shares. Certainly, the era of guided economic growth inspired by the Soviet model that accompanied post-war booms in Japan and France was long over. But as much as laws and regulations, Japan was governed by an "iron triangle," an informal and powerful alliance of politicians from the ruling Liberal Democratic Party, business leaders and bureaucrats. The alliance was drawn from the weight of history and conventions—notably the networks where University of Tokyo graduates were at the fore-front—the homogeneity of elites and a political continuity that is unique among democracies. The system may not have been as ines-capable as it was in the second half of the twentieth century, but it had many remnants.

Need for an Outsider

In ancient Greece, a metic was a foreign resident of Athens—most often from another Greek city—who did not enjoy the benefits of being a citizen of the city state. Metics largely contributed to the glory of Athens, starting with Aristotle. The term did not have the xenophobic or racist connotations it acquired in France in the twen-tieth century, which seems to have been reincarnated in the "devel-oped" world in the early twenty-first century.

When an organization gradually lets itself be overtaken by the sclerosis of habits, vested interests and outdated working practices, recourse to the observations and actions of outsiders can sometimes be the only way to avoid a fatal outcome, opening the windows and doors to let the air in, imposing a different vision and finding a new path.

At the end of the 1990s, Nissan Motor Company Ltd. was close to bankruptcy. There was no internal solution. Nor was there a "Japanese" solution in a country where the intensity of corporate culture—and the complex interlocking shareholdings between families of companies—made any rapprochement between large industrial companies about as imaginable as peace between Athens and Sparta. That's why the Japanese government's crazy idea of merging Nissan with Honda in 2020 was rejected outright by both companies.

Carlos Ghosn, born in the Brazilian city of Porto Velho to parents of Lebanese origin, was educated in French-speaking religious schools in Beirut and the grand public schools in Paris. He was the perfect outsider. This was evident in Japan where a *gaijin*— literally, outsider—was propelled to the top of one of the country's industrial jewels. But it was no less true in France, where Carlos Ghosn graduated from the Paris School of Mines but, being a foreigner, was excluded from the prestigious Corps des Mines along with the École Nationale d'Administration, which formed part of the caste system that dominated the boards of recently privatized national companies in the late twentieth century. It was this nomenklatura which greeted Carlos Ghosn's arrest with a resounding silence, not even questioning the way he was treated by the Japanese judicial system. He was the metic who had been hit by a scandal.

The odyssey that Carlos Ghosn made from the Upper Amazon Basin to Renault to the bright lights of Ginza is recounted in our book *Shift: Inside Nissan's Historic Revival* in 2004 (first published in France as *Citoyen du Monde* in 2003). It's worth referring to if one wants to know who the real Carlos Ghosn is, rather than the caricature rehashed by certain French and Japanese media.

In the years of Ghosn's training, as well as professional and personal development, two things stand out. One was Michelin, the French tiremaker whose humanoid mascot and restaurant guides were known the world over. It was under the leadership of François Michelin, the mentor of Carlos Ghosn and so many other young French engineers fresh out of college, that the manufacturer based in Clermont-Ferrand embraced globalization to become a multinational company; at one stage the world's biggest tiremaker before it ceded the title to Japanese rival Bridgestone.

Michelin, especially the Michelin of "Monsieur François," was not a typical French company. It was tightly controled by a French family which was as religious as it was paternalistic to its workers from cradle-to-grave. Pious, rural and diligent, its foreign workers often came from Portugal, which made Clermont-Ferrand a great Lusitanian town. The company worshipped the customer. And it was suspicious of the French government, always threatening from the distant capital in Paris.

While turning around the French tiremaker's ailing operations in Brazil and overseeing a merger with American rival Uniroyal-Goodrich, Carlos Ghosn experimented with techniques at Michelin that he would later apply to the recovery of Renault, the rebirth of Nissan and the building of the Alliance.

The U.S. period was important for Carlos Ghosn. He was based in Greenville in the Bible Belt of South Carolina, where the last three of his four children were born. It was here that he flourished in both the professional and family spheres. America's attractiveness would never fade for him. But as number two at Michelin, responsible for 40 percent of the company's turnover, he knew that he would never be number one. That role was destined for Édouard, the youngest son of François Michelin, who would be sent to train in the United States under Carlos Ghosn.

Renault-Nissan Alliance

Like many human enterprises, the Alliance was a product of chance and necessity. The first accident was the failure in 1993 of a merger between Renault and Swedish automaker Volvo, largely caused by the French government's clumsiness as a shareholder. So, by necessity, Renault's chairman Louis Schweitzer was forced to find another partner for the company which was too small, too French, too unprofitable and too focused on Europe.

Schweitzer's opportunity was the 1998 widely celebrated "merger of equals" between Daimler and Chrysler, which forced the German manufacturer of Mercedes to abandon a simultaneous takeover of Nissan, a move that was favored by the Japanese automaker's management. They left the stage to Renault alone, with Carlos Ghosn as Louis Schweitzer's trump card.

The two men had different visions of the Alliance. For Schweitzer—a former senior civil servant known internally at Renault as E.T. or Loulou—it was a Franco-Japanese venture that could not be indifferent to the relations between the two countries and the two peoples, their history and culture. It was a binational company with remnants of trade ties from the past. In post-war Tokyo and Osaka, Renault's 4CV model briefly dominated taxi fleets in a Japanese automobile market not yet closed to foreigners.

For Carlos Ghosn, the Alliance was the basis for building a global company brick-by-brick with more than 100 plants on five continents, employing people from dozens of nationalities. He headed the "commando" team of thirty Frenchmen arriving in Tokyo in April 1999, but he would recruit senior executives from the four corners of the earth.

The very nature of the two companies did not make things easier. At Nissan, Japanese social norms of lifetime employment and promotion by seniority prevailed. In France, it was no longer internal problems at Renault, but a perception by the country—and a good part of its elites—of globalization and its impact on the business climate. This would be seen in 2010, when Carlos Ghosn chose Morocco as the site of a second plant for Dacia, the ground-breaking low-cost brand Renault built on the remains of a large industrial site in communist Romania. The decision was bitterly criticized in political circles in Paris.

On the capital structure of the Alliance, there was no less divergence between the two men. In 2018, Louis Schweitzer confirmed his long-held belief that the French government's withdrawal from Renault as a shareholder would inevitably lead to Nissan taking control. But as early as 2003, before he replaced Schweitzer as Renault chief executive, Carlos Ghosn was thinking of a new capital structure—to ensure the durability of the Alliance, reduce the massive discounts at which Renault and Nissan shares were traded and open itself to a new partner—from North America, for example. Mainly due to obstruction from the French government, this issue would be left pending and lead to the crisis of November 2018.

Despite the obstacles and difficulties, the Alliance got as close as possible to being the world's first truly global automotive corporation in 2017 when it became the world's largest auto producer with more than ten million units sold. In his memoirs published in 1984, the former Ford president Lee Iacocca recounted how he was obsessed with such an idea in 1978 after being brutally fired by Henry Ford II.

"My dream was to build a consortium of manufacturers in Europe, Japan and the United States. Together, we would build a firm capable of challenging the dominant position of General Motors," Iacocca wrote. Volkswagen was a possible partner in Europe, and eventually Fiat or Renault. In Japan, Mitsubishi, but why not Nissan or Honda? In America, the only partner could be Chrysler. General Motors was too big and Ford was out of the question. Iacocca was soon called in to take up the challenge of rescuing Chrysler, on which he would build his legend. His dream would fade, though, until Carlos Ghosn came along. The world had meanwhile entered a new era of globalization.

Emerging with the Emerging Markets

In the second globalization (after the first one between the end of the 19th century and 1914), the turning point came in 1989. On one side, the fall of the Berlin Wall and the collapse of the Soviet empire. On the other, the decision by China's communist leaders to continue with economic reforms after the bloodbath on Tiananmen Square on June 4. A few years later, Shanghai Mayor Zhu Rongji would succeed Li Peng, the "Butcher of Tiananmen," as prime minister and become the most important economic reformer since Deng Xiaoping. It was Zhu who urged Carlos Ghosn to form a joint venture between Nissan and Dongfeng, opening the Alliance to what would become the world's largest automobile market ahead of the United States and the European Union.

In terms of growth, Russia was not China but it was one of the world's leading emerging economies. Despite political tribulations, its economy had not crumbled under the weight of Western economic sanctions and Russia had a respectable market with a population of 150 million people. By taking control of top automaker AvtoVAZ, Renault was taking a risk and buying into the global history of automobiles. Reviving the giant plant in Togliatti was also an industrial and social challenge commensurate with its ambitions.

Togliatti, named after a former general secretary of the Communist Party of Italy, was seen as the "Detroit on the Volga" in the same way as Thailand was considered the "Detroit of Southeast

Asia." By taking control of its distributor Siam Motors in 2004, Nissan established a manufacturing beachhead in Thailand that was considerably reinforced when the Alliance was joined by Mitsubishi, which was better represented in this part of the world.

Under Carlos Ghosn, the international expansion of the Alliance exposed the three partners to enormous growth opportunities. In 2018, Dongfeng and Siam Motors produced 2.4 million vehicles out of Nissan's overall production of 5.6 million units and almost all its growth in sales over the previous decade.

Carlos Ghosn School of Management

Carlos Tavares, a former senior executive with Renault and Nissan, turned French automaker PSA Peugeot-Citroën around in record time. He also acquired and brought Opel and Vauxhall, the European brands of General Motors that had been losing money for twenty years, back into the black. Didier Leroy, who was quickly spotted by Carlos Ghosn after his arrival at Renault, is now number two at Toyota, alongside Akio Toyoda, heir to the company's founding dynasty. José Muñoz, purged by the Nissan Old Guard after the judicial coup d'etat of November 19, 2018, is number two at Hyundai, the largest automaker in South Korea, and also head of its North American operations. Finally, Thierry Bolloré, who was purged from Renault, now heads British automaker Jaguar Land Rover, part of the Indian conglomerate Tata.

These are four of the dozens of executives who worked under Carlos Ghosn. The guiding management principles, applied to the recovery and building of highly complex industrial organizations, are detailed in *Shift* and dozens of management books and studies published in Japan and abroad, reflecting a desire to learn about an industrial venture that has no equivalent in the first two decades of the twenty-first century.

Carlos Ghosn may have been reduced to media labels such as "Cost Killer" and "Davos Man," but his management principles stood the test of time with their pragmatism, transversal cooperation and systematic benchmarking of performance. Carlos Ghosn is not a management theorist, but a practitioner of prescriptions tested by reality throughout an exceptional career that lasted until November 19, 2018.

Social Benefits of the Alliance

Notwithstanding the melodramatic obsession with Carlos Ghosn's salary among journalists, politicians and self-proclaimed champions of small shareholders, was it possible to make a social assessment of the Alliance? From the Nissan Revival Plan of 1999, lazy journalists reported on factory closures and job cuts even though there were no layoffs. Through globalization, the auto industry had indeed gotten rid of jobs in some old industrial areas. This was primarily from productivity gains, the time needed to make a car having been divided by four, over thirty years. But it was also a result of production sites moving closer to markets. According to Carlos Ghosn, globalization and localization went hand in hand. In fact, the industry created hundreds of thousands of jobs in emerging economies, the transitional economies of Eastern Europe and developing economies as well. These jobs generally required greater skills and were better paid.

Advanced economies also benefited. The largest automobile plant in North America is Nissan's factory in Smyrna, Tennessee, with more than 8,000 workers. Within the Alliance, the two largest facilities are the research centers in Atsugi (Nissan) and Guyancourt (Renault), where thousands of engineers are employed.

As for Carlos Ghosn's compensation, the issue is not at all taboo if only because it was put forward by the architects of the November 19 coup. But it warrants serious consideration without the "indignation" draped over the heads of contemporary self-righteous people.

First of all, public policies were behind the uncontrolled inflation of a whole series of asset classes, including salaries for top executives as countries borrowed money to finance deficits after the ruptures of the 1970s. Today, the world's leading central banks are flooding the markets with liquidity, fueling the deepening of inequalities as money chases money. The remuneration of corporate bosses was almost stable between the 1940s and 1970s, but soared in the last two decades of the twentieth century in correlation with ballooning valuations of listed companies.

Secondly, an international market exists for a very small number of top managers. This was the case for Carlos Ghosn, who the Obama administration tried to hire in 2009 as General Motors was being rescued from bankruptcy. If the head of the Alliance had considered only his financial interests, he would have accepted the offer. He would today be a free man and not targeted by a political-judicial machine trying to destroy his career, life, family and reputation.

Was he overpaid to run three companies employing 450,000 people across the world? Everyone has the right to think so. But in twenty years at the helm of Nissan, Renault and the Alliance itself, Carlos Ghosn brought considerable dividends and fiscal receipts to the French government as the main Renault shareholder compared with the vast losses of so many state-owned companies.

Can the Alliance Outlive its Creator?

A bit like the European Union, the Renault-Nissan-Mitsubishi Alliance was a daily miracle—whatever the strength and rationality of the grouping, abandoning sovereignty is never easy. Also, with progress in implementing the Alliance, the areas involved became more sensitive and the compromises more delicate, often involving inevitable misunderstandings. It was a long way to go from joint purchases from suppliers, shared platforms and initial exchanges of technology and knowhow, to creating a genuine convergence in engineering.

Nissan is a very "technocentric" company dominated by engineers, as can be seen at the Nissan Engine Museum in Yokohama. Other operations like purchasing, marketing, finance and customer relations are subordinate to engineering, which partly explains the dramatic situation the company faced in March 1999.

Japanese teams resented what were seen as unequal technological exchanges with Renault, which took a less fundamentalist approach to automotive manufacturing with greater focus on the customer. How this, and no doubt other sensitive issues, could not be dissipated by twenty years of close cooperation illustrates the challenge.

In the most favorable circumstances, Carlos Ghosn's succession would have been perilous. It was made impossible by the plotters behind November 19, 2018, and their instigators and political accomplices in Tokyo and Paris. The crisis triggered massive losses in share prices, distrust between management teams, the return of political influence on Renault, and the manifest absence of a strategic vision shared at headquarters in Billancourt and Yokohama—as witnessed by aborted negotiations with Fiat-Chrysler Automobile which has since merged with PSA Peugeot-Citroën.

Jean-Dominique Senard, who the French government parachuted in as Renault chairman, thought the Alliance could be based on consensus. But Hiroto Saikawa, who succeeded Carlos Ghosn as chief executive, read things differently.

"From now on, each entity will decide what it wants to do and not do," Saikawa said. The so-called Japanese consensus is, in any case, a myth; the source of dreams for Western managers faced with social conflicts from the 1980s.

In reality, the history of the automobile industry, including in Japan, is a testament to the role played by larger than life personalities who show real leadership. The Alliance and other industrial empires were not built by faceless bean-counters or mundane diplomats.

Will the Auto Industry Survive Beyond 2050?

Throughout the history of the automotive industry, dozens of legendary car brands have disappeared, although some like Datsun and Alpine have been reborn under the Alliance. What's striking in the global auto industry is the resilience of the incumbent manufacturers, not only within the Alliance itself with Renault (founded at the end of the nineteenth century) and Nissan (established at the beginning of the twentieth century), but also elsewhere. Companies like Ford, General Motors, Fiat, Daimler, Volkswagen and Toyota all have track records going back a century or thereabouts.

The revolution the industry now faces is electric mobility. A recent German documentary did not hesitate to evoke the "twilight of the gods," a world of disruption embodied by Tesla, whose atypical creator Elon Musk comes from Silicon Valley. Starting from a clean slate, Tesla is part of the auto industry but is valued as a high-tech company, surpassing market leader Toyota in 2020. The challenges are not limited to technology. With humanity approaching ten billion and more than half of the world's people living in mega cities, private cars could disappear in the long term.

For the established players, the years and decades ahead will require colossal investments, hence the categorical imperative for critical mass. There will also be social upheavals both upstream and downstream, with electric mobility not being a big job creator, and resistance to new entrants. At the same time, companies will have to deal with legacy costs—the financial and social weight of the past which brought Detroit to the brink.

Can these unprecedented upheavals in the industry allow newcomers to leapfrog the giants that have dominated for decades? Could the big names of today share a fate similar to Kodak, whose business was eroded by digital photography, and Nokia which missed the smartphone revolution? Do Tesla and start-ups in China hold the fate of the global auto industry in their hands?

The battle promises to be exciting. Carlos Ghosn will no longer be a player, but an informed observer. By betting on electric vehicles in 2009, he took the Alliance to the top ranks of global production. He armed the Alliance for the battle. And now?

Philippe Riès
Castelo de Vide, June 2021

CHAPTER ONE

19 November

For Joseph R.—as he would later be described in the French press—Monday, November 19, 2018, was a special day at work, as it was every time "Monsieur Ghosn" arrived on one of his regular visits to Japan.

Joseph had been, for 17 years, the computer specialist in charge of technical support for the chairman of the Renault-Nissan-Mitsibishi Alliance. He was the only person in the Alliance to be employed by all three companies. Based at the Nissan headquarters in Yokohama, he also oversaw the Renault head office in Billancourt near Paris, as well as offices in Beirut and Amsterdam, to ensure that the devices used by the head of the Alliance worked without bugs in optimal security conditions.

Joseph arrived very early at the Nissan headquarters, where his office also served as a storage space for computers and other equipment that would be needed during the chairman's visit. That Monday morning, he received a strange email from Christina Murray.

"Hari Nada wants to see you this afternoon, at 4:30 or 5:00 at the latest," Murray had written. Joseph was surprised by the message from the American head of internal audit and compliance, as she was not part of his chain of command. Nor was Hari Nada, who ran the CEO Office, a part of the horizontal structure around the chief executive officer.

Later that morning, the computer specialist received an email from Maya, the youngest of Carlos Ghosn's three daughters. She informed him that the Internet was not working at the accommodation that Nissan had long been providing to the chairman, an apartment in a building in the Azabu district of Tokyo, known locally as the Mushroom Tower.

"I'd passed by the previous Friday," Joseph recalled, "but didn't check if the Internet for guests was working. I went back and found that the router was dead. It had to be changed. I sent an email telling Ohnuma, who's my direct superior." Since 2012, Toshiaki Ohnuma had been in charge of the Nissan secretariat, holding the rank of vice president. "The equipment was for private use so it would be billed to Carlos Ghosn," Joseph said. He had lost time replacing the router, and knew it would be difficult to return to Yokohama in time to see Hari Nada. And on the following day, Tuesday, November 20, Joseph was scheduled to spend all day at the headquarters of Mitsubishi in Tokyo with Carlos Ghosn, who had, in recent years, turned the company around as chairman of the board.

As the afternoon wore on, Joseph sent a message to Christina Murray: "I won't be able to get to the meeting at 4:30. We'll see each other Wednesday." Her reply came back immediately.

"Hari Nada absolutely must see you this evening," Murray said. Surprised by her urgency, Joseph R. replied that it should be possible, but not before 5:00. "OK. Do your best to be there on time," she wrote.

Joseph got back to his office in Yokohama at 4:30, earlier than he expected. Towards 4:45, the office door flung open and out walked a visibly disturbed old man. It was Carlos Ghosn's regular driver, with whom Joseph, who spoke fluent Japanese, had a friendly relationship. "Something fishy's going on. It's scary," he said to Joseph before leaving.

Since Joseph had a few minutes before the 5 p.m. meeting, he headed up to the twenty-first floor to retrieve some computer equipment left for him by Ghosn's driver. He assumed the Nissan chairman had already reached the company headquarters, which was just a short drive from Haneda airport where he was scheduled to arrive around 4 p.m.

"Whenever Carlos Ghosn landed in Tokyo, I would receive the iPads he used on the road from his driver. So, I decided to go up to the twenty-first floor to get the equipment which would have been left in the chairman's office," Joseph explained. "Carlos Ghosn's personal assistant, Fumiko, was shocked when she saw me enter the room that led to Ghosn's office."

"What are you doing here? Shouldn't you be seeing Hari Nada?"

she asked Joseph. He wondered how, and by what means, she could possibly know about the meeting.

"You better go and see Hari Nada," she insisted. Yes, he agreed, but the meeting was not until 5:00.

Men in Black at Nissan's Headquarters

Top executives were located on the twenty-first floor of the Nissan headquarters, including Hari Nada, who headed the CEO Office. At exactly five o'clock, Joseph headed towards Hari Nada's office where, as he approached, he witnessed an alarming scene. The area, to which access was strictly controlled, had been invaded by a cohort of men and women, many young, and all dressed in black.

"In the corridors, the presence of all these outsiders had triggered incredible turmoil," Joseph recalled. Joseph was led to the meeting room often used by Hiroto Saikawa, the chief executive officer at Nissan who Carlos Ghosn had appointed in 2016.

"Three people came in—Hari Nada, flanked by a woman who I later found out was Christina Murray, and Rui Kamei, the head of security," Joseph recalled.

They had barely entered the room when Hari Nada told Joseph to hand over his personal phone.

"When I asked, 'what's going on?' Hari Nada pretended to be surprised and said: 'Your boss has been arrested. He's done some very serious things and you have to work with the investigation. The authorities will take care of you and you'll do what they ask'." The computer specialist, Joseph, was then led to another room and a security guard employed by Nissan was posted at the door.

It was around this time that senior executives of the Japanese automaker would hear—through a different channel—the news that would soon be broadcast across the planet.

The Nissan operations committee had been meeting since the early afternoon. The committee comprised the main members of the executive committee along with Saikawa and the four key executive vice presidents who oversaw performance, planning, competitiveness and finance.

"It must have been almost 4:30 when Saikawa suspended the

meeting and asked members of the executive committee to meet him in his office," recalled José Muñoz, the executive vice president in charge of global performance. He was also in charge of Nissan North America, which enjoyed record sales in 2016 and 2017.

"The ambiance at the meeting of the operations committee was not good. It was very tense. One thing struck me. Arun Bajaj was sitting opposite me. During a break, before Saikawa called us to his office, Arun disappeared. And to this day, I've never seen him again," said Muñoz. Later it was discovered that Bajaj, the director of human resources at Nissan, had suddenly been "put on leave" by Hari Nada.

Hiroto Saikawa's Surprise

"When the executive committee members regrouped in his office," Muñoz continued, "Saikawa announced—as if it was a big surprise—that Carlos Ghosn had been arrested. 'We don't know why, we don't understand what's going on,' Saikawa said.

"When we came back from the meeting, we couldn't talk about anything else. The atmosphere was even more tense. I tried to find Arun to ask what he thought. But he'd vanished." José Muñoz now suddenly remembered that Arun Bajaj had asked him a question several months earlier: "Do you trust Hari Nada?"

A little before 4:00 that Monday afternoon, a Gulfstream G650, landed at Haneda airport, whose runways reach out into Tokyo Bay. The private jet's registration number was N155AN to resemble the automaker's name. On board was Carlos Ghosn, who chaired the boards of Nissan Motor Company Ltd. and Mitsubishi Motors Corporation in Japan and Renault S.A. in France, where he was also chief executive. He also served as head of the overall Alliance between the three companies, the world's leading automaker since 2017 in terms of the volume of cars built. The plane could fly 8,000 miles without refueling and could accommodate nineteen seated passengers, or a dozen in beds. But Carlos Ghosn was often the sole passenger. The plane was an extension of his homes and offices around the world.

"I'd been in Beirut and was coming to work for a week in Japan," Ghosn recalled. "We had a very busy schedule apart from the Nissan board meeting. I was alone in the plane. When I got out, there

remain silent," a right nevertheless guaranteed under the constitution. "A defendant's refusal to sign the minutes of an interrogation is considered proof that the defendant wants to destroy the evidence." Moreover, "the rate of release on bail of defendants who refuse to confess has been declining for thirty years, from twenty percent in 1984 to seven percent in 2014." And judges, supported by the Supreme Court, "are not required to justify the motive for accepting or denying release on bail." Ultimately, "the confession is to facilitate the work of the prosecutors and judges, who don't have to provide evidence of charges or question witnesses." It saves time. And from this, "the charge is not required to prove what it alleges." At the end of the day, Takano said, the Japanese judicial system overturns the basic principles of human rights.

In response to allegations made by Carlos Ghosn in Beirut on January 9, 2020—less than two weeks after he fled Japan—an indignant Japanese justice minister commented: "If defendant Ghosn has something to say about his penal case, he should make his arguments openly before a Japanese court and bring concrete evidence with him." But even in Japan, it is incumbent upon the prosecution to provide evidence. The minister's ill-considered remarks were later retracted.

The basic liberties which characterize a nation are exercised in Japan with nuances and distinctiveness. Norms imported from abroad are translated to fit Japanese traditions and social realities. The current Constitution of Japan was drawn up by American occupiers after World War II, at the same time as several radical changes such as land reform. But the country's elite technocrats "Japanized" the new constitution. Nothing surprising or shocking about that. As French political philosopher and historian Alexis de Tocqueville noted in *The Old Regime and the Revolution*, continuity hides behind every rupture.

Character Assassination

In Japan, freedom of the press is somewhat constrained by "reporters' clubs" known as *kisha kurabu*. The clubs bring together journalists accredited to public and private institutions. Ministries and Japanese corporate giants each have their own clubs. Nissan has its own, as does the Tokyo Public Prosecutors' Office and the Ministry of Justice. Journalists registered by their media organizations are provided workspaces by the institutions they "cover," spending days, evenings and often nights with their sources who force-feed them with information, irrespective of its importance or relevance.

This unscrupulous practice of "embedding" journalists in the institutions they cover is by no means exclusively Japanese. But in no other democracy has the system become so widespread and institutionalized. The system discriminates intrinsically. The clubs admit only "respectable" media such as mainstream newspapers and television stations. Weekly magazines, considered uncontrollable mavericks, are not members. For decades, reporters working for foreign media were excluded. For foreign media to take part in briefings at certain clubs, it took many years of lobbying by Foreign Press in Japan, an association affiliated with the Foreign Correspondents' Club of Japan that groups more than 100 media organizations from more than 20 countries.

Such institutionalized deceit was reflected in the smear campaign against Carlos Ghosn, launched by Nissan chief executive Hiroto Saikawa at his news conference hours after his arrest in November 2018. Day by day, the big names of Japanese media increasingly questioned the character of the man that had once been their corporate idol.

Widespread Leaks

On January 1, 2017, *Nikkei* started running a series of autobiographical articles by Carlos Ghosn. The title of the 30-part series, which dates back to 1956, was *Watashi no Rirekisho* or "My Personal History." The chairman of the Alliance was in good company. Over the years, similar memoirs had been published for people ranging from former British prime minister Margaret Thatcher and Japanese conductor Seiji Ozawa to notable Americans such as former Federal Reserve Board Chairman Alan Greenspan and Jack Welch, the former chairman of General Electric.

But on November 21, 2019, two days after his arrest, the very same *Nikkei* ran an editorial stating that the case had "shocked the global business community" and that Ghosn "should be held responsible for taking advantage of his position at the automaker for personal gain" if allegations were correct. "There is no question that the downfall of one of the auto industry's most powerful executives stemmed from his lack of respect for ethics and the law." And for good measure, Japan's leading business newspaper added: "Nissan's internal governance system shares part of the blame, as it failed to prevent the charismatic chairman from running out of control."

The *Nikkei* reminded its readers not to confuse Carlos Ghosn with Japanese executives whose financial malpractices, fraud and other scams were always making headlines. "While Japanese executives have often committed crimes to protect corporate reputations or destinies, they have rarely crossed the red line out of pure greed," the newspaper said.

This image of a "greedy dictator" would quickly replace that of the "cost killer" who rescued Nissan from the brink of bankruptcy two decades earlier, at least in the minds of the Japanese public. It was not unlike how Stalin swayed Soviet popular opinion against the former companions of Lenin accused of being agents of American imperialism or the Nazis in Germany.

"The character assassination pursued by the law firm Latham & Watkins, the prosecutors and Nissan was very professional," Carlos Ghosn said. "With repeated leaks coming out day after day for weeks, public opinion was whipped up in a very calculated way. They zeroed in on the reception at Versailles and replayed video loops as if to ask: 'Who does this guy think he is?' Then there was the house in Beirut, the apartment in Rio, private jets and other things. People got the idea that this guy had completely lost the plot. It's worth noting that these accusations against me had nothing to do with the charges. The targeting of specific media, how they were bought by supposed scoops, they did everything. Like professionals."

Les Échos is, to a lesser extent, the equivalent of the *Nikkei* in France. On January 14, 2019, the newspaper—controlled by Bernard Arnault, the chairman and top shareholder of LVMH, the world's biggest luxury goods company—interviewed Hiroto Saikawa, the Nissan chief executive. Nicolas Barré and David Barroux, the top two editorial managers, traveled to Yokohama.

Both had worked in Japan early in their careers and met up with Yann Rousseau, the newspaper's then correspondent in Tokyo. On November 19, 2018, Saikawa told the Nissan board that he knew nothing about Carlos Ghosn's arrest. To the French journalists, however, he was now saying that he launched an incriminating internal inquiry into the chairman of the Alliance back in October and shared "very serious facts" uncovered with other board members. It was not clear which ones. It was just another lie and not particularly important. But the article published by *Les Échos* on January 15 was significant.

The headline read: "How Carlos Ghosn pampered his close associates at Nissan's expense." The newspaper cited "new documents seen by *Les Échos*" to report a series of "revelations" on salaries paid to Claudine Bichara de Oliveira, one of Carlos Ghosn's sisters in Brazil, and details of Nissan's purchase and renovation of a house he used in Beirut. For France Info, a 24-hour public television news channel affiliated with *Les Échos*, Yann Rousseau said he had a "chance to consult" the documents.

It was a chance that Carlos Ghosn's lawyers did not enjoy. In a good number of cases, Japanese prosecutors routinely violate the penal code and basic rights by refusing to share alleged evidence with defense teams. In this case, the "revelations" by the French journalists—and many others in the Japanese and international media—did not have a direct impact on the case. But they found their way into the moralizing questioning by prosecutors.

Such moralizing changed with the wind. "Seki once dared to assert to me, his eyes closed: 'From our side, we prosecutors never leak.' But leaks were everywhere including from their side. He was brazenly lying to me. Based on simple and obvious cases easily identified by my lawyers, I asked him: 'Do you speak to the press?'" His reply: 'Not at all.' Carlos Ghosn's lawyers drew up a partial leak inventory in a 39-point motion to halt the proceedings dated October 17. Among other reasons, it argued that the prosecution's active participation in the smear campaign against Carlos Ghosn was illegal, and a crime under Article 100, paragraph 1, and Article 109, paragraph 12 of the National Public Service Act.

Following the example of Nissan, which was behind many "revelations," the prosecution's contributions were limited to "evidence" collected at great expense by the Japanese automaker and its lawyers. The prosecutors chose their communication channels, notably the *Asahi Shimbun* and its television affiliate, which had privileged access—as seen in the event staged on the tarmac on the day of Carlos Ghosn's arrest.

When the defense team lodged a comprehensive document substantiating the earlier motion to throw out the case with the Seventeenth Chamber at the Criminal Affairs Bureau of the Tokyo District Court on October 21, 2019, there was only one leak—to the *Asahi Shimbun*. An editor nonchalantly rang the office of Carlos Ghosn's lawyers to confirm the authenticity of the documents, scheduled to be made public at a court hearing on October 24.

By the time of the hearing, the defense had effectively been reduced to silence. Carlos Ghosn had been under arrest for eleven months, subjected to a barrage of questioning jointly orchestrated by Nissan and the public prosecutors. For almost an entire year, the defendant was only able to speak for ten minutes before the judge, conduct two fifteen-minute media interviews and allowed less than ten minutes to make a video recording released by the defense team under dramatic circumstances.

On April 3, 2019, Carlos Ghosn tweeted that he would be holding a news conference the following week at the Foreign Correspondents' Club of Japan, an appearance for which the world media had been waiting for months. But on April 4, investigators arrived in the early morning hours at the small apartment in Shibuya owned by a Franco-Japanese couple where he had been staying since his release on March 6. The tweet said: "I'm preparing to tell the truth about what happened. Press conference Thursday, April 11." The prosecution decided otherwise and he was arrested for the fourth time. The search of the premises was particularly rough and humiliating for Carlos Ghosn and his wife Carole.

Collusion

Throughout the bid to destroy Carlos Ghosn, the professors of morality in the prosecution team were under the formal authority of Hiromu Kurokawa, chief of the Tokyo High Public Prosecutors' Office. He was number one at the office, just below Japan's

Prosecutor-General Nobuo Inada. The government of Prime Minister Shinzo Abe wanted to elevate Kurokawa to the position of prosecutor-general, but there was a problem. He was scheduled to reach the mandatory retirement age of sixty-three in early 2020. So, the government extended the retirement age by six months, adding prosecutors to the list of public officials who could retire later, which is at its discretion. But the maneuver, perceived as benefiting Kurokawa, himself, and not the position, triggered an outcry, and the government backed down.

Then on May 20, the *Shukan Bunshun* carried a bombshell that was picked up by Japanese newspapers, moving Covid-19 off the front pages for the first time since the pandemic had begun. According to the weekly, Kurokawa violated Japan's ban on gambling and Covid restrictions on gatherings to take part in mahjong parties at people's houses on several nights in April and May. Originating in China, mahjong is to East Asians what poker is to Americans. But illegal gambling during a period of restricted gatherings was only one part of the story. It turned out that a reporter at the daily newspaper *Sankei Shimbun* had held one of these gambling parties and that a journalist from the *Asahi Shimbun* was also implicated. The *Sankei* is by far the most conservative of Japan's national newspapers and widely read by prosecutors, who are not really known for their progressive views.

"My interrogator, Seki, once gave a spirited defense of the death penalty," Carlos Ghosn recalled. The day before the fourth arrest—which took him back to the Tokyo Detention House on April 4—*Sankei* benefited from a "tip-off" which rang alarm bells within the defense team. As for the *Asahi*, it had been the main recipient of leaks about the former head of the Alliance all along.

Kurokawa was not forced to resign. The report by *Shukan Bunshun* resulted in him getting a simple "warning" from the justice minister which was backed up by the Prime Minister's Office. In the ritualistic excuses that the *Sankei* felt it owed to its readers, the daily said two of its journalists had been playing mahjong with a "special source of information" for years. The *Asahi*, meanwhile, admitted that its keen mahjong player had long been covering the Tokyo prosecutors' beat. The Kurokawa affair was a valuable confirmation of two things—political control over the appointments of senior prosecutors and collusion between the prosecutors' office and Japan's leading newspapers.

Defense Speaks

Appearing before eighty journalists and the cameras of fifteen television stations including the six main networks on October 24, Junichiro Hironaka and his colleagues spoke on behalf of the "global defense team of Mr. Ghosn." The team comprised lawyers from Japan, the United States, France, Lebanon and the Netherlands. The media coverage was generally factual and balanced—unlike the negative reactions with which the *Sankei* had bombarded its readers for eleven months. The newspaper nevertheless admitted that "this case has put the Japanese judicial system in the global spotlight. Some critics consider that recourse to renewable detentions and questioning without the presence of lawyers amounts to 'hostage justice'," it wrote.

In reality, the memorandums of lawyers laid bare the various mechanisms and tricks prosecutors could use which went against the rights of defendants.

The statute of limitations was a primary example. The prosecution's excuse for arresting Carlos Ghosn at Haneda was not only groundless, but also the charge would no longer be valid after November 27, 2018. Yet Ghosn was not indicted for alleged violations of the Financial Institutions and Exchange Act until December 10.

Prosecutors then decided that the seven-year statute of limitations could be extended to take into account the time Carlos Ghosn had spent outside of Japan. But as the defense lawyers noted, that point of Japanese jurisprudence applied only to cases where it was impossible to locate and communicate with a defendant. That was not the case with Carlos Ghosn, who had an office at the Nissan headquarters and a personal address in Tokyo.

In democratic countries, the exclusion of illegally obtained evidence is a basic principle of justice. Japanese prosecutors trampled over this principle by seizing a computer and hard disk in Beirut that belonged to Carlos Ghosn's childhood friend Fadi Gebran, a Lebanese lawyer who was his legal advisor in Lebanon until his death in August 2017. Within hours of the arrest at Haneda in November 2018, Nissan employees and lawyers from the Chicago office of the American law firm Latham & Watkins invaded the Beirut office of Amal Abou Jaoude, who had been Fadi Gebran's assistant. Now employed by Nissan Middle East, she continued to manage the legacy affairs of her late boss. The people who barged into the Beirut office in close coordination with Tokyo prosecutors had no right to do so in a foreign country. Indeed, such behavior is explicitly outlawed under Article 25 of the Constitution of Japan. But the individuals involved threatened Mrs. Abou Jaoude and forced her to hand over the equipment which contained innumerable documents protected by attorney-client privilege.

In the proud spirit of the Watergate break-in half a century earlier, the same team then moved to the Christian quarter of Achrafieh in Beirut where Nissan had made available a house for Carlos Ghosn. A wild search ensued. On the other side of the world, a few hours later, a Nissan employee in Brazil—obviously also without a warrant—entered the apartment where Carlos Ghosn stayed during visits to Rio de Janeiro. By threatening Ghosn's assistant in Brazil, the Nissan employee had obtained a mobile phone, a computer and all the documents he could lay his hands on. He kicked out the housekeeper in Ghosn's apartment, Rafia Rufino, and the apartment was effectively placed under a "private" seal. Around the same time, the "third team" sent by Nissan and the American law firm had less success when it arrived at the apartment used by Carlos Ghosn in Paris. It was vacant and the key could not be found.

Similar to when the Stalinist machine was eliminating Soviet citizens, the dreaded moment was the early-morning knock at the door. And Carole Ghosn, with that same sense of dread, will never forget dawn on April 4, 2019. That was when prosecution investigators arrived at the apartment where she had been living with her husband for less than a month. Throughout the search, which ended with her husband's re-arrest, a woman in black—who accompanied her to the toilet or bathroom—did not leave her for a second. This gross and gratuitously humiliating violation of her privacy was complemented by the unauthorized seizure of her computer, mobile phone, passport and correspondence with lawyers. Traumatized and terrorized by such "legal" violence, she fled Tokyo the same day with the help of the owner of the apartment.

For the Japanese upholding the tradition of Stalin's prosecutor Andrey Vychinski, attorney-client privilege is a foreign notion. After the spectacular flight of Carlos Ghosn from Tokyo to Beirut, prosecutors arrived at the office of defense lawyer Junichiro Hironaka on January 8, 2020, determined to illegally seize the computer on which his client had been preparing his defense. Hironaka threw them out. But the seizure was later authorized by a judge who was only too willing to please.

Criminal Intent?

Behind the repeated violations of Japanese law, the nation's constitution, its penal code, judicial proceedings, civil rights and attorney-client privilege was a simple requirement. As the initial charge was weak, other charges had to be found. This was not only to prolong the detention of the defendant indefinitely, but especially to prepare for the trial, which had become a game of politics, finance and even survival for the Nissan Old Guard and the Tokyo prosecutors.

Not a single yen had been spent, promised or budgeted for. Nissan did not make provisions to justify Carlos Ghosn's imprisonment until after his arrest. The litigation against the builder of the Renault-Nissan-Mitsubishi Alliance was for alleged criminal intent. But the initial charge was a fabrication, pure and simple. There was no crime, no body and no weapon. In its 39-point memo dated October 17, 2019, the defense team tore to pieces the charade made up by the special investigation team to justify imprisoning Carlos Ghosn and Greg Kelly. There was no underreporting of income, an infraction under the Financial Institutions and Exchange Act. Moreover, the memo said, "even if the prosecution allegations were true, it would amount to no more than an omission from annual reports, a matter of civil law resulting at worst in an administrative financial penalty" rather than a criminal proceeding and 130 days in prison.

"From the beginning, I wanted Nissan to resolve this issue internally," Prime Minister Shinzo Abe told a meeting of Japanese business leaders in January 2020, according to former chief cabinet secretary Takeo Kawamura. That would have been simple and made sense.

Where's the Victim?

But what about the second charge of misusing company funds? This was another gross fabrication, stemming from a Nissan board decision ten years earlier in the interests of the company and Carlos Ghosn in his capacity as an employee.

"In a number of multinational companies, expat employees are paid in the currency of their choice. We had people paid in British pounds. It was also common for part of the salary to be paid in yen and the rest in other currencies, sometimes in the country of origin," Ghosn explained.

Many foreigners love Japan. They may wish to live in the country and work for years or even decades but they don't necessarily want to retire or invest their money in Japan. Carlos Ghosn's children were still young at the turn of the century but they would eventually leave Tokyo for college in the United States. In Lebanon and Brazil, Carlos Ghosn had family ties and financial interests. Since the dollar remained the world's reserve currency and dominant investment currency, there was no surprise in wanting to be remunerated partly or wholly in dollars.

"When I officially took over Nissan's management in 2001, they thought the head of a Japanese company couldn't be paid in dollars. I didn't want to argue so I accepted that my salary would be paid in yen. But from 2002, I took out forward cover on the exchange rate with Shinsei Bank in Tokyo. At first, the yen never appreciated above 102 yen to the dollar, and never went below 130 yen. Under the agreement with Shinsei, a clause provided for margin calls if the yen appreciated above 80 yen to the dollar. This was virtually unprecedented and the risk seemed low, if not zero, taking into account the general state of the Japanese economy.

"The collateral I used for the contract was Nissan shares which rose to 1,300 yen. With the arrival of the financial crisis of 2008, the yen suddenly became a refuge currency like the Swiss franc. The yen climbed to 75 to the dollar and the Nissan share price plummeted to 400 yen, even a bit lower. My collateral vanished and my exposure soared. 'Mr. Ghosn, margin call,' the bank said.

"I had two choices—either to get out of the contract and cut my losses, which to my memory corresponded to 1.8 billion yen over ten years, or to increase the collateral, which, financially speaking, was not easy to achieve. The bank suggested that Nissan put the contract on its books with a clause protecting the company from any future loss. I knew the foreign exchange market would eventually stabilize and I had no doubt about Nissan overcoming the crisis. But the whipsaw trading on the foreign exchange market nevertheless continued for more than two years."

On October 31, 2008—six weeks after the failure of U.S. investment Lehman Brothers triggered the onslaught of the global financial crisis—the Nissan board adopted a resolution to authorize Toshiaki Ohnuma, the vice president in charge of the secretariat office, to conclude contracts to cover currency exposure for non-Japanese senior executives. These contracts provided for the company incurring no losses.

Three months later, on January 30, the following year, Carlos Ghosn suffered a loss of 62.5 million yen when a yen-dollar swap matured. If need be, any Nissan exposure to the loss would be covered by his retirement package. The arrangement cost Nissan nothing and the company did not even have to deposit collateral with Shinsei Bank. So, there was no loss, and not a single yen was withdrawn from Nissan's coffers.

"We reached an agreement but Japanese market regulators opposed it on the basis of a conflict of interest and it was rejected. By this stage, it was February 2009. When the Japan's Securities and Exchange Surveillance Commission rejected the agreement, the only option was to find a friend who could provide the collateral guarantee. Obviously, you don't find people like that on the street. But in Asia, notably in the Middle East, deals based on friendship are not uncommon. And that's how Khaled Juffali agreed to help me, without hesitating. If I hadn't found such a solution, the truth is that I would have had to leave Nissan. My bonus on retirement would have largely covered my exposure. But how could I abandon ship in the middle of the worst financial crisis since the 1930s? Misuse of company funds goes against the interests of the company. Again, this arrangement cost Nissan nothing."

Khaled Juffali, who had known Carlos Ghosn for twenty years, issued a letter of credit for three billion yen. It was deposited with Shinsei Bank, which put it in a safe where it would stay until stability returned to the foreign exchange market.

Arabian Sands

The sleuths at the prosecutors' office did not see things the same way. Courtesy of the Nissan Old Guard, they drew a third charge out of their hat at the precise moment they had to re-arrest Carlos Ghosn. The new accusation involved the prisoner at the Kosuge detention centre Ghosn and Juffali, the Saudi Arabian businessman. In other words, one fictitious breach of trust to cover up another fictitious breach of trust.

The Middle East is a big market for Japanese carmakers. Its importance can be seen in news images or television series like *Homeland* or *The Bureau*, a French spy thriller. Big Japanese pick-ups and large SUVs are robust, agile and pliable for transporting anything from live animals and bags of cement to heavy machine guns. And the customers range from non-governmental organizations, like charities, to jihadist groups. The market is enormous, and a major source of earnings for the market leader, Toyota Motor Corporation.

The decision by the Nissan Old Guard and its prosecutor friends to "go after" Carlos Ghosn's business dealings in the Gulf was not innocent. Nor was it without innuendo. But once again, it was a curiously selective pursuit.

"If people really wanted make a big fuss, they'd investigate why jihadist groups are huge users of Japanese vehicles," Carlos Ghosn said. "How did Daesh come to have Japanese pick-ups? It's because Daesh was born in Iraq, with people who used to be in the Saddam Hussein regime. In Iraq, the Japanese dominate the automobile market. Toyota ranks first, but there's also Nissan, Mitsubishi and others. How are the vehicles distributed? Toyota's main base is Saudi Arabia, and the Abdul Latif Jameel Group is one of the best Toyota distributors in the world to the extent that they've penetrated markets in Africa. The pick-ups are usually delivered to Dubai, then sent to Iraq. Toyota washes its hands.

"Despite U.S. and international sanctions, Toyota also has a presence in Iran. The Abdul Latif Jameel Group sells vehicles to brokers who officially sends them to Africa with a certain number ending up in Iran. Bahwan does the same thing with Renault cars," Carlos Ghosn said, referring to Omani distributor Suhail Bahwan

Automobiles. "The Americans can't ignore this, but what's in it for them? Go after Toyota, a large employer in the United States? And how could Toyota's complicity be proven? If there was public criticism, it could be very embarrassing for those concerned, especially in Japan," Ghosn remarked.

The Nissan managers who brought the company to the brink of bankruptcy in 1999 had skimped on this part of the world. Nissan languished behind its Japanese rivals and, more recently, South Korean competitors, especially in Saudi Arabia. The Nissan brand was hostage to a distribution agreement in 1957 with Alhamrani United Company, whose poor performance was a source of frustration for the Japanese automaker. With internal divisions within the Alhamrani family, Nissan was at impasse.

From May 2008—well before Carlos Ghosn asked his Saudi friend for help—Nissan started negotiating with Khaled Juffali Company to relaunch distribution in the Gulf region. The talks were led by Gilles Normand, the executive in charge of sales in the Middle East, Africa and Latin America since 2006. Assisting him on the ground was Atsuo Kosaka, managing director at Nissan Middle East.

Khaled Juffali Rides to Nissan's Rescue

Nissan set up a joint venture with businessman Nasser Watar's company Al Dahana FZCO in the Jebel Ali Free Zone in Dubai in July 2008. The new company, Nissan Gulf FZCO, would oversee distribution in the four Gulf markets of Saudi Arabia, Abu Dhabi, Kuwait and Bahrain. The brand relaunch in Saudi Arabia would involve cooperating with Khaled Juffali.

"Juffali," recalled Carlos Ghosn, "started doing business with Nissan in 2008. But it wasn't by chance. At the time, everyone was trying to source money in the Gulf, which was one of the markets that had suffered commercially but had not collapsed."

With their oil revenues, investors from Gulf monarchies were indeed highly sought after as the global financial crisis accelerated with problems emerging in the international banking system and global liquidity drying up. Carlos Ghosn should be congratulated and thanked for introducing Nissan to Khaled Juffali.

"We were not satisfied with our distributor in Saudi Arabia. And we couldn't get out of this relationship without a local partner. We asked Juffali to help us. He agreed as long as he could be involved in distribution. He already represented brands like Mercedes and Siemens. It's one of the largest private companies in the country. The truth is that Nissan needed him more than he needed Nissan. I'd known him for a long time and trusted him. He was a respected businessman, a corporate heavyweight in Saudi Arabia. Describing him as a petty businessman who used Nissan at the company's expense was part of the smear campaign against me," said Ghosn.

"In fact, Nissan paid him the sum of 14.7 million dollars over four years, which confirms the accusations aren't justified." Ghosn continued. "Moreover, each payment was checked by ten people, including three members of the company's executive committee."

On May 21, 2009, the committee decided to transfer three million dollars to Khaled Juffali Company to cover expenses incurred and a commission. On June 1, Gilles Normand, who oversaw the Middle East, approved the withdrawal from the "CEO reserve"—the alleged "slush fund" triumphantly brandished by Carlos Ghosn's accusers. Before Carlos Ghosn gave his approval, it was countersigned by CEO Office chief Greg Kelly, head of financial planning and accounting Emmanuel Delay, and Colin Dodge, the executive vice president who oversaw markets outside of Japan. Colin Dodge, Gilles Normand and Stephen Ma, financial controller for the Middle East, later gave their approval for the funds to be disbursed.

"It was always like that," Ghosn said. "The 14.7 million dollars received by KJC included 11 million dollars that it had spent on Nissan's behalf—things like legal services, market research and promotions. The rest was remuneration which was quite reasonable. To prepare my defense, we gathered all the invoices for services provided by Juffali. He sent them to me, not Nissan. The charge asserts that he was 'compensated by Mr. Ghosn' for the collateral in the Shinsei Bank affair. That's rewriting history, a gross fabrication that completely belies what happened next."

Nissan's tie-up with Juffali rapidly led to a surge in sales by its old distributor Alhamrani United Company, which largely exceeded the 50,000 units forecast for the 2009 financial year. In July 2009, Nissan renewed its agreement with Alhamrani family, avoiding costly litigation and commercial damage to the brand. Between 2008 and 2013, Khaled Juffali was closely involved with Nissan's research into opening a plant in Saudi Arabia, an idea that was eventually shelved as it did not meet the criteria for profitability. In 2014, however, Nissan started distributing its vehicles directly to the Saudi market in partnership with Juffali's group.

By the first quarter of 2019, Nissan's market share in the Gulf had climbed to a record 16.9 percent, up 2.9 percentage points in two years. This was ignored by the Japanese and international media, which were no doubt too busy with the "revelations" being leaked by the Nissan Old Guard and the Tokyo prosecutors' office. It was a rare ray of sunshine for the company's global performance, which had become increasingly gloomy after Hiroto Saikawa assumed the top job at Nissan and which would later turn into a disaster.

"Finally, We've Got Him"

In terms of leaking and manipulating information, the fourth charge of "aggravated misuse of company funds" is worthy of a case study. With the Omani affair—known as the "SBA case" in reference to local distributor Suhail Bahwan Automobiles—prosecutors sent Carlos Ghosn back to prison on April 4, a week before the news conference scheduled for April 11. The *Financial Times* duly reported on May 9 that a "laptop in Lebanon" obtained a few weeks earlier had information on Carlos Ghosn's financial transactions, allowing investigators to corner him again.

In fact, the laptop was among the equipment illegally spirited away more than five months earlier in the raid on Mrs. Abou Jaoude's office in Beirut. As early as December 2018, rumors about the Omani affair emerged among traders on the Japan desks of the big international banks in Dubai. As part of the global hunt to get more dirt on Carlos Ghosn, Nissan and its American law firm made inquiries.

"It was pretty fantastic, this Oman affair, which, according to the media, led the prosecutors to say, 'finally, we've got him'," Ghosn said. "They asserted that Nissan, which had a commercial arrangement with SBA, transferred money to the account of the chief executive of the distributor, which belongs to the sultanate's largest private company. But in reality, the media alleged, this money went to Carlos Ghosn and his family to buy a boat and shares in an investment company."

As part of Nissan's reconquest of the Middle East market, Suhail Bahwan Automobiles became a distributor for the Japanese automaker in 2004. The partnership was not only for sales in Oman but also other markets through its Arata International Trading subsidiary. These markets included Iraq, Libya, Saudi Arabia and even China. "For geographic and historical reasons," Carlos Ghosn recalled, "the Omanis had inherited an age-old trading tradition." The partnership benefited Nissan considerably.

By 2008, the initial annual sales of 2,000 units generating revenues of thirty-three million dollars had skyrocketed to 23,000 units with revenues twelves times higher at four-hundred million dollars. The Nissan Old Guard questioned the relationship with the Omani company, who had been accused of being involved in Carlos Ghosn's alleged misuse of company funds. As of late 2020, however, SBA was still Nissan's distributor in this part of the world.

The document lodged by Carlos Ghosn's defense lawyers on October 24, detailed the business relationships between Nissan's global headquarters, the Nissan Middle East venture in Dubai and its distributors, notably when rules were modified at the height of the global financial crisis in 2009. There were ten levels of decision-making including Nissan Middle East managing director Toru Hasegawa, general manager in charge of accounting Takahiko Ikushima and financial controller Alain Dassas. The same rules applied to the chief executive's reserve.

"First of all," Carlos Ghosn said, "this reserve had nothing to do with an alleged 'slush fund'—it was an annual budget line which was voted on and published regularly. As we showed, ten signatures were required each time funds were withdrawn from the reserve. And it wasn't cash, it was an authorization to draw from the company's budget. And this money was spent by executives in charge of operations following procedures that were completely codified.

"Second, all the funds transferred from Nissan to SBA resulted from contractual obligations." Between mid-2012 and mid-2018, Nissan transferred to SBA, once or several times a year, bonuses linked to achieving pre-determined commercial targets. It was

Hiroto Saikawa who approved the final transfers in 2017 and 2018.

"The charge questioned the role of a company called GFI (Good Faith Investments) whose owner was Divyendu Kumar." He was managing director of an Omani family company called Bahwan International Group Holding and was credited with considerably improving its management over a period of about fifteen years.

Carlos Ghosn said Nissan and the American law firm "spent a lot of money to research all banks in the region. They were unable to find any transfer from SBA to GFI. Not one. All the money transferred to GFI came from an account of Kumar, located in Switzerland. At the end of the day, they were unable to find any link between the money Nissan paid to SBA and the investments made by Kumar. Our defense team asserted that no transfer from SBA benefited me or my family directly or indirectly. It was up to the prosecution to prove what they were saying, and they couldn't.

"Unless mistaken, Mr. Kumar was free to spend his own money," Ghosn continued. "He was a director of SBA who had been recruited from Tata Motors in India, but was not a shareholder in SBA. It was at the level of the regional director of Nissan Middle East that contracts were negotiated—in complete transparency—for automobile concessions with distributors. In the charge sheet, I was described as a beneficial owner of GFI. I was not a shareholder and never had a management position. Despite our repeated demands, the prosecutors were unable to produce a single email exchange between Kumar and me. Not one."

Reliable Witnesses Only

"But there's even more," Ghosn said. "They sent a team to Oman to interview, for an entire day, Ahmed Suhail Bahwan Al-Mukhaini, the son of the founder of Suhail Bahwan Automobiles who headed the company and was also responsible for the group's modernization. As the questioning contradicted their theory, they asserted that they didn't produce any record of the conversation. Of course, my lawyers insisted before the judges that they produce this document, as SBA's lawyers had told us about it. They finally acceded to the demand, but it was a day of questioning they would have liked to hide."

Therein was a fundamental question for the Moscow show-trial treatment of Carlos Ghosn in Tokyo—could there be witnesses for the defense?

Similar to the way in which the statute of limitations had been interpreted, the Japanese justice system posed a major handicap on the defense, as only sworn statements by witnesses physically present in the court could be accepted. This could lead to discrimination against foreign defendants. For months, Carlos Ghosn's lawyers argued that video recordings of testimonies or depositions registered by foreign magistrates should be accepted. By December 29, when Carlos Ghosn fled Japan, a response was still pending.

At the same time, the world had learned of the hitherto unknown aspects of the Japanese judicial system through the "Carlos Ghosn affair," and that was enough to dissuade non-resident witnesses from appearing physically before the trial. When the head of a global industry giant is imprisoned and held in isolation for 130 days on the basis of flimsy charges, the international business community starts asking questions.

Foreign Minister Taro Kono experienced this firsthand when he took part in an Australian Leadership Retreat in 2019. Flying to the state of Queensland in late May to promote Japan at this Australian mini-Davos, Mr. Kono was flanked by Yoshito Hori, the founder of Japanese business school Globis, when he faced a barrage of questions and criticism of how the chairman of the Renault-Nissan-Mitsubishi Alliance had been treated. The head of a foreign company asked Mr. Kono if it was still possible to travel to Japan without a team of lawyers.

Mr. Kono and Mr. Hori could have recognized the need for at least some serious explanation to restore the country's tarnished image, but as part of the Japanese establishment, they chose victimhood and denial instead.

Discrimination Based on Race, Nationality and Social Status

It should be pointed out that the term "hostage justice" was not coined by foreigners with bad intentions. On May 10, 2019, more than one thousand professionals from the Japanese legal world, including lawyers, academics and jurists, met in Tokyo to issue a "call for the elimination of hostage justice." They noted that the

Japanese system "uses detention well beyond the purpose of guaranteeing the presence of defendants in court and violates human rights guaranteed by the Constitution of Japan, including physical freedom, the right to remain silent and the right to a fair trial. The consistent practice of denying bail to those who deny what they are accused of may flout the prohibition against torture as it uses prolonged detentions and interrogations to extract confessions. It is also a violation of international norms governing human rights, including the presumption of innocence, the prohibition against torture and the assistance of counsel during questioning."

Some defenders of "hostage justice" argued that Carlos Ghosn had not been treated differently from anybody else in Japan who refused to confess, affirming that confessions were indeed the cornerstone of the judicial regime. But this ignored reality.

Take the well-known postal fraud case of Atsuko Muraki, a former vice minister at the Ministry of Health, Labour and Welfare. She spent more than five months behind bars for refusing to "confess" to a "crime" based on "evidence" fabricated by the Osaka prosecutors' office.

But three senior executives at Tokyo Electric Power Company, which ran the Fukushima nuclear power plant, were cleared of allegations of "professional negligence" on September 19, 2019. They never confessed, nor did they spend a single day in prison. Moreover, despite years of public protests, prosecutors have refused to take action to find out who was responsible for this global disaster. In pronouncing their acquittal, the judge ignored reports—including internal ones from the company—and warnings, notably from a U.S. energy services company, that had long expressed concern that the dykes of the Fukushima plant were not high enough to protect it from a tsunami and the poor installation of generating units to keep the four reactors cool in case of an accident.

The truth is that the business elite's nomenklatura enjoy quasi-impunity in the judicial system—as long as they comply with rituals of public apologies with their ninety-degree bows in front of the television camera and other formal displays of contrition.

Recent scandals involving companies like Toshiba, Takata, Kobe Steel and Olympus have been bigger and more serious, lasting longer than those involving Carlos Ghosn and Greg Kelly. One can only conclude, as Carlos Ghosn's lawyers did in their request to have the case thrown out, that the discriminatory proceedings were "based on race, nationality and social status."

A striking illustration of such discrimination is the complete immunity that prosecutors and judges gave Hiroto Saikawa, who was directly linked to many of Nissan's decisions that justified the charges and who was even one of the beneficiaries.

Many corrupt Japanese businessmen have benefitted from deals "offering" parole in exchange for confessions. But such a deal was never offered to the chairman of the Renault-Nissan-Mitsubishi Alliance.

"Otsuru said this was hypothetical, not a deal," Carlos Ghosn said. "In any case, I refused to play that game. Irrespective of what was going on in Japan, my international reputation was at stake. No way."

CHAPTER FOUR

Why?

Japan takes things easy during "Golden Week," a series of public holidays in late April and early May. In a country known for "death from overwork," *karoshi* in Japanese, both the public and private sectors force their employees to take vacations. Not so at the Ministry of Economy, Trade and Industry (METI) during the spring of 2018, where there was no time for officials to relax, especially at the ministry's Manufacturing Industries Bureau.

"After Carlos Ghosn was ordered to make the Alliance irreversible, the Japanese side grew noticeably restless," a French diplomat recalled. "In the middle of Golden Week, we were summoned by METI. Their behavior was somewhat hysterical at the time." According to the diplomat, discussions were led by Akihiro Tada, the director general for manufacturing industries who reported directly to Economy, Trade and Industry Minister Hiroshige Seko, who held the position between August 2016 and September 2019.

On the French side was Pascal Faure, director general for enterprises at the Ministry of Economy and Finance and especially Martin Vial, the commissioner of the French Government Shareholding Agency, better known as the APE. The agency was the powerful arm of "France Inc." where government equity in companies persisted despite the "neo-liberal revolution," which the country went through in the 1990s with no fewer than eighty-eight companies now listed. The government shareholding of 15.01 percent in Renault was the jewel in its stock portfolio which had a market value of about seventy-five billion euros in 2019. Moreover, the APE had two seats on Renault's twenty-member board.

A few months before Golden Week, on February 18, the French government made Carlos Ghosn's last term as Renault chairman conditional upon him "selling" to the Japanese side a strengthening of the links between the French automaker and Nissan. In early April, Martin Vial, whose title at Renault was "director designated by the French State," made a very discreet visit to Japan to explain to Nissan management the official French vision for a permanent Alliance. The visit, confirmed by a Renault board member in 2019, was later reported by the Japanese media.

The person who met Martin Vial at the Nissan headquarters in Yokohama was Hemant Kumar Nadanasabapathy, a Malaysian lawyer who was the Japanese company's senior vice president in charge of legal affairs. He was known among colleagues as Hari Nada. Politically, it was curious to say the least. According to Carlos Ghosn, "Martin Vial did not inform the Renault board, had no mandate and his integration project was not a Renault plan."

Irreversible?

Hari Nada summarized details of the talks in an email. "Mr. Vial asked me if Nissan preferred the status quo," he wrote. "I said Nissan would prefer shareholdings to be rebalanced based on principles that had been discussed for several weeks. This would involve Renault reducing its share in Nissan's capital and Nissan increasing its stake in Renault. This would ensure that neither party could take control of the other. Added to this was the withdrawal of the French government. Mr. Vial replied that such a rebalancing would be too great a sacrifice for Renault if a real step towards merging was not taken."

A source who took part in the talks later recalled Hari Nada's increasingly antagonistic behavior. He expressed hostility towards the plan—unless it succeeded in rebalancing the Alliance to the benefit of Nissan. Towards Carlos Ghosn, he barely hid his contempt. "He was indicating to us that Nissan had now been strengthened by taking Mitsubishi on board and no longer needed Renault," the source said.

According to Hari Nada, the METI director general Tada would soon be sending a letter of response to his French government counterpart Martin Vial. Hitoshi Kawaguchi, the senior vice president in charge of public affairs at Nissan, warned that Minister Seko was impatient and ready to write a letter himself.

After a week of tense exchanges during Golden Week—with diplomats from both sides trying to calm things down—the Japanese sent a document to their French counterparts.

"Cat's piss," was how the French diplomat described the memorandum of understanding that was supposed to be the basis for an agreement between Tokyo and Paris. The Japanese side affirmed that "strengthening the Alliance requires respecting Nissan's independence," and that "the intentions expressed by Renault executives will never affect the freedom of Nissan executives to take decisions." This amounted to strengthening the amended Restated Alliance Master Agreement, known as Rama II. Under this accord, the French accepted the weakening of Renault's rights as Nissan's main shareholder back in 2015.

According to the *Journal du Dimanche*, a weekly French newspaper, public affairs chief Kawaguchi sent this document to Nissan's top management, including Carlos Ghosn, on May 22, explaining what had been discussed by French Government Shareholding Agency commissioner Martin Vial and Akihiro Tada, the METI director general. Kawaguchi thought METI was going "a little too far." According to Nissan chief executive Hiroto Saikawa, the government's Chief Cabinet Secretary Yoshihide Suga—the right-hand man of Prime Minister Shinzo Abe—was being more reasonable than the Ministry of Economy, Trade and Industry. Towards Nissan, Suga had shown "very solid support but is more discreet and less talkative," Saikawa said. "We have to find a more subtle way to get Suga to better control METI."

Hiroshige Seko, the Japanese minister, spoke with his French counterpart Bruno Le Maire in Paris, but the talks were inconclusive. "Silence then fell," the French diplomat said. But not Nissan's unease. In June, Kawaguchi met a French official on the sidelines of a French film festival in Yokohama for which the Nissan executive was the main sponsor. It was clear that an agreement to make the tie-up between Nissan and Renault irreversible would not happen anytime soon.

Macron's Maneuver

The mistrust had come from afar, especially three years earlier when the APE raised the French government's stake in Renault to 19.7 percent by purchasing shares on the open market on April 22, 2015. In a statement, the agency said the move "marks both the state's wish to defend its interests as a shareholder by pushing for the introduction of double voting rights in the governance of Renault and the strategic character it attaches to participating in the capital of this large industrial company."

More specifically, the French government was aiming to defeat management at Renault's upcoming annual shareholder meeting, which had to vote on the introduction of double voting rights for "stable" shareholders of more than two years under a new law. Sixty-six percent of shareholders could oppose the change, as Carlos Ghosn would recommend to the general assembly, to avoid upsetting the fragile alliance with Nissan.

Known as the Florange Act, the new law was pure political opportunism. François Hollande, the Socialist Party candidate in presidential elections in 2012, had promised workers in the northeastern town of Florange to prevent the partial closure of a local steel mill. He failed, of course, but after assuming the presidency in May, his socialist government passed the new law on double voting rights for stable shareholders, "aiming to get the real economy back."[5] In France, tradition dictates that governments, not consumers or markets, determine economic reality.

---

5. In an editorial published on April 8, 2015, the *Financial Times* said the new law was "misguided," describing it as a "vehicle for large existing investors to entrench control . . . that threatens to raise the cost of capital for French enterprises." It recalled the origins of the law in 2012, when Indian-run steel group ArcelorMittal decided to close two blast furnaces in Florange. In passing the legislation requiring companies to make every effort to find another buyer before closing a plant, the editorial noted that French lawmakers had "built another objective" into the new law—double voting rights for shareholders of more than two years. But "French corporate law already allowed anyone owning shares in a company to do this," the newspaper said, "as long as the company's constitution was amended to permit it. The Loi Florange in effect reversed the presumption. Double votes are now the norm after two years unless specifically disapplied."

"The best is sometimes the enemy of the good," Carlos Ghosn remarked. "The French government held 15 percent of Renault's capital with voting rights, and Nissan held the same with no voting rights. They wanted to increase their voting rights to 28 percent with Nissan staying at zero. This was a wake-up call for the Japanese at Nissan, who thought that enough was enough. When I warned French leaders, they didn't listen. They thought I was manipulating the situation: 'Ghosn's using the Japanese for his own interests.' They didn't understand—or didn't want to understand—that this would have big repercussions on the Japanese side, which is exactly what we saw when the Japanese killed me off because they thought I was betraying them.

"I spoke to Economy and Finance Minister Emmanuel Macron directly during this period, but it was like speaking to a brick wall," Ghosn continued. "To get out of the crisis with Nissan, what mattered most to the government was re-establishing control over Renault much more than preserving Renault's influence on the Alliance. So, they got their double voting rights, but the upshot was that Renault could no longer oppose decisions by the Nissan board. This was to reassure the Japanese that the French government had no intention of interfering in decision-making at Nissan. It was a complete aberration."

A temporary ceasefire was concluded with the signing of Rama II, an amended version of the initial Restated Alliance Master Agreement of 2002. Neither agreement was publicly disclosed. What the new accord did was to effectively transform Renault into a sleeping partner of Nissan. The Japanese automaker's main shareholder could no longer question Nissan board decisions about the appointment, dismissal or remuneration of directors, or of those that had not been approved by the board.

Nationalist Reaction in Japan

"The right attitude would have been to respect the wishes of the Renault shareholders and not create double voting rights, as the law passed by the French government allowed," Carlos Ghosn said. "Honestly, I still ask myself today what the French government was trying to achieve. In this case, there was a crying lack of strategic vision. The government won in the short term, but France was the loser in the long term. The decision taken by Renault was a strategic blunder, resulting in Nissan being rendered totally independent.

"The French caused what happened next. They never believed the Japanese could have their own view or their own position independent of me," explained Ghosn. "As I was very popular in Japan, they saw me maneuvering behind Nissan's protests. For a very long time, they thought Japan didn't exist or count in this affair, and that there wouldn't be a nationalist reaction in Japan.

"They thought it was all a 'set-up' by Ghosn to trick us. Since they thought I was in cahoots with the Japanese, they were surprised by my arrest. Even more seriously, they didn't say anything to me when tensions with the Japanese resumed during the first half of 2018."

According to the official Japanese version, there was no background or context to the second "Ghosn shock" two decades after the first. It was all about power and ambition. The political climate in both Japan and France was irrelevant. It was simply a story of a man ensnared by his own greed—the madness of the powerful who lose sight of reality—unveiled by whistleblowers who confided to those incorruptible guardians of justice at the Tokyo prosecutors' office after being seized by guilt for having assisted in wrongdoings. Fancy receptions in Versailles, crystal chandeliers in the pink house with the blue shutters in Beirut and the sands of Copacabana provided "optics," but did not explain anything to a public eager to believe the bigger they are, the harder they fall. The downfall of the mighty keeps the public happy with morality safe in the best of all possible worlds.

What We Now Know

We don't claim to know everything. Many in the know are not talking and have never had to bother with the Japanese justice system or be interrogated. Nor have they had to deal with media that mostly regurgitate whatever falls into their mouths from the Nissan Old Guard and the Tokyo prosecutors' office. What we do know, is that the internal inquiry was launched by senior Nissan management at the height of tensions over the permanence of the Alliance in the spring of 2018.

"The affair started just after my term as Renault chairman was renewed," Carlos Ghosn recalled. "I hesitated a lot. I wasn't really keen to resign myself to the conditions imposed by the French government. I was told that there was still work to do. But I knew perfectly well it would be complicated to align the Japanese, the French government, Renault and Nissan given the requirements of each. I told the French authorities that I would not force anything through. It would have been pointless to have an agreement that was not respected. I'd led the Alliance to the top rank in the world, a demonstration of what I was capable of doing. I didn't have anything to prove.

"I didn't see making the Alliance irreversible as the issue. I basically don't believe for a second that the permanence of companies should be guaranteed, at least not by virtue of legal provisions. Making the Alliance irreversible was all about performance.

"But the French government insisted. They promised: 'We'll help you.' I was ready to tell them that I was maybe not the right man for the job in January or February 2018, that they should choose someone not involved with the history of the Alliance, someone with a fresh eye. And I shared my feelings with Renault board members Philippe Lagayette, Patrick Thomas and Marc Ladreit de Lacharrière.

"I was considering a change of life. I didn't want to be reappointed at any cost. It's now clear that nothing would have happened in Tokyo if I had left at that time. The French government pushed me into being reappointed and Nissan trapped me immediately after that."

Sounding the Alarm

On the surface, there were two whistleblowers. One was Toshiaki Ohnuma, chief of the Nissan secretariat, who was seen as relaxed while holding a phone on the top floor of the Nissan headquarters as men in black from the Tokyo prosecutors' office raided the building on November 19, 2018. The other was Hari Nada, in charge of legal affairs, who was informed that morning what was about to happen at the immigration counter at Haneda airport in the afternoon, and that a similar fate awaited his "friend" Greg Kelly who he had put so much energy into convincing to come to Japan.

Japan's official narrative states that Ohnuma and Nada "sat down" with prosecutors and entered into an "exchange and agreement program," a form of plea bargain that was added to the Japanese penal code in 2016. This "spontaneous" action by two Nissan executives closely associated with the CEO Office for years coincided with the crisis over cementing the Alliance with Renault.

As if by chance at the same time, of course, a newcomer arrived at Nissan as an independent director—Masakazu Toyoda, a former vice minister for international affairs at the Ministry of Economy, Trade and Industry. As part of corporate governance reforms, Prime Minister Shinzo Abe had been pushing for Japanese companies to have more independent directors since coming to power for a second time in 2012.

"As it was now an obligation, we were looking for two independent directors," Carlos Ghosn recalled. "So I said to the team: 'Very well, propose some Japanese names as possible board members.' Kawaguchi drew up a shortlist and showed the candidates to Saikawa. They came to me to say that we had to meet Toyoda and a few others. We'd hired former METI officials as auditors in the past. I knew it was a way to recycle former senior officials. I wasn't suspicious. I met Toyoda, who was being pushed by Kawaguchi. He fit the mold—if that made people happy, why not? But obviously, he was on a mission."

On Assignment

It is customary for Japanese bureaucrats to seek a second career in the private sector when they retire. The practice is called *amukadari* in Japanese, which translates as "descent from heaven." But in a country where the bureaucracy enjoys a certain amount of prestige, going back to a tradition imported from China, those who descend are not necessarily angels. To be sure, they help grease the wheels of commerce with their government contacts. But they also keep a watchful eye over Japanese capitalism for their former masters. In the "Carlos Ghosn affair," the former vice minister would carry out his assignment to perfection.

"Toyoda was elected a director at the shareholder meeting in June 2018, but his appointment was semi-official, dating back to

February or March," Carlos Ghosn said. "He was a director-elect of sorts, but not yet crowned."

Hitoshi Kawaguchi was the interface between Japanese authorities and Nissan's management including Carlos Ghosn. Graduating from the reputable Hitotsubashi University in Tokyo, he joined Nissan in 1976, and had long worked for the company in Europe after completing an internship at the European Commission in the early 1980s. Since 2009, he had been in charge of external affairs and government relations as a senior vice president.

"I'd meet Kawaguchi every month," Carlos Ghosn recalled. "He had very high-level government meetings to explain what was going on at Nissan. He obviously told me what he wanted to tell me, but I didn't attach too much importance to it. For me, it wasn't an issue as there was no government interference in the running of the company.

"What it showed was complete transparency between the Japanese hierarchies of Nissan and the Japanese government. I experienced this in 2015 when Paris launched its double voting rights offensive and there were exchanges between the French and Japanese governments. The French government wasn't telling me anything. Neither was Martin Vial. Important information was coming to me from the Japanese government, which was speaking to Kawaguchi.

"When Nissan started considering this internal inquiry into me, it's quite impossible to imagine that the Japanese government was not informed. Kawaguchi would have been dead scared of keeping METI out of the loop. He almost certainly requested and received the green light. It wouldn't have been possible to do what they did without the agreement of the Japanese government."

Japanese Authorities Enter the Scene

"It's not very difficult to imagine what motivated the Japanese government to get involved," Ghosn continued. "They would have told themselves: 'Watch out, Ghosn could leave at any moment and we'll need to be concerned with Nissan.' Kawaguchi was spokesman for the Japanese position. He's a political figure. He told me that people at METI weren't very happy and that a solution would have to be found—without warning me how serious the situation was, which would have put me on edge. Until 2015-2016, they considered there was no problem, as I managed to prevent any French government interference. From 2018, the question arose in Paris about my term being renewed and making the Alliance irreversible. Their reasoning would have been that 'Ghosn won't be here forever, so it's up to us to see what's going on.' We know what happened next."

Up to what level was the Japanese political world implicated? What's known is that Kawaguchi was very close, even friendly, with Chief Cabinet Secretary Yoshide Suga, the prime minister's right-hand man since 2014. Suga represented the second electoral district of Kanagawa Prefecture which includes Yokohama, where Carlos Ghosn had moved the global headquarters of Nissan. Suga was serving his sixth parliamentary term and had his eyes on succeeding Shinzo Abe as prime minister, which he did in September 2020.

According to an unidentified Nissan source quoted by the Japanese website Lite-ra, Suga and Kawaguchi had been "in frequent contact in recent years, taking part in dinners and meetings. It's unbelievable that the Ghosn case wasn't raised in advance." Moreover, "the common feeling at Nissan is that Suga covers Kawaguchi's ass."

It was reported in January 2020 that Prime Minister Abe belatedly distanced himself from the plan to use the Japanese judicial system to bring Carlos Ghosn down. According to several sources, however, it was Abe's close associate Akihide Kumada who brought together the Nissan Old Guard, its METI backers and the special team at the Tokyo prosecutors' office. Kumada was himself a member of the special prosecution team before becoming a lawyer. The weekly *Shukan Bunshun* described him as "guardian of the administration and wisdom" of the ruling Liberal Democratic Party.

Apart from Kawaguchi and Toyoda, there was also Hidetashi Imazu, a Nissan veteran who was almost seventy years of age. The auditor was said to have been shocked when he discovered, through Nada and Ohnuma, the "embezzlement" that was supposed to have been committed by Carlos Ghosn and Greg Kelly. That was about as believable as Kawaguchi acting without METI advice.

"My conviction is that Kawaguchi, Toyoda and Imazu were behind the affair," said Ghosn. "Toyoda was the brains, without a doubt. Kawaguchi was motivated by personal ambition and was temporarily rewarded with a promotion to the Nissan executive committee. They took the initiative under the tutelage of Seko, the METI minister. It wouldn't have been hard to make Imazu realize he'd be compromised as internal auditor. And when they realized they needed Hari Nada, they would have gone to him with a gun to his head: 'My friend, either you cooperate or go to prison.' He acted under threat as he was implicated in the transactions which served as a basis for the accusations. This was where the plea bargain—which had just been legislated in Japan—came into play. It was the same for Ohnuma."

Guilty Plea Diverted

In seeking to get the proceedings thrown out, Carlos Ghosn's defense team argued that the hijacking of plea bargains was behind the action taken by the Nissan Old Guard, METI and the Tokyo prosecutors' office. Hari Nada and Toshiaki Ohnuma "weren't the real participants," Carlos Ghosn said. "They were lawyers employed by Nissan and their bosses took the case to the Tokyo prosecutors and they cooperated with them, negotiating an agreement. They did not take the initiative themselves. They were persuaded by Nissan . . . and simply signed a written agreement that was basically a company order. This practice violates the purpose of plea bargaining and is illegal."

In preparing for the trial in 2019, Carlos Ghosn's defense team repeatedly asked the judge to get the prosecution to be more transparent about the plea bargain. Apart from the two made public, how many other Nissan officials benefited from such an arrangement? In particular, did the prosecutors extend a plea bargain to Hiroto Saikawa, who was implicated in the several cases of embezzlement allegedly involving Carlos Ghosn and Greg Kelly? With the support of pliant judges, prosecutors ignored these requests.

"Apart from Mr. Saikawa," said Ghosn, "there were numerous senior executives and employees implicated in acts that were the basis of the accusations. Threatened by Nissan and the prosecutors with criminal charges, they were forced to testify how Nissan and the prosecutors wanted them to give evidence—namely, the dictatorial behavior of Mr. Ghosn and how it was impossible to go against his authority when forced to do improper things."

Hiroto Saikawa was effectively first among equals when it came to the numerous Nissan executives who benefited from the financial arrangements that were the excuse for arresting Carlos Ghosn and Greg Kelly.

The List

At a Nissan board meeting on October 8, 2019, Thierry Bolloré, chief executive of Renault and also a director of the Japanese automaker, stated he was astonished by a report in the *Wall Street Journal* four days earlier. The report referred to a document drawn up by Christina Murray, the American head of internal audit and compliance who played a prominent role on the day Carlos Ghosn was arrested the previous year. The document was a list of eighty Nissan employees "she believed enabled alleged wrongdoing by former Chairman Carlos Ghosn," the newspaper said. Murray "planned to create a committee to consider disciplining them, but Nissan quashed her plan after a leading target said it wasn't necessary."

A letter signed by Thierry Bolloré, and drafted by Renault's lawyers in full knowledge of Jean-Dominique Senard, who the French government had appointed Renault chairman, was important for several reasons. The document gave an idea of what would have been an honest approach to charging Carlos Ghosn and Greg Kelly as individuals and Nissan as a company—if the aim was to comply with company financial law rather than the hasty removal of the head of the Alliance. In September, Thierry Bolloré received letters from three anonymous whistleblowers at Nissan, who implicated Ohnuma and Nada in the embezzlement for which Carlos Ghosn and Greg Kelly had been accused. These letters expressed surprise that Nada had led Nissan's internal inquiry and was still in a senior position.

The document illustrated the extent to which the Nissan Old Guard kept board members from Renault, the main shareholder, in the dark about what was going on in Yokohama both before and after Carlos Ghosn's arrest almost a year earlier.

Thierry Bolloré learned only on September 23 through the *Wall*

Street Journal that Nissan's general counsel, Ravinder Passi, had on September 9 expressed concern to independent directors—led by Toyoda, the former vice minister at METI—about conflicts of interest related to Hari Nada and the American law firm Latham & Watkins. Nissan had hired the firm to probe the same transactions it previously advised the company on to ensure legal compliance. One whistleblower alleged that Michael Yoshi, an associate at the Tokyo office of Latham & Watkins, had been working for Hari Nada for years.

Mr. Passi was subsequently excluded from all questions related to Carlos Ghosn on the basis of conflict of interest and replaced by Kathryn Carlile, a special advisor to the Nissan board who was a protégé of Hari Nada, and Kimio Kanai from the board's secretariat. He was later demoted and exiled to a small office in London, himself and his family being put under surveillance through private goons hired by Nissan.

At the request of Christina Murray, under pressure from audit committee chairman Motoo Nagai, the list of 80 suspects was neither made public nor shared with Renault. The American lawyer, who played a key role in Carlos Ghosn's downfall, was no longer with Nissan when the board met on September 9, a day after Nissan announced that Hiroto Saikawa was resigning as chief executive.

In an interview with the weekly *Bungei Shunju*, Greg Kelly alleged that Saikawa had received unjustified remuneration of 440,000 dollars. But there was no question of touching Hari Nada, who received 280,000 dollars under the same scheme arranged by his fellow "whistleblower" Toshiaki Ohnuma, or other beneficiaries who Nissan would rush to clear.

"Numerous and substantial elements show that the internal inquiry was perverted to the detriment of the company, its employees and its shareholders," Thierry Bolloré concluded in the October 8 document. "I request that the board launch a completely independent external audit on the conditions in which the internal inquiry was carried out and the revised report by Latham & Watkins and, more generally, any conflicts of interest of senior Nissan executives or external advisors involved in the inquiry."

The courageous initiative of Thierry Bolloré and his embarrassing questions to the Nissan Old Guard cost him his job. Upon his return to Paris from Japan with Renault chairman Jean-Dominique Senard, he learned about his demise in *Le Figaro*, a conservative French daily. The Renault board ended his term "with immediate effect" on October 11.

It turned out that Thierry Bolloré had fallen into a trap set by Senard with the complicity of Jean-Benoît Devauges, director of legal affairs at Renault who had long worked alongside Hari Nada at Nissan. The chief executive of Renault took on the Nissan Old Guard and was then fired. "The Japanese don't want to work with you anymore," one board member told Bolloré, a day after expressing his support.

Purge

Purges were the essence of the Moscow show trials in the 1930s. At Nissan, almost nine decades later, executives deemed to be too close to Carlos Ghosn were quickly let go. In the rush to arrest the chairman of the Alliance, dozens of non-Japanese executives were targeted. A handful of Japanese executives were later earmarked for different reasons.

"The first thing Saikawa did after my arrest was to fire José Muñoz, one of the most promising executives," Carlos Ghosn recalled. "He'd come from Toyota and was hired in Europe, spending his career with Nissan ever since. He could have become chief executive of Nissan, working alongside an Alliance chairman. Then we saw the departure of Daniele Schillaci, also coming from Toyota, who was the member of the executive committee in charge of sales and marketing. He also had great potential.

"Two executive committee members, that's a lot. Christian Meunier, who was in charge of the Infiniti brand, then left for Jeep. The list was long."

Daniele Schillaci, who had worked for Renault, Alfa Romeo and Toyota, returned to his native Italy where he was hired as chief executive at Brembo, a world leader in automotive braking systems based in Bergamo. As for José Muñoz, he was quickly snapped up by Hyundai as number two of the South Korean automaker's global operations. He was also put in charge of the crucial North American market.

"If you want my advice, José, you'd do best to leave Japan as soon as possible," said an American friend after Carlos Ghosn's arrest on November 19, 2018.

"I stayed in Tokyo for a few days because I had meetings," said Muñoz.

"Between meetings on November 20, I left the building to go for a walk along the waterfront of Yokohama port. I didn't want to take the risk of being overheard talking to my attorney in America. His advice was the same—leave Japan as soon as possible. On November 26, I used an Alliance board meeting in Amsterdam as an excuse and I left. But instead of using one of the company's private jets, which I was authorized to do, I asked my assistant to book me a seat on a KLM flight. In Amsterdam, Saikawa switched the time of the meeting without telling me. By excluding me, the message was clear.

"Retrospectively, what was interesting was that Nissan had been putting pressure on me to give up my U.S. laptop, which had a special security system managed from outside the company like Carlos Ghosn had," recalled Muñoz. "They insisted I use a Toshiba like other executives.

"I left Amsterdam for America with my return to Japan planned for December. But we had to prepare an announcement with Waymo, the Google affiliate working on self-driving cars, and I sent a message to Saikawa telling him that I had to meet with the head of Waymo in Silicon Valley. He agreed. After that, I took part in all management meetings online from the Alliance research center in Sunnyvale.

"At the end of December," said Muñoz, "I'd just boarded a Nissan jet for Europe when I received an email from Christina Murray asking me to return to Japan immediately. She said there was nothing to worry about. It would be just a few days working with internal auditors and maybe the prosecutors. My attorney advised me to find an excuse not to go. When I arrived in Paris, I noticed they were inquiring about my presence in France, thinking I was conspiring with Renault, which I wasn't. From the Nissan office in Paris, I took part in a board meeting of Dongfeng, whose operations in China were overseen by me. Then I went to Madrid for the Christmas holidays.

"I got back to Nashville on January 2. And someone strongly advised me to refuse any meetings with the human resources people. 'They'll jump on the first chance to get rid of you,' I was told. I later learned that to avoid firing me, Marlin Chapman—who had been at Nissan for thirty years and headed the unit in charge of my contract—quit a week before he was due to retire. The job fell to Mark Stout, another American who was in charge of human resources outside of Japan. He told me I'd be put on paid leave, but that I had to return all my electronic equipment to him. He came to my house with a security guard to seize my iPad and other equipment."

Offer Made to José Muñoz

José Muñoz said Stout "put a document under my eyes, which I still have, in which Nissan offered me the 12.8 million dollars I was due as long as I went to Japan to cooperate with the prosecutors for eighteen months without working. They took my personal phone with all my contacts and insisted on handing me over a new one. I refused, luckily, as I found out later that the phones could be used remotely to locate where you are and eavesdrop on communications.

"My attorney told Nissan that all negotiations had to take place in America or Europe—and especially not Japan. And do you know who was leading the negotiations for Nissan? It was Kathryn Carlile, the British lawyer close to Hari Nada. All they wanted was for me to go back to Japan.

"On January 11, they leaked that I had gone on personal leave and that an inquiry had been launched. I decided that was it and I resigned. After 15 years with the company, I left with nothing," said Muñoz. But there was something—a strong desire for revenge. Hired by Hyundai, the primary aim of José Muñoz became overtaking Nissan in the North American market, the market crucial for Asian automakers that he knew so well. By the spring of 2021, he had reached that target, for Hyundai alone, without counting its Kia affiliate.

CHAPTER FIVE

Capitulation

When British Prime Minister Neville Chamberlain returned from a meeting with Adolf Hitler in Munich in 1938, Winston Churchill reportedly stated: "You were given the choice between war and dishonor. You chose dishonor and you will have war." Meeting with the German Chancellor alongside French head of government Édouard Daladier, Chamberlain had yielded to Hitler's demands in an agreement that ceded German-speaking Sudetenland from Czechoslovakia to Germany. Czechoslovakia, which considered the agreement as a betrayal by Britain and France, ultimately capitulated.

Such was the appeasement adopted by French authorities eight decades later in reacting to the act of war perpetrated by the Nissan Old Guard, the company's acolytes at the Tokyo Public Prosecutors' Office, and certain Japanese political supporters.

"We were briefly dumbfounded and then had to work out how to react," recalled a French diplomat. On Tuesday, November 20, 2018—a day after Carlos Ghosn's arrest—Agnès Pannier-Runacher, junior minister at the French Ministry of Economy and Finance, met Japan's Economy, Trade and Industry Minister Hiroshige Seko in Tokyo. French Finance Minister Bruno Le Maire himself later spoke by phone with his Japanese counterpart. A brief statement noted, "the importance of French and Japanese government support to the Renault-Nissan Alliance, the top automobile manufacturer in the world and one of the largest symbols of Franco-Japanese industrial cooperation, and their shared wish to maintain this successful cooperation."

With the statement noting the French priority "to avoid a Franco-Japanese dispute," low-level diplomatic work began. It would last for months. The statement reaffirmed the "presumption of innocence" of

Carlos Ghosn, without questioning how the head of the Alliance had been treated by the Japanese judicial machine. Nissan was asked for evidence supporting the accusations against him, but it was either not released or trickled out much later. Concern was expressed about the running of Renault, since its chairman and chief executive was now "prevented" from doing his job. As for Nissan, the rights of Renault as its leading shareholder would be systematically trampled on in the weeks and months ahead.

Re-Japanizing Nissan

Appeasement was out of the question for the Nissan Old Guard. In fact, quite the contrary was true, as Takaki Nakanishi told the Foreign Correspondents' Club of Japan on November 29. Nakanishi, the dean of auto industry analysts in Japan, had no doubt about what was going on.

"The appropriate expression to describe this is 're-Japanizing' Nissan," Nakanishi said. He noted the "passion" of management around Hiroto Saikawa to regain Nissan's independence, and "their belief that they can move forward without Renault."

Saikawa's confession may have come late, but it was still a confession. A year later, he admitted that nationalist forces at Nissan had hurt the Japanese automaker. "There were people inside Nissan who held deeply rooted conservative views that the company should go back to before it faced its financial crisis in the late 1990s," the outgoing chief executive told the *Financial Times* in an interview published on November 28, 2019. Before the crisis meant before the arrival of the French, before Carlos Ghosn assumed the helm at Nissan. "These forces were unleashed when the Ghosn system fell," Saikawa said.

Nissan launched an all-out offensive in the wake of Saikawa's news conference denouncing Carlos Ghosn on the Monday evening of his arrest. On that Thursday, as Hiroshige Seko and Bruno Le Maire held ministerial talks in Paris, Nissan called a board meeting which proceeded to dismiss Carlos Ghosn with immediate effect.

The vote on November 22 was unanimous, with the two French board members representing Renault aligning themselves unreservedly with the Japanese directors. One was Jean-Baptiste Duzan, a veteran of Renault and the Alliance, notably in running the joint purchasing system for Nissan and the French automaker. He may have graduated well before Carlos Ghosn from the École Polytechnique in Paris, one of France's leading public universities, but the two were on familiar terms. The other was Bernard Rey who joined Nissan in the spring of 1999 and eventually became one of Carlos Ghosn's closest colleagues in managing Renault. Both Duzan and Rey served on the Nissan board as independent directors designated by the French automaker as leading shareholder.

"Since they were in Paris, we saw these two gentlemen to discuss things," recalled Thierry Bolloré, the deputy chief executive of Renault at the time. "Duzan didn't stop telling us that Saikawa was a good man and that he trusted him. If he'd made such accusations, there must have been something to them. We told them that we didn't understand what was going on, that we had no information from Nissan and that the only possible stance was to presume Carlos Ghosn was innocent. We also said, 'Given that we haven't seen the charge, you should in no case vote for his removal.' Duzan and Rey left our meeting telling us that they agreed. But afterwards, we learned of the unanimous vote like the rest of the world did. We called them back to ask if they hadn't understood what we'd told them. That's when they told us about an incriminating document of hundreds of pages prepared by Latham & Watkins," said Bolloré.

At Nissan headquarters in Yokahama, a video conference was presented to the board, dominated by five Japanese directors and the American law firm Latham & Watkins. The meeting started at 4:30 p.m. and lasted close to four hours. What exactly transpired during this meeting is unknown. Did Philippe Klein, the chief planning officer at Nissan, show the two French directors documents that he had previously assured the Renault senior management he did not have? Japanese media reported Duzan and Rey asked numerous questions but, in the end, they responded "okay" to Hiroto Saikawa's proposal to dismiss Carlos Ghosn effective immediately. Visibly relieved, one of the Japanese directors reportedly said that they had been "persuaded that there was no conspiracy."

"In the best case scenario," Carlos Ghosn noted, "those two were simple-minded people who didn't see the fire in the Japanese game at the best of times. In the worst-case scenario, they were traitors."

Chaos in France

And at the Renault headquarters in Billancourt? "Despite the huge shock suffered by the company, I wasn't worried about management continuity at Renault, as Mr. Ghosn had handed me the reins,"Thierry Bolloré said. "At the board level on the other hand, we very rapidly saw many who started to see which way the winds were blowing and asking how this affair would end. Despite this, we succeeded in making the presumption of innocence the corporate line for members of the board and the company. In any case, the initial contacts with the APE and the finance ministry—the minister and his cabinet chief Emmanuel Moulin—apparently went the same way."

But this is not how things turned out for several reasons. According to the dominant popular belief in France, the government is not only the sole defender of public interest, but also, by decree of quasi-divine origin, entrusted with long-term visions and strategic ambitions—not short-term considerations, tribal selfishness or the mercantile interests of economic agents. This founding dogma, uniquely French, was seriously undermined by the government's management of the crisis triggered by Carlos Ghosn's arrest.

According to Thierry Bolloré, "we quickly learned that the government's reasoning was: 'We don't like this gentleman, we don't control him and his remuneration poses a problem, as does his ability to build an impregnable alliance.' In other words, 'this crisis could serve our interests.'"

"At the same time," said Bolloré, "it coincided with the yellow vest movement which was in full swing and causing a panic that was perceptible at the top levels of government. I felt straight away that the support for Carlos Ghosn was incredibly timid. Given the yellow vests, they neither wanted nor could support him. There was also this avalanche of elements fueling daily media accounts."

The supposedly "peripheral" protest movement against President Emmanuel Macron and the "Paris elites" started on Saturday, November 17, two days before Carlos Ghosn's arrest at Haneda. In a country where occupying public areas is both a mark of identity and a national sport, the movement initially reacted to a hike in fuel prices by occupying streets and roundabouts (for which France holds the European record of more than 40,000).

These Saturday gatherings—organized through social media by protestors wearing fluorescent vests for road safety—quickly spread to city centers and descended into violence. As the Bastille fortress served as the battleground when it was stormed during the French Revolution in 1789, the Champs-Élysées in Paris became the new symbol at stake for "the people" and those in power. The violence peaked with an attack on the Arc de Triomphe and widespread pillaging in chic neighborhoods of the capital. The scenes were broadcast across the world, giving rise to soul-searching political commentary and anthropological studies.

But the movement attracted only a minority—about 260,000 people at its peak, out of a population of sixty-seven million—and the wave of protesters steadily fell to a trickle.

Weight of Ignorance

Amid such political hysteria, it would have been suicidal to defend a "plutocrat," even based on the basic principles of law. The vision of many French people is blurred by the sort of "class hatred" embodied by populist left-wing lawmaker François Ruffin, who represents the party France Insoumise ("France Undefeated") in the National Assembly.

In early December 2018, Emmanuel Moulin, the finance minister's cabinet chief, received a foreign private equity manager at the Ministry of Economy and Finance. The former investment banker knew the Renault-Nissan Alliance well—as he did Japan and the rest of Asia, where he had been based for thirty years. Organized by a mutual friend, the meeting was scheduled for thirty minutes. It lasted two hours. Moulin was a graduate of the ESSEC Business School and the École Nationale d'Administration, the elite public graduate school that serves as the top training ground for French bureaucrats. He was accompanied by Malo Carton, advisor on enterprises and government shareholdings in the same cabinet. Carton was a graduate of the Institut Polytechnique and the Paris School of Mines, the country's top graduate school for engineers.

As far as the Alliance went, these two distinguished representatives of the nomenklatura that rules France knew very little: "Samsung? In the auto sector?" Well, er, yes. During the Asian financial crisis of

1997 and 1998, Renault chairman Louis Schweitzer—who was negotiating the capital tie-up with Nissan at the time—picked up an ultra-modern plant in Busan that the South Korean electronics giant had built with help from Nissan to realize its dreams in the auto sector. Today, Renault remains the controlling shareholder of Renault Samsung Motors.

The name of Dongfeng Motor Company did not ring a bell either. Established by Nissan and China's biggest manufacturer of heavy vehicles in 2005, the joint venture had been making major contributions to the Japanese automaker's growth and earnings for 15 years. Furthermore the Chinese state-owned enterprise had opened the doors of China's auto market to Renault in 2013. Siam Motors in Thailand? "Never heard of them either." But how else could one refute the Japanese argument that the Alliance favored Renault without recognizing Nissan's growth in emerging economies, the credit for which went to Carlos Ghosn.

The private equity manager said he felt perplexed when he left the meeting at the finance ministry. How could a government with strategic ambitions be "paralyzed by the fear of doing anything that upsets the Japanese?" he asked Moulin, the finance minister's cabinet chief.

"Monsieur, our hands are tied," Emmanuel Moulin said when the private equity manager had listed all the legal reasons for pushing aside the amended Restated Alliance Master Agreement (Rama II) to reassert Renault's rights as Nissan's main shareholder. "That would be a declaration of war."

"But you're already at war," the private equity manager replied.

"From this confusion," the private equity manager said, "came a dominant line with the theme: 'In government relations with Japan, we have interests to protect'." Really? Whose interests? And how?

These interests could be seen in the sad episode of 2015 when Emmanuel Macron's initiative ended with a compromise—Rama II, which considerably weakened Renault's position as Nissan's leading shareholder. "I managed Rama II," Carlos Ghosn said, "but I didn't realize that certain Japanese were going to assassinate me." Nor did the French authorities.

Calamity of French State as Shareholder

The history of state ownership in French companies is littered with examples of endless industrial disasters and vertiginous losses covered by taxpayers ranging from the bank Crédit Lyonnais and power companies Areva and EDF to Renault before it was privatized in 1996. The government does not sit on boards to defend company interests, but instead to promote political objectives that are sometimes foreign to businesses and often harmful. And political horizons are now drawing closer as the field of vision narrows— the pressure comes not from the next election but the latest public opinion poll or the political chatter on 24-hour news channels.

A recent episode illustrating the conflicts of interests related to public shareholdings involved a company called GM&S Industry France. In May 2017, Emmanuel Macron emerged as the surprise winner in French presidential elections. In the first six months of that year, the Renault-Nissan-Mitsubishi Alliance became the world's top auto producer in terms of volume. But the media and public opinion preferred to focus instead on a socio-industrial psychodrama, a pastime in which France excels.

A series of GM&S owners had mistreated the modest auto subcontractor with 277 workers based in La Souterraine, a small town in the Nouvelle-Aquitaine region of central France. The town is located in Creuse, the poorest region in France, with the country's lowest real-estate prices. Facing court-ordered receivers, the workers went on strike, occupying the plant and threatening to, "blow it to bits"—the title of a 2019 documentary on the incident by American filmmaker Lech Kowalski which was screened at the Cannes Film Festival in 2019.

What workers did was threaten to use gas cylinders to destroy equipment at the plant. In the campaign for the presidential elections, the French political class marched through the town which came to dominate television news with the vital "David and Goliath" angle. In this case, there were two Goliaths—the automakers Renault and PSA Peugeot-Citroën, which were both partly state-owned companies. Once in office, the new Finance Minister Bruno Le Maire—from the right—spent a lot of time on the case. The solution was to squeeze the arms of the evil carmakers to artificially boost their orders. Yet GM&S was poorly managed, badly located and had only two customers as it had not diversified as Renault and PSA had long been urging. It was not viable.

Thierry Bolloré came under pressure from the new government, which went as far as asking Renault and PSA to fully finance a new "social plan" for the subcontractor. "I told Benjamin Griveaux, who was at the finance ministry at the time, that there was no way—not only because it was not allowed under the law, but also because it would set a precedent in sending a very bad signal to our suppliers."

For the senior Renault executive, such "transfers of site activities" have to be addressed as early as possible. "It's a question of listening to each other to show that one can anticipate and deal with situations to avoid any drama," he said.

A happier outcome occurred with the planned closure of a company called ACI, a producer of chassis parts for a Renault plant in Le Mans. ACI had been located for more than a century in the heart of Villeurbanne, in the greater Lyon area, and the local town hall had its eyes on several dozen hectares that were no longer suitable for industrial activities.

Renault invested eighteen million euros to develop tooling and prototyping activities at a new site in the Lyon metropolitan area with management transitioning, massive training and social support.

"The program lasted four years," Thierry Bolloré said. "We prepared and negotiated for two years in a union environment dominated by the CGT."[6] For Thierry Bolloré, the agreement with unions signed in July 2019, was the model for the auto industry to manage complex and faster-than-expected technological changes which are accelerating with the demise of diesel engines.

6. Traditionally the most militant grouping of trade unions in France, the Confédération Générale du Travail ("General Confederation of Labor") is now the country's second-largest union federation and only recently cut its ties with the French Communist Party.

Increasingly Narrow Horizon

"When they force us to fly to the rescue of GM&S, or take other measures that are not economically justified, there's no deliberate political wish to ruin Renault," Carlos Ghosn said. "But they believe we'll be able to do what's necessary to deal with the consequences of a decision they know is wrong. They say they're not responsible for corporate earnings and they're not wrong. They have a social responsibility towards the country. It's simply a contradiction for them to have shareholdings in these large companies which rely on earnings for their long-term health.

"Advocates always claim that the government has a long-term vision. That's sweet talk. Let's take a look at the companies in which the government has played a role over the past thirty years. In France, we have to deal with ideologues—people with big principles who never evaluate the results. I'm not dogmatic, I'm a pragmatist, and I noticed that the results are disastrous every time the government gets involved." Airbus is always cited as an exception to the rule. But the aircraft manufacturer is a European consortium, not a French company, and it has not been emulated.

"On the Renault board, the APE representatives behaved like simple spokesmen," Carlos Ghosn said. "It was impossible to imagine they made any decisions themselves. They often requested breaks in meetings to make phone calls. When they made comments or voted they were on remote control. Their contributions to the workings of the board were generally quite minimal. For important decisions that had to be discussed, they were informed in advance and arrived with instructions."

The extent of intervention by officials depended on who was president. "Under Jacques Chirac, there was a certain neutrality that did not disrupt the board's work," Carlos Ghosn said. "Things got more active with Nicolas Sarkozy. But they remain civil servants."

So, the president set the course, the minister implemented the course and the representatives on the board transmitted it.

"You might think they carried a strategic vision, ideas or suggestions. There was none of this, and it's obviously saddening. I'm not taking an ideological position. It's the observations of reality under four different heads of state. One could legitimately expect government shareholders to be engaged, active and make a contribution as they claim to do. In my opinion, if they made a contribution, it was rather negative."

Renault's Failed Merger with Volvo

When it came to Renault, the French government was as recidivist as the worst repeat offender. In July 1999, the painful failure of the French automaker's proposed merger with Volvo forced Renault chairman Louis Schweitzer to look towards Asia to find a partner.

"I'll never forget that terrifying, horrible ordeal," Schweitzer confided at the time. "I consider the French government to be 95 percent responsible for the ultimate failure. They made us wait, and humiliated the people at Volvo in unimaginable ways."

As soon as Renault started looking at Nissan in Japan, the former cabinet chief of Laurent Fabius—when he was finance minister and ultimately prime minister—warned the government whose social-democratic sensitivities he shared and where he had friends. At the beginning of summer in 1998, Prime Minister Lionel Jospin had been advised, and Industry Minister Christian Pierret and Finance Minister Dominique Strauss-Kahn were duly informed. The situation seemed fine, at least at the political level.

But that was not enough. "As soon as the deal was finalized, the directors on the Renault board representing the finance ministry and the trade ministry were seized by a violent desire to intervene like they did in the Volvo episode: 'Is this really a good deal? Wouldn't it be better to do it like this or like that?' I knew that if we delayed, the deal would be dead," the former Renault chairman said.

Louis Schweitzer recalled being subjected to a "police-style interrogation" in the office of a senior finance ministry official from 8 p.m. until 10:30 p.m. one Friday evening. "But I refused to give them access to my colleagues or our bank advisers. I was respectful but didn't let them exert any influence. It was a bit tense, but ended amicably as I was politically covered. I called for help from the political powers that be to order them to back off and vote to approve the deal."

Two decades later, in January 2019, the Renault headquarters near Paris was awaiting the return of the company's chairman, who had been in prison in Tokyo since November 19. In Carlos Ghosn's office, not a paper clip had moved. The company had been operating on an interim basis, with independent director Philippe Lagayette presiding over board meetings held in an atmosphere of deep crisis. Once a senior finance ministry official, Lagayette had served as cabinet chief to Finance Minister Jacques Delors during a period of austerity in the early 1980s before Delors became president of the European Commission. He was typical of the French government nomenklatura, where age and financial appetite push people who retire to reinvent themselves by consulting for companies or sitting on their boards.

At the operating level, Renault was being managed, decisions were being taken and objectives met with Thierry Bolloré designated as joint chief executive.

"To manage the crisis, I quickly surrounded myself with a SWAT team, which notably included the small investment bank of Ardea, former Goldman Sachs bankers who'd worked a lot with Mr. Ghosn," Thierry Bolloré recalled. "We had to anticipate a possible attack against the company itself. We were equally well supported by bankers from Société Générale and Claudine Pons, who specialized in crisis management . . . and our lawyers too, of course."

Nissan's Blackmailers

The Nissan Old Guard adopted a blackmail strategy—no information, no communication and no cooperation, as long as Carlos Ghosn remained as chairman and chief executive at Renault. Such internal pressure within the Alliance was reinforced externally by streams of leaks fueling a smear campaign against the prisoner back in Tokyo. On the sidelines of meetings in Billancourt, Yasuhiro Yamauchi—the Nissan representative on Renault's board—reproached Thierry Bolloré over the French automaker's support for Carlos Ghosn.

Not wanting to make a decision themselves, Renault board members decided in January 2019 that Carlos Ghosn had to be approached as he was now in indefinite detention. "The guideline," Claudine Pons recalled, "was that we had to make Carlos Ghosn understand—without appearing to let him go—that it was in the company's interest that he give up the chairmanship." When the question was raised about who would go, nobody volunteered except Thierry Bolloré, but that was impossible as far as the Japanese were concerned."

It was Claudine Pons herself who went to Tokyo in her capacity as an external consultant. "I went with everyone's blessing and even carried some personal messages for Carlos Ghosn—one from a board member and another from a senior executive. But I went to Tokyo without an official mandate and came back without any instructions."

Carlos Ghosn did not "resign" from Renault, as reported, but exercised his option to retire as chairman, with the French government noting that he had been "prevented" from carrying out his duties. On January 21, a board meeting chaired by Jean-Dominique Senard unanimously accepted the decision and Thierry Bolloré became chief executive.

Back in Yokohama, the Nissan Old Guard was triumphant. "We welcome these management changes at Renault," said Hiroto Saikawa. "Over the past 20 years, each company has respected the other's identity and autonomy, and by combining our strengths we have created synergies and achieved profitable growth. These mutually beneficial activities will not change in any way. In fact, we believe they need to be accelerated. We are very pleased to be able to open a new chapter in our historic partnership."

French Finance Ministry in Driver's Seat

During the period between Carlos Ghosn's arrest and his departure as chairman of Renault, the French automaker became a puppet of the Ministry of the Economy and Finance. It was not a return to its fully government-owned status as Régie National des Usines Renault ("Renault Factories National State-Owned Company"), which was how the company founded by two brothers in 1898 was known for half a century after it was nationalized in 1945. In a way, it was worse.

The minister himself dictated the financial conditions of Carlos Ghosn's retirement to "independent" members of the Renault board. "As shareholder of reference, I can tell you that we shall be extremely

vigilant about the departure conditions set by the board of directors," Bruno Le Maire reportedly said.

The ministry had already done its groundwork. Less than two
weeks before his decision to retire was accepted by the Renault
board, the daily newspaper *Libération* reported that Carlos Ghosn
had not been a resident of France for tax purposes since 2012.
Instead, he paid income taxes in the Netherlands, where Renault-
Nissan B.V. was based. Initially set up by Louis Schweitzer, the
former Renault chairman, Carlos Ghosn had transformed the
Dutch company into a pillar of the Alliance. To its credit, *Libération*
did mention that Carlos Ghosn paid taxes on income earned in
France. But that small detail faded as the newspaper report was
picked up by other media. In character assassinations, substance is
less important than the signal conveyed. The smear campaign
launched against Carlos Ghosn by Nissan on November 19, 2018,
had now spread to France, where the Japanese automaker had hired
no fewer than three communications firms.

On November 23, four days after Carlos Ghosn's arrest, the
Audit, Risks and Ethics Committee at Renault began looking at
payments to the chairman. No irregularity was detected between
2010 and 2018.

Following what Renault explained as leaks from Nissan in Tokyo,
the committee started looking at other transactions on January 14.
It found a "gift" of fifty thousand euros linked to a Renault sponsor-
ship for the Palace of Versailles. And then on March 14, it came
across "financial flows between Renault and an importer based in
the Middle East." The company, which alerted French judicial
authorities, spoke of "possible violations of ethics rules" at Renault.

Finally, on February 4, Renault and Nissan began auditing
Renault-Nissan B.V. in Amsterdam. Notwithstanding the principle
of confidentiality, it soon transpired that the French and Japanese
automakers had given the job to French audit firm Mazars, the
biggest in Europe. Details of an interim report, which Renault did
not legally own, found their way into the French media in April. The
auditors—which would not hear from the main interested party,
Carlos Ghosn himself, until the eve of their final report in July—
had reportedly found "unjustified" expenses amounting to eleven
million euros. Most were related to the alleged private use of Nissan

corporate jets. Also leaked was the guest list to a Versailles reception commemorating the 15th anniversary of the Alliance. This was reported as a party to celebrate Carlos Ghosn's 60th birthday on March 9, 2015. The leaks were by design. Although it contained nothing of a personal nature, the speech at the event was not made available to the media.

One employee of the Dutch venture was surprised to be asked by auditors about a residence of Carlos Ghosn in a country where he used to work. It had nothing to do with the scope of the inquiry. He protested, the auditors backed off—and never sent him the minutes of their conversation.

One witness noted "harassment" by the auditors and said board member Philippe Lagayette was becoming irritated at the lack of progress to implicate Mouna Sepehri, the executive vice president who ran the Office of the CEO. She developed an argument based on the amended version of the Restated Alliance Master Agreement to mount a vigorous counter-offensive defending Renault's rights as shareholder. In his zeal, Lagayette went as far as suggesting a reduction below 40 percent of Renault's stake in Nissan to appease the Japanese. This was seconded by Pierre Fleuriot, another eminent member of France's financial elite who had previously served as a senior finance ministry official, secretary general of the country's stock market watchdog and chief executive of Credit Suisse France. He later assumed Lagayette's mantle as lead independent director and joined the Nissan board as well in January 2020.

The Diplomat

To toe the line in capitulating to Nissan, the French government logically chose a diplomat. That was how Jean-Dominique Senard liked to be seen, although it was actually his father Jacques Senard who pursued a diplomatic career culminating in a brief period as France's ambassador to Italy. Like Carlos Ghosn and Thierry Bolloré, the younger Senard came from Michelin, one of the world's largest tiremakers. Before that, he worked in finance for French industrial giants such as Total, Saint-Gobain and Pechiney. In 2005, Michelin's managing partner Édouard Michelin hired Jean-Dominique Senard as chief financial officer. The newcomer quickly attracted the critical eye of the Commandeur—Édouard's father François Michelin, who had recently retired as co-chairman. The elder Michelin did not believe the desire to please at any cost was a quality for a business leader. But Édouard's tragic death at forty-two in May 2006 would be a game changer.

Édouard Michelin was unexpectedly succeeded by Michel Rollier. He came from the other family associated with the company, but who had long lived under the shadow of Michelin. Rollier's father, François, was a cousin of "Monsieur François," who headed the tire company for forty-seven years. Michel Rollier assumed the chairmanship of Michelin five years later, leaving management to Jean-Dominique Senard, who became the first managing partner not related to the family which founded the company in Clermont-Ferrand in central France in 1889.

The Anti-Ghosn

Jean-Dominique Senard could not have been more different from Carlos Ghosn. He was from an aristocratic family (his mother was descended from a lord in Saint-Rémy-de-Provence in southern France) and grew up in a fancy neighborhood near Paris. Carlos Ghosn was born in the Brazilian town of Porto Velho in the Upper Amazon region and was schooled in Beirut. Jean-Dominique Senard was heir to a fortune, whereas the young engineer from Lebanon owed his meteoric rise at Michelin to merit. Jean-Dominique Senard was perceived as "emotional" and "egocentric" compared with the man he replaced as Renault chairman, who was seen as "rational and pragmatic."

At Michelin, Jean-Dominique Senard continued the modernization and restructuring started by Édouard and continued by Michel Rollier, inevitable after a half-century long reign of François Michelin. Jean-Dominique Senard may have shown courage, but he lacked imagination and ambition. The company's foray into the Indian market remained a drag, and he failed to expand its presence in China which had been started by François Michelin. Adjusting the industrial base in France was too little, too late.

"He doesn't understand what nemawashi means," said a Renault board member, referring to the Japanese concept or process of laying the groundwork for achieving a "consensus" that Jean-Dominique Senard would adopt in his relations with the Nissan Old Guard. In Japanese companies, *nemawashi* ("compromise") is often the way in which one person's will is imposed on the rest. Otherwise, it is often a recipe for conservatism or immobility.

At a news conference in Yokohama on March 12, 2019, the Renault chairman joined his chief executive Thierry Bolloré, Nissan counterpart Hiroto Saikawa and Mitsubishi Motors chief executive Osamu Masuko to announce plans for a "new start" for the Alliance. This included establishing an "Alliance Board" with Jean-Dominique Senard as chair, and the three chief executives as the other members. Hiroto Saikawa said the new arrangement would have "absolute respect for our cultures and brands" and "represent a true partnership between equals." He said operating decisions taken by the Alliance board would be "consensus-based" with a "win-win" approach. "Doing something or not doing something means that each party has to agree," the Nissan chief said. "Over the past three years, we have been too focused on convergence at the expense of projects."

Carlos Ghosn had relaunched the convergence strategy for the Alliance in 2012 to generate synergies in the four key areas of engineering, manufacturing and supply chain management, purchasing and human resources. But now, the "new start" for the Alliance was accompanied by Renault's capitulation as the main Nissan shareholder. "Mr. Senard is ready to respect Nissan's new governance," Hiroto Saikawa said.

The Japanese automaker's new governance evoked a return to the golden age of "administrative guidance" by the Ministry of Economy, Trade and Industry where the interests of leading shareholders were often ignored. Jean-Dominique Senard accepted the vice chairmanship with undefined responsibilities. After some hesitation, the Nissan chairmanship went to Yasushi Kimura, the former boss of JXTG Nippon Oil and Energy Corporation, a second-tier player in the global oil and gas industry. He was also a vice chairman at the Japan Business Federation, the country's main business group. Ranking third in Nissan's new hierarchy behind Jean-Dominique Senard, was Masakazu Toyoda, the former METI vice minister who was the company's lead "independent" director. This leading architect of Carlos Ghosn's downfall had a big say in nominations.

The icing on the cake was Bernard Delmas as lead outside director. If personal—almost visceral—hostility towards Carlos Ghosn was the criterion for selection, Jean-Dominique Senard could not have found a better candidate in the former local Michelin representative who had long chaired the French Chamber of Commerce and Industry in Japan.

In Paris, and especially at the Ministry of Economy and Finance, the word was out—it was time to turn the page on Carlos Ghosn. The deteriorating commercial and financial performance of the three Alliance partners would take care of that.

The exchanges between Yokohama and Billancourt to repair the performance and prepare for the future gave rise to some curious decisions. According to Thierry Bolloré, "the government suggested Nissan engage French bank Rothschild & Co as advisor, which was surprising, given the former links between this bank and the President of the Republic." A senior civil servant, Emmanuel Macron had indeed acquired some investment banking experience with Rothschild before rejoining the political fray to win the Presidency in 2017. Moreover, Rothschild managing partner Grégoire Heuzé had actively taken part in the failed primary campaign of Finance Minister Bruno Le Maire to become the candidate for the right in the French presidential elections of 2017.

From Resistance to Appeasement

Despite the appearance of being united, the French camp was deeply divided during this period. On one side were those who supported appeasement, who were guided by the government and fears that the Alliance would implode. On the other side, were those who advocated resistance and wished for Renault's rights at Nissan to be respected. They wanted to clean up Yokohama and resume work on consolidating the Alliance.

The first group wanted to navigate by the stars, while the second had a plan based on the idea of a holding company, which is what Carlos Ghosn had favored. The plan was developed under the leadership of Thierry Bolloré as Renault chief executive with a small team led by Christopher Cole at London-based investment bank Ardea working with the French automaker's lawyers. In Japan,

Renault was advised by investment bank SMBC Nikko Securities, whose executive deputy president Noriyoshi Suzuki had been introduced to Thierry Bolloré by Claudine Pons, the external consultant for Renault who traveled to Tokyo to persuade Carlos Ghosn to retire. A detailed study resulted in a proposed capital tie-up that was almost perfectly balanced. In exchanges with the Japanese, it was referred to as the Goju-Goju ("Fifty-Fifty") Plan.

"We worked with our lawyers and letters were sent to Saikawa in November and December to protect Renault's interests and ask for explanations, which were never forthcoming," Thierry Bolloré said. "The Nissan management around Saikawa failed at two levels, by placing Nissan in difficulty and by being unable to deal with possible accounting issues without causing a tragedy. The entire team had to go.

"The question was how to do it without being trapped by the provisions of Rama II. There were two possibilities—holding an extraordinary general meeting, which I requested but could not impose under Rama, or waiting for the annual ordinary meeting of shareholders after the financial results were published. The results would not be good, possibly even disastrous, and replacing management would be perfectly legitimate. Our advisors said we could do this with 50 percent of the votes at a general meeting, and I called Dieter Zetsche, the boss of Daimler, to get involved."

It was easy to forget that the Mercedes manufacturer was a discreet partner in the Alliance. Under a strategic partnership agreement signed in 2010, the Stuttgart-based automaker acquired 3.1 percent of Renault and 3.1 percent of Nissan, which each acquired 1.5 percent of Daimler. Since November 19, 2018, Saikawa and his men had treated the minority, but prestigious, German shareholder with the same contempt, lack of disclosure and refusal to clarify as it did with its French shareholder. It would not have taken much for Renault and Daimler to muster up enough votes to get their way at the general meeting.

"The idea was to have a full new board of directors and an executive committee in the room ready to get to work," Thierry Bolloré said. "We were going to affirm our disagreement with the current management and get the shareholders to vote for a new board and designate a new executive committee. It wasn't without risk, but it was legal. I presented the option to the Renault board on two occasions—in January 2019 and then again after the arrival of Senard."

Japanese Political Diversity

But those who wanted to appease Nissan saw things differently. "Senard saw himself as the diplomat who was going to make allies out of the people whose recent behavior recalled Pearl Harbor," Bolloré said. "I supported a stronger approach because the Alliance could not advance, as Carlos Ghosn wanted, with people who were so deeply hostile to that very idea. But the board did not want to hear anything about such advice as it was singularly lacking in determination with Lagayette as with Senard. The approach was deemed to be too aggressive and impossible for the Japanese. I discussed this with the APE and the minister, who was fretting about a possible negative reaction from the Japanese government to which I replied: 'The Japanese government is not homogenous.'

"Even among Japanese politicians classified as nationalists, some were attracted by the Goju-Goju Plan, a holding company with a single board and one management," said Bolloré. "Exchanges of documents and emails attest to this. We were dealing with people directly linked to Shinzo Abe who were always loyal and remained committed to what they had to do including changing the head of MITI." In September 2019, Economy, Trade and Industry Minister Hiroshige Seko—in power at the time of the coup d'état against Carlos Ghosn—was replaced by Isshu Sugawara for no apparent reason.

At the end of September, Nissan announced the resignation of Hiroto Saikawa as chief executive, which offered an opportunity for Renault to reshuffle the cards.

"At the beginning of October, we had a long working meeting with SMBC Nikko including Suzuki-san, who had just retired and set up his own consulting firm," Bolloré said "He was a childhood friend of Abe. He was also a close friend of Isao Iijima, special advisor to the prime minister who was involved with the work. Their message was unambiguous: 'You have to move and hit hard.' At the end of the meeting, Suzuki told me: 'The prime minister wishes to invite you to dinner with Mr. Senard as soon as Ashwani Gupta is appointed to head Nissan. And Mr. Abe would also like to play a round of golf with you'."

With chief performance officer José Muñoz gone, Ashwani Gupta was, without a doubt, the best candidate for the job of getting Nissan out of the rut where Saikawa had led the company. Carlos Ghosn had appointed him to address problems at Mitsubishi Motors.

"The Nissan board meeting on October 8, 2019, was the occasion to clear things up at the Japanese automaker, starting with the publication of the list of employees compromised by Christina Murray's inquiry," Thierry Bolloré said. "An extraordinary meeting of the board in late October would then shortlist the candidates and allow Ashwani Gupta to be appointed as chief executive. I reached an agreement with Ashwani on the team of ten executives we would need in order to replace those who were being let go. As part of the process, we were going to put the holding company for the Alliance into place. But Jean-Dominique Senard put an end to all that."

Senard, the diplomat, had other plans. "At a meeting of the nomination committee ahead of the board meeting, a triumvirate was decided on by the people who, I understand, still pull the strings at Nissan today," Thierry Bolloré said. "Gupta was to serve as deputy to Makoto Uchida, who was named chief executive officer, and be flanked by Jun Seki as vice chief operating officer. As he was leaving the room, Senard triumphantly told me: 'I won.' What he'd won was my departure, after a compromise which turned Ashwani into a guarantor for a balance of power that hadn't changed. It's now clear that Senard was playing a double game, appearing to accept the strategy that involved creating a holding company, but sabotaging its implementation in agreement with its fiercest opponents. The price of this betrayal was my departure. It's obvious that I was targeted for supporting the continuation of Carlos Ghosn's strategy."

In Paris, the daggers had been drawn. Taking part in the crucial Nissan board meeting, which could have changed the course of events, was Thierry Bolloré's final act as chief executive of Renault.

Low-Intensity Democracy

The end of this story has not yet been written. It is too early to fully assess the impact of the appeasement of Nissan for the Alliance and Renault. The same goes for Nissan. One thing is clear—the "diplomacy" of Jean-Dominique Senard, who confronted Nissan with a fait accompli of a merger "between equals" of Renault and Fiat-Chrysler Automobiles. Nissan's de facto veto delivered John Elkann, the Agnelli family member who served as the Fiat-Chrysler chairman, into the arms of Carlos Tavares, the chairman and chief executive of PSA Peugeot-Citroën. Elkann in any case would have the chance to feel the weight of the French government on the operations of Renault—enough to scare anyone into running away.

"What was striking in this affair," said Thierry Bolloré, "was how other shareholders were silent and how independent directors were passive. People were paralyzed because they knew who decides things in France, that you can't oppose the state or its leader who decides everything. Speech is not free and it's in this sense that this affair goes well beyond Renault and the Alliance."

The private equity manager, who visited the French finance minister's cabinet chief Emmanuel Moulin in December 2018, liked to dream.

"In a democratic country, such state meddling would lead to a collapse of government, or at least cause difficulties," he said. If democracy in Japan leaves much to be desired, democracy in France is low intensity with its presidential monarchy and a legislative branch that is little more than a rubber-stamp parliament. When the fate of one of France's biggest industrial groups and 50,000 French workers was called into question, lawmakers from the National Assembly and the Senate were preoccupied with a minor scandal involving Alexandre Benalla, a former bodyguard for President Emmanuel Macron. As for the political-judicial success in "re-Japanizing" Nissan, the lawmakers did not even bother to summon the finance minister to a hearing.

CHAPTER SIX

Two Visions of the Alliance

On March 27, 2001, the Alliance was two years old. To celebrate the anniversary, the Renault Foundation organized a cultural conference in Tokyo. It focused not only on the corporate cultures of Renault and Nissan, but also on national cultures of the two countries involved in an unprecedented industrial adventure. Renault chairman Louis Schweitzer was keen to finance a Franco-Japanese version of the Erasmus program of the European Union that allowed thousands of students to spend a year at a university in another E.U. country. Created by Jacques Delors, president of the European Commission between 1985 and 1995, Erasmus is often cited as one of the best examples of European cooperation.

In a speech, the Renault chairman said the Alliance was "not a merger or acquisition, but the creation of a binational Franco-Japanese group with a common strategy of profitable growth with mutual respect for the corporate cultures and national identities of our two groups." He recalled the ties between France and Japan going back to the Meiji era including industrial cooperation. He noted that Louis Renault, the founder of the French automaker, set up a subsidiary in Japan in 1908. Schweitzer also cited prophetic remarks by diplomat and dramatist Paul Claudel who, as French ambassador to Japan, expressed his wish for an "alliance between Renault and a Japanese company" in 1926. He also recalled how, between 1953 and 1957, the French automaker collaborated with Hino—now part of the Toyota empire—to allow the Japanese heavy vehicle manufacturer to assemble 50,000 units of the Renault 4CV car and other passenger vehicles.

"To successfully create a binational group, we must achieve a true cultural alliance," the Renault chairman said. It was not a question of making Nissan more French or Renault more Japanese, but of creating a "common platform of understanding and respect for our French and Japanese values. To be deployed forcefully in the long term while maintaining our roots, our project must be based on the increasingly closer bonds we weave between our two companies and countries." For the former senior government official— who would years later return to the public sector after a long period at Renault—the industrial partnership was also political. The objective was a Franco-Japanese group, admittedly a little more French than Japanese, that embraced globalization like other multinational automakers such as Volkswagen and Toyota but also somewhat different.

Schweitzer and Ghosn

"There were two concepts for the Alliance," recalled Carlos Ghosn. "One, which we could call Schweitzerian, was for an Alliance dominated by Renault with the French government as guarantor of French national interests."

Louis Schweitzer never changed his view on this point. In an exchange in 2017, when he was serving as commissioner general at the General Secretariat for Investment under the French prime minister, he said: "If the French government withdrew its equity in Renault, the Japanese would have quickly taken control of the Alliance." He had made the same remarks in an interview in Tokyo on October 31, 2002: "How can Renault remain French if the government withdraws? It's something to think about ... The discussion in France and elsewhere is not so much about a third party taking control but about the balance being reversed." But with Renault raising its stake in Nissan from 36.8 percent to 44.4 percent in February 2002 (later reduced to 43.4 percent), "the idea of reversing the balance seems almost impossible," he said.

"I was opposed to this vision," said Carlos Ghosn. "It couldn't work in the real world. It was a guarantee for disaster, ensuring the Alliance could not survive. In my opinion, the only way of moving forward was to be global with French and Japanese influences, of course, but with each in their place—no power relations, no domination of one by the other or over others. That's how I ran the Alliance during the first six years. Despite differences in cross-shareholdings, there was never any grief or bitterness. I didn't let Renault interfere in the running of Nissan, nor vice versa. The companies retained their autonomy. Performance was the barometer.

"First and foremost, the Alliance was there to facilitate synergies within the group but it was neutral—neither French, nor Japanese. That allowed different segments to develop—not only for a French company like Renault or Japanese companies such as Nissan or Mitsubishi, but also for a Russian company like AvtoVAZ or a Chinese one like Dongfeng. It was a win-win situation. There would be no conflicts if we maintained this line. By its very nature, French domination would have turned the Japanese into second-class citizens, which would have been hard to accept even when they were in difficulty and impossible when they started to generate the most earnings. It was as simple as that.

"The French government tended to crow and wave the flag to take advantage of it in the eyes of French public opinion," Carlos Ghosn said.

In fact, "that's exactly what we did," admitted French Treasury director Jean Lemierre in 1999.

Carlos Ghosn said: "I told them: 'You're going to kill the Alliance if you behave like that. The Japanese will never accept a situation that leads them to believe they're ceding part of their sovereignty to France. Never.'

"The idea of the Alliance was very simple—strong national entities that retained their national characteristics and even pride. The Alliance was there to encourage coordination between segments and synergies to strengthen each side. It oversaw a global whole whose parts preserved cultural heritage, history and strong national ties. Louis Schweitzer did not share this vision for the Alliance and the French government even less so—hence me being criticized more or less openly for not defending French interests. That was wrong because I was convinced the Alliance would hit a wall if that vision was not respected."

Gamble of 1999

The conditions under which the Alliance was born in March 1999, are fairly well known (and covered in detail in *Shift*). In November 1998, the announcement by Daimler and Chrysler of a "merger between equals" shook the global auto industry. A decade after the fall of the Berlin Wall, globalization had become unavoidable. The race for critical mass was a categorical imperative (at the time, the threshold for survival was set at producing four million vehicles a year).

Speaking four months after the Alliance was launched, Renault chairman Louis Schweitzer said: "The Daimler-Chrysler affair helped because two factors had to be brought together for all of Renault's management to agree to the project. The first was that there was no question of doing nothing. Success with Nissan would ensure the future of Renault. If not, we would end up as a subsidiary of Daimler-Chrysler. The second was that if we did nothing, the French government would one day sell its equity in Renault which would become a subsidiary of Daimler-Chrysler."

The irony was that the German-American auto giant's withdrawal from the competition to help save Nissan would leave the door open for Renault, which was "smaller, poorer but *nicer*," Schweitzer said. "Becoming part of Ford or Daimler-Chrysler "would have been much less humiliating than being saved by Renault. On the other hand, the French automaker could say to Nissan 'we can offer you a future other than being a regional colony of Daimler-Chrysler.' But there were completely false analyses in the press saying that we'd be softer than Daimler. In fact, we had less cash so we'd be more rigorous in the revival plan," the Renault chairman said.

Equity markets also played a role in bringing Renault and Nissan together after Japan's speculative bubble economy burst at the end of the 1980s which plunged the country into the "lost decade" of the 1990s. "The market value of Nissan was below that of Renault between March 1998, and March 1999," Schweitzer said. "We had only a year to make an offer to Nissan, not one month more."

And then there was the human factor. "A lot of people at Renault were heartbroken by the failure with Volvo and wanted something new and exciting. Making money is fine, but a great project is something else. Nissan was obviously a great project," Louis Schweitzer said. Above all, was the individual factor. "To put things simply, I wouldn't have done it if I didn't have Carlos Ghosn," the Renault chairman said. The previous September, Louis Schweitzer told Carlos Ghosn that he would "find a pretext to cancel the whole deal" if he did not go to Japan. "Our analysis was that Nissan suffered from management problems. The company was basically healthy, but had been very poorly managed. But you can't turn a business around from the outside. We therefore needed an extraordinary manager, someone who could train the people at Nissan. Through a headhunter, we had miraculously come across a first-class candidate." When Renault hired him in 1996, Carlos Ghosn was a senior executive at French tiremaker Michelin.

At the outset, little separated Renault and Nissan in terms of production volumes and revenues. But as far as earnings went, the French automaker was in the black and the Japanese company was close to bankruptcy. Yet Nissan had a presence in the North American market, the world's most profitable, and benefited from advances the Japanese auto industry had made in manufacturing, quality control and robotics. In the European market, Renault was known for its flair for new concepts like its minivans of various sizes.

Nissan had world-class gasoline engines but had long been overshadowed by Toyota. It had too many models, too many platforms, too many engines, too many suppliers and too many dealers. Among forty-two models the number two Japanese automaker offered customers in 1999, as many as thirty-nine were losing money. Nissan's market share in Japan had been falling for twenty-six consecutive years and it had been in the red for eleven out of the past twelve fiscal years. It was being crushed by debts amounting to more than two trillion yen, about 18 billion dollars at the time.

Two Mules Don't Make a Horse

General skepticism greeted the unveiling of the Alliance in Tokyo on March 27, 1999. According to *Business Week*, Renault would need at least ten years to see a return on its investment. The French media did not seem to be particularly interested. The almost unanimous consensus, Carlos Ghosn later recalled, was that "two mules don't make a horse." Bob Lutz, the loud-mouthed vice chairman of General Motors, said Renault would have done better to put the five billion euros invested in Nissan into a container and let it sink in the Atlantic.

So, it was with some surprise in 2001 when *Time* magazine nominated Carlos Ghosn as the world's best chief executive after *Automotive News,* the Detroit-based automobile industry weekly, named him business leader of the year. Bob Lutz had to eat humble pie, admitting that his prediction had not taken Carlos Ghosn into account. What was the impact of the spectacular success of the Nissan Revival Plan?

Beyond the personality cult around Carlos Ghosn—fueled by the same media that later took part in assassinating him—the Japanese were interested in what lessons the government and companies could draw from Nissan's unexpectedly rapid recovery. Dozens of management books were published to decipher the unique experience. The Japanese also took note of certain business practices Carlos Ghosn had pioneered, such as the unwinding of the *keiretsu* system of cross-shareholdings in companies of little strategic significance, that weighed Nissan down instead of protecting it.

"When I arrived in Japan in 1999, the trend was more towards opening to the world," Carlos Ghosn recalled. "Prime Minister Koizumi sincerely wanted to reform the country." In a nation where politics is often a hereditary affair, Junichiro Koizumi hardly had a revolutionary profile—his grandfather and father were both lawmakers and one of his sons would become a member of parliament too. What brought him to power were grassroots members of the ruling Liberal Democratic Party (LDP) who were allowed for the first time to elect the LDP leader, a privilege previously reserved for LDP lawmakers. In running for the party presidency in 2001, his slogan was: "Change the LDP, change Japan." He even vowed "to destroy my party if my party destroys my reforms."

Despite being immensely popular, Koizumi—known as "Lionheart" for his unconventionally long hair—did not destroy the LDP and his reformist ambitions came up against the powerful vested interests of the ruling party. But with Heizo Takenaka, an academic economist who became his state minister for economic and fiscal policy, he managed to purge the banking system that had been dragging down the anemic economy since the financial and real estate bubble exploded a decade earlier.

Example for Japan

"Look at what Mr. Ghosn has done at Nissan," Koizumi said in April 2001, during his campaign for the LDP presidency, which automatically brings with it the premiership in Japan. After becoming prime minister, he invited Carlos Ghosn to join a temporary commission on structural reforms, the sole political appointment he had ever accepted.

"I distrust all generalizations," Carlos Ghosn said. "I don't think there's one France but several Frances. And there's not one Japan but several Japans."

France tends to be openly protectionist, even nationalist, as it dreams of sheltering behind walls. But numerous French people are perfectly at ease with globalization. Japan is similar—open to the outside world, but with a nationalist fringe. One difference is that France belongs to Europe which has provided a peaceful and cooperative environment for three quarters of a century. On the other hand, Japan is an archipelago located in a difficult, even hostile, region—where Japanese themselves have contributed to past hostilities.

"I don't think people fell in love with the Alliance, but they recognized a lot of its benefits," Carlos Ghosn said. "The Alliance especially had no domination of one party over another, no citizens of different categories, but was based on performance and helping each other take advantage of economies of scale. It was a rational structure; a marriage of convenience. My conception of the Alliance was very rational.

"There was no evidence of any nationalism. Globalization is rational whereas nationalism is emotional. We all have split personalities. On the one hand as nations, villages and tribes with their own ethnic groups, religions and other things. On the other hand, recognition that the marketplace was global and that nothing could be achieved without cooperation. That's all. I played the rational card, never the emotional one. There was no need to have winners and losers, first and second-class citizens. Everyone was in their own company with its own brands, but we were stronger if we worked together. It's simple. I knew that crossing the line of this rule would eventually lead to disaster. And that's what happened in the spring of 2018.

"When Saikawa paid tribute to the former Nissan management on the evening I was arrested, he was expressing a view that's quite certainly always existed in Japan without being expressed publicly: 'We don't need or no longer need these people who come from outside.' But this was the same management that had led Nissan to disaster. The message he sent was that performance didn't matter much. What counted more than everything was the sense of belonging. But if we came to Japan, it was because the situation at Nissan was so untenable that they swallowed their national pride to ask us to help. But once the mission was accomplished, the temptation was strong to go back to the good old days of isolation, which is absurd. By contrast, Toyota is trying to recruit foreign executives into the group—and not only Didier Leroy, the former Renault executive who's now number two. Withdrawing in on oneself will always go backwards. The speech by Saikawa also provided evidence of the influence exerted by some government officials which is not the sort of behavior you see in the corporate world."

Japanese Industry

In its broadest sense, performance was what constrained nationalist pressure inside Nissan, but also in business and government circles for 18 years. The company, founded by Choshu Domain descendant Yoshisuke Ayukawa, did not start making vehicles under the Datsun brand until the early 1930s. But it had roots similar to the *zaibatsu*, which dated back to feudal Japan before the Meiji Era to become huge industrial conglomerates that were ultimately broken up by the Americans after World War II.

Ayukawa brought fresh eyes to Japan's industrialization and was not reluctant to throw himself behind the emerging new auto industry. American writer David Halberstram described him as, part Henry Ford, part Alfred P. Sloan. In *The Reckoning*, his book on Japanese-U.S. rivalry in the automobile sector published in 1986, he wrote that Ayukawa had connections, talent and awareness of the possibilities offered by the time.

As a businessman and politician, Ayukawa played a role in Japan's post-war reconstruction after its defeat in 1945. Elected to the House of Councillors, the upper house of parliament under a new Constitution dictated by American occupiers, he served as supreme economic advisor to the government of Nobosuke Kishi (1957-1960), the maternal grandfather of future prime minister Shinzo Abe. The obsession of Abe, following his return to power in 2012, was to achieve what his grandfather did not—to reform the Constitution that was seen by nationalists as overly pacifist.

The destinies of Nissan and Prime Minister Kishi, who agreed to a revised U.S.-Japan security treaty in 1960, had already crossed paths in Manchukuo, the puppet state established by the Japanese army in the northeastern Chinese provinces of Manchuria in the 1930s. Kishi was at the time a young civilian administrator in charge of industrializing the territory and appointed Ayukawa to help him carry out the task. Nihon Sangyo, the name from which Nissan was derived, literally meant "Japan Industry," and the company would drive the region's industrial development through a venture known as Manchuria Heavy Industries Development Corporation. Kishi served in the cabinet of Prime Minister Hideki Tojo during World War II, and was charged by the Americans as a class-A war criminal. He was detained in the Sugamo prison in Tokyo, which would later be replaced by the Tokyo Detention House in Kosuge. As for Ayukawa, he was detained for 21 months before being released, and prohibited from public office or managerial positions until 1951.

In terms of industrial heritage and the weight of history, Nissan was largely to the Japanese what Renault was to the French. In a country which made yogurt a strategic sector when French food giant Danone faced foreign acquisition, it's not difficult to imagine what would have been the reaction to a former Japanese *zaibatsu* taking over Renault, a company which developed a reputation as a "fortress of the workers" as a fully state-owned enterprise after 1945. It seems this never crossed the minds of the French government nomenklatura.

Seeking a Better Balance

It was clear from the early days of the Alliance that control over a Japanese industrial flagship by another sovereign state as "reference shareholder" in Renault was not going to fly. That's why the initial agreement provided for Nissan to acquire equity in the French automaker.

"There was a gentlemen's agreement between Schweitzer and Hanawa," said Dominique Thormann, referring to the Renault chairman and Yoshikazu Hanawa, the chairman of Nissan at the time. Thormann was from Renault Credit International and was picked by Carlos Ghosn to join the small group that accompanied him to Japan in 1999 to help turn Nissan around. He spent the first decade of the twenty-first century doing just that, initially in Japan, then in the United States and finally in Europe before succeeding Thierry Moulonguet, a key person among the early Renault arrivals in Tokyo, as chief financial officer for the French automaker.

When Renault exercised warrants to boost its stake in Nissan to 44 percent in the spring of 2002, the Japanese acquired 15 percent of its French partner in two stages. Nissan's renaissance had been so rapid and spectacular that its share prices had jumped to about 800 yen, twice the level of 400 yen when the Alliance was announced. Investors and minority shareholders had thus pressed Renault to increase its shareholding by exercising the warrants based on the lower share price back in 1999.

But this was subject to the agreement of the French securities market watchdog. "In Paris and at the European Commission in Brussels, Nissan was considered a subsidiary of Renault," Dominique Thormann said. "The reasoning was that a shareholding of more than 40 percent gave Renault de facto control over the annual general meeting of Nissan since even in Japan it was exceptional for

80 percent of shareholders to be present or represented. The Commission des Opérations de Bourse (COB, which became the Autorité des Marchés Financiers in 2003) concluded that Nissan's acquisition of equity of Renault created a loop of self-control between a parent company and its subsidiary."

The upshot was that Renault shares held by Nissan would not have voting rights. "The COB ruling was late in being communicated to Nissan and the news didn't go down well in Tokyo," Dominique Thormann said. Nor did it go down well with institutional investors or financial analysts who could not understand how Nissan could justify its money being immobilized and not having any influence on Renault in exchange for its investment. "They criticized our contradictory attitude. On the one hand, we were proceeding to dismantle the *keiretsu* system in Japan by selling off hundreds of sterile cross-shareholdings which pleased them. On the other, we had just taken on one with Renault, which they didn't like. But the agreement of 1999 had to be respected and Nissan's recovery welcomed."

How to Get Rid of the French State

The other gentlemen's agreement, aimed at facilitating the formation of the Alliance, provided for the French government to reduce its shareholding in Renault. When the Alliance was announced in 1999, the government held 44.4 percent in what used to be a wholly state-owned enterprise. France nationalized the privately-owned Usines Renault in 1945, officially to punish founder Louis Renault for collaborating with the Nazis during the German occupation of France. The status of Régie Nationale des Usines Renault was changed to a public limited company in 1990, with Swedish automaker Volvo later acquiring a shareholding of 20 percent.

In 1994, the government of Prime Minister Édouard Balladur launched a vast program to "denationalize" French companies including financial institutions that had become state-owned following Liberation in 1945 and the Socialist Party's victory in presidential elections in May 1981. Balladur opposed the full privatization of Renault, but the government's stake was nevertheless reduced from 79.2 percent to 51 percent.

A commentary in the *Wall Street Journal*[7] at the time noted that "the fortress of workers has become the paradise of shareholders" with 70 percent of Renault's 75,000 employees subscribing to shares offered at preferential rates. A protest against the privatization was organized by the French Communist Party and the CGT, the party's trade union affiliate that was the main force for workers at Renault headquarters in Billancort. But only a few hundred workers took part in the protest at Place Nationale, a traditional site for displays of the revolutionary struggle of French workers.

In 1995, the government finally reduced its stake in Renault to below 50 percent by selling slightly less than 6 percent of the company's equity. Under Finance Minister Francis Mer, the government further reduced its stake to 25 percent in 2002, although it retained voting rights amounting to 30.48 percent. The government shareholding dropped to 15 percent the following year. "They kept their word," said Dominique Thormann. "The question is to know why the French government never wanted to go further and completely withdraw."

The residual yet cumbersome presence of the French government as a Renault shareholder weighed heavily on the fate of the equity balance within the Alliance and sowed the seeds of a crisis that started in 2015.

"They were warned," said Dominique Thormann. And for years, a way out was sought. A final attempt was made in 2007 to reduce the stake below 40 percent to comply with the regulatory objection and assign voting rights that would normally have been attached to the shares held by Nissan. But the COB's successor agency, the Autorité des Marchés Financiers, was not convinced. And then the Global Financial Crisis erupted with the Lehman Brothers collapse in September 2008, putting the issue on hold indefinitely.

Far from being anecdotal, the equity issue was related to the very existence of the Alliance—to seize more easily future opportunities for expansion and address the situation that would inevitably occur when the builder and guarantor of the Alliance left the scene.

7. Commentary by Phillipe Riès.

Dr. Courtis

Kenneth Courtis first met Nissan board member and chief financial officer Thierry Moulonguet at *La Tâche*, a modest yet renowned restaurant near the former site of the International French High School in Tokyo. It was the early 2000s. The Japanese chef had named his French restaurant after a vineyard in Burgundy attached to the most expensive agricultural plot on the planet, the Romanée-Conti vineyard.

Before arriving in Tokyo in the early 1980s, Dr. Courtis—which is how he has been known in Asia for four decades—studied at the INSEAD business school in Paris before completing his doctorate at Sciences Po, the top French public university specializing in social sciences. The booming Japanese economy seemed irresistible in the 1980s. But then the bubble burst in 1990, bringing to an end the biggest speculative mania in history.

Originally from Canada, Dr. Courtis was the regional economist for Deutsche Bank. In conquering markets across Asia for the German bank, he worked with the legendary Simon Murray, a former soldier with the French foreign legion who became the right-hand man of Hong Kong billionaire Sir Li Ka-Shing, known locally as "Superman" for his business acumen. The Asian financial crisis of 1997-1998 and the Global Financial Crisis ten years later put an end to Deutsche Bank's dreams of rivaling the financial titans of Wall Street.

But the Frankfurt-based bank was above all a financial institution for German industry, especially the auto industry, the strongest in the world. Ken Courtis had long been associated with the international advisory board of Daimler AG and developed an intimate knowledge of the automobile industry. He worked with Daimler chief executive Jürgen Schrempp in Japan when the company started looking at Mitsubishi Motors Corporation after Chrysler—the German automaker's American partner—forced his ambitious boss to give up plans to acquire Nissan.

As the world prepared to enter the twenty-first century, Ken Courtis joined the New York-based investment bank the world loved to hate—Goldman Sachs. It was October 1999, and he was now the firm's vice chairman for the Asia-Pacific region, the most dynamic in the world. He brought with him a deep understanding of the region, a high public profile and a voluminous contact book, notably in China and Japan. Among those contacts was Carlos Ghosn. Both loved Japan, both were pillars of the annual World Economic Forum in Davos, and both were at ease with French culture. They were made for each other.

"We started working regularly with Carlos in 2003," Ken Courtis recalled. "I assembled a global team that brought together the smartest people at Goldman at the time in brainstorming sessions at least once every quarter for strategic assessment of the global automobile market. We had to be really careful. Carlos used to arrive at the underground carpark at the Okura Hotel in the late afternoon. Meetings took place in a private room on the twelfth floor of the east wing, near the Belle Époque restaurant, and he always booked under a discreet name." The team also included a young Christopher Cole. "I found he was smart and brought him into the group," Courtis said of Cole.

Among the items discussed at the 2003 meetings were the equity arrangements for the Renault-Nissan Alliance. There was no question yet about Carlos Ghosn succeeding Louis Schweitzer as Renault chairman. But while Nissan was gaining in strength and earnings, investing massively in America and entering the Chinese market, Renault—the Japanese company's main shareholder—was failing to benefit from its own global expansion. Renault's market capitalization reflected the growing disequilibrium. The French automaker was barely worth more than its stake in Nissan, sometimes less. In strictly equity market valuation terms, Renault and foreign automakers in the French group, like Dacia in Romania and Samsung Motors in South Korea, were together worth nothing, or even less than nothing.

Risk of a Hostile Takeover

"The normal baseline was that Nissan was worth more than Renault," Schweitzer said in 2002, dismissing the risk of a hostile takeover if the gap grew too embarrassing or even to dangerous levels. "For a financier, it would be a high-risk transaction," he said. "For another manufacturer, it would have to ask itself if it could create value compared with current market capitalization." Moreover, the Renault chairman said, all recent mergers in the auto sector had contained "nasty surprises."

"Faced with a group that was running very well, it would not be a very intelligent calculation to take control and seriously question the spirit of the Alliance between Renault and Nissan," said Dominique Thormann. Nevertheless, "Schweitzer was terrified of a hostile takeover," he said.

In 2005, Thierry Breton, the finance minister who is now European Commissioner for the Internal Market, led the passage of a new law. The legislation required any hostile suitor to also make a bid for any listed affiliate of Renault in France or abroad that was at least 33 percent owned by the French automaker. At the time, Renault's market capitalization was some 21.5 billion euros, barely half that of Nissan, which was valued at about 40 billion euros. The recourse to a legislative weapon was a sign of weakness and small shareholders were outraged by the new law, with some even speaking of a "psychosis."

The dilemma was that the Alliance itself did not have any listed securities that investors could buy to take advantage of its growth opportunities. So, when Renault acquired a stake in Russian automaker AvtoVAZ, Nissan became a shareholder in Mitsubishi Motors. Still, the combined market value of Nissan and Renault always suffered a steep discount to Toyota's market capitalization, even when the Alliance was producing more vehicles than Japan's top automaker in 2017 and 2018.

"In 2004, we had a discussion with Carlos about a holding company idea which had been floating around in Billancourt two years earlier," Ken Courtis said. "Carlos was strongly opposed. He was convinced that it would blow up everything. But I told him: 'You've got a problem because if an opportunity comes up, especially in the United States, you don't have a bargaining chip.' My American and European colleagues at Goldman were arguing for a full merger. They didn't understand the hybrid nature of the Alliance—and, of course, it was in their interests given the fat commissions they would have earned for arranging a merger. Carlos had to repeat several times that such a deal was doomed to fail."

Louis Schweitzer, the Renault chairman, liked the idea of a holding company already conceived by French law professor Guy

Carcassonne and Darrois, a corporate law firm based in Paris. The plan—codenamed *Metis*, after the French word for mixed race—was overseen by Georges Douin, who played a key role in approaching Nissan. In 1999, Renault's stake in Nissan was fixed at a level so Renault could avoid consolidating the huge debts of its Japanese partner on its balance sheet. But with unexpected speed, Carlos Ghosn overcame this obstacle—Nissan and Renault shareholders would own the holding company.

Before the APE was created by Finance Minister Francis Mer as the French Government Shareholding Agency in 2004, state equity in enterprises was "managed"—if that's the right word—by officials at the Treasury Department in the Ministry of Economy and Finance. And the Treasury imposed a condition, namely a dominant position for Renault.

"The Japanese were already not very keen and that put them off completely," said a person involved in the negotiations. So instead, the French and Japanese companies formed a joint subsidiary in the Netherlands. Renault-Nissan B.V. was not set up for tax reasons, as many have claimed. It was established because Dutch laws are more flexible. The two companies each held 50 percent of the new company in Amsterdam, the headquarters of the Anglo-Dutch energy giant Royal-Dutch Shell and one of two head offices of Unilever until 2020 when the dual-headed structure was unified under a single company in London. But in case of a split board, Renault could cast the decisive vote. It would never be exercised.

Holding Company as Only Alternative

But if the Alliance was going to owe its existence to a corporate structure rather than a single man, the options were limited. A merger was considered out of the question, even harmful. The only option left was a holding company. So it was, in 2004, that Ken Courtis and his team came up with the idea of a financial holding company made up of different parts of the Alliance. The plan would resurface with adjustments at regular intervals over the years, with somewhat esoteric names—Project Caterpillar in 2013, Orange in 2017 and Strawberry in 2019 (for Fiat-Chrysler to join the Alliance), followed by Fruit Salad (a combination of the Orange and

Strawberry projects) and finally, after Carlos Ghosn's arrest, Goju-Goju or Fifty-Fifty.

"The suits were always the same, the only things that changed were the colors of the shirts or the ties," Ken Courtis said.

"Three demands had to be met—improving the Alliance's strategic management, notably in terms of allocating capital and making major investment decisions including eventual activities for external growth, creating a common currency as a unique financial instrument to receive and make investments, and creating a medium of exchange for negotiating the entry of new partners into the Alliance," the Canadian economist said. "By far, the first was the most important. With the unprecedented technological revolution that the auto industry faced, it was becoming even more so."

But because of the permanent "structural" blockage of the French government and how to get rid of it, there was no concrete progress over ten years. And then other things got in the way. In 2005, Louis Schweitzer asked Carlos Ghosn to come to Billancourt to succeed him as chairman and chief executive of Renault while retaining the same position at Nissan. It was the first time in history that two Global Fortune 500 companies were led by the same man. Any thoughts about strategic actions were absorbed by a tentative approach with General Motors in 2006. The Global Financial Crisis then started in 2007, exploding in full force when Lehman Brothers collapsed in September 2008. Then there was a scandal in France over false accusations of industrial espionage in 2011, which seriously destabilized Renault and its chairman. A new major impetus on the operations of the Alliance did not occur until 2012. But, once again, the question was over the equity arrangements between the French and Japanese partners.

The Alliance had meanwhile not stopped expanding and diversifying. "When we were thinking about it at first, there were only four companies involved—Renault, Dacia and Samsung Motors on one side and Nissan on the other," Ken Courtis said. "Then Nissan invested in Dongfeng in China, Siam Motors in Thailand and finally Mitsubishi Motors in Japan as Renault was gradually assuming control of AvtoVAZ in Russia."

Like so many others before and after him, Ken Courtis left Goldman Sachs in 2006 over a conflict with chief executive Hank

Paulson, the future U.S. Treasury Secretary under President George W. Bush. Christopher Cole took on Carlos Ghosn as a client for Goldman Sachs.

"Carlos Ghosn requested complete confidentiality," said Robert Falzon, who worked with Cole. "Chris never went through the Paris office, as he had direct personal ties. It was how he worked, using the Goldman machine."

It was this small Goldman Sachs team that came up with Project Caterpillar, a holding company listed in Paris and Tokyo with severely rationalized manufacturing activities and a headquarters on neutral ground in London. But the political and social obstacles were considered insurmountable, as confirmed by the sudden emergence of Emmanuel Macron in the name of the Florange Law in 2015, like a bull in the China shop the Alliance represented.

Veterans from Goldman Sachs

In 2016, Christopher Cole left Goldman Sachs to set up his own mergers and acquisitions firm in London, a boutique company known as Ardea Partners. He brought with him his closest former colleagues—Robert Falzon, who had overseen the European industrial sector for Goldman, and James Del Favero, who had been in charge of cross-border deals for the U.S. investment bank.

Carlos Ghosn and Renault became Ardea's main clients in Europe, and the Alliance project was its main activity. A small team from both Renault and Ardea began working with the chairman of the Japanese and French companies.

"This project involved a holding company listed in Paris and Tokyo," Carlos Ghosn recalled. "It would have been the sole listed company with a single board of directors. If it had nine board members, three would have been from Renault, three from Nissan and the other three would have been independent directors. To avoid complication, Mitsubishi was going to remain a Nissan subsidiary. It didn't amount to a merger because the companies and, of course, the brands would continue to exist and function. Employees would remain with their companies and keep their social contracts and cultural environments. The Alliance would be irreversible as it would be impossible to unravel.

"The status quo was considered dangerous because it wasn't known who was going to succeed me. Conflict was a big risk. I was acceptable to all companies. But that wouldn't necessarily be the case with a successor. So, I was going to be executive chairman of the holding company with a chief executive at each of the three companies. The operational structure would have been the same as the Alliance, but with the holding company at the top. We gave it a financial structure that would make it impossible to fall apart. Purchasing and technological development would have still been undertaken jointly, and plants would have been shared but remain autonomous. The only way to prevent it unravelling after I left was to create a common share, common equity.

"The holding company would have made it possible to not only raise the enormous sums of capital that the industry needed, but also to unleash a tremendous process of revaluation, with the new shares increasing by 15 to 20 percent compared with the combined value of the old shares. It would have benefited shareholders, including the French government. On November 19, 2018, the day of my arrest, the combined market value of the two companies was 67.4 billion dollars. The holding company would have provided an increase of at least 10 percent, a very conservative estimate that would have boosted the market value to almost 75 billion dollars. Chris Cole and Ardea worked on the plan."

Ken Courtis, who is still in friendly contact with Carlos Ghosn, did not stop looking at the Alliance after leaving Goldman Sachs. He estimated the revaluation of the Alliance would have been around 40 percent with the market capitalization of the holding company approaching 100 billion dollars, bringing market value in line with book value. The shares of Nissan, and especially Renault, were generally undervalued by the market.

"Our work initially involved simplifying the situation," recalled Robert Falzon. "Mathematically, it was pretty simple to resolve valuing the respective contributions to the holding company to get a balance. The market value of Nissan was twice the value of Renault. But Renault held 43.4 percent of Nissan's capital, and Nissan only 15 percent of Renault. At the beginning of 2017, we were ready."

But the deal depended on one thing. "I imposed the withdrawal of the French government as a condition," Carlos Ghosn said. "If the French government exchanged its Renault shares for shares in the holding company at the valuation agreed, it would have become a direct shareholder in Nissan, which was something the Japanese weren't about to stomach. We thought about this for a long time, but didn't start the preparatory work until the beginning of 2018, after I was renominated as head of Renault for a mandate whose objective was to make the Alliance irreversible. It was advisory work, but also allowed for the plan to be refined. Obviously, the French government was not very warm to the idea of withdrawing. My counterpart was Martin Vial, who headed the APE, but everyone knew it was not him who would make the decision, but the president. Not even the minister.

"On this issue, the position of the French government could change according to the administration and how much they interfered. They didn't say 'no' at first. They asked to look at the conditions. I don't think they had another plan. It suited them to remain shareholders with a diluted state of 6 or 7 percent, down from 15 percent. But I refused. It was unthinkable for the Japanese management, which was supported by METI. When I spoke to Saikawa and Kawaguchi, I knew it would go straight back to METI.

"I was convinced that it was a good time for the French government to withdraw. But I think certain Japanese saw a chance to get rid of the French by eliminating me. They had to sell that to their friends in the Japanese government—that I had to be removed to end the French government's influence on Nissan and that they no longer need Renault, they could manage Nissan themselves. We saw how that ended."

Goju-Goju Project

After Carlos Ghosn's arrest, Renault's former chief executive Thierry Bolloré revisited the "Ghosn plan without Carlos" in early 2019, and made revisions with the team at Ardea, the boutique investment bank in London.

"The holding company would be equally owned by the two companies (Goju-Goju or Fifty-Fifty) which would continue to exist with their own general management and executive committees, and Renault and Nissan shares still listed in Paris and Tokyo," said Robert Falzon. "For governance and operations, a single body at the level of the holding company was planned. For strategic functions like purchasing and product planning, along with research and development, there would have been four or five teams of about 200 top people working directly for the board of the holding company." Moreover, "if the French government still wanted to be represented on the board of the Alliance, it could have only one director on a temporary basis. The idea was that the government would finally realize the value created by the new structure and quickly get rid of its residual shareholding that was now devoid of influence," Falzon said.

The industrial and financial logic behind what Ken Courtis and his Goldman Sachs team began thinking about in 2003 was implacable.

"The way the whole thing was handled was incredible," said Robert Falzon. "Consolidation in the auto industry is inevitable and the Alliance was ready to take part. A few years from now, what Carlos Ghosn asked us to put together will be the evidence. Beyond a certain nationalism in Japan, which never got over the humiliation of 1999, Japan has many well-intentioned people who know the country needs friends."

On February 17, 2020, Claudine Pons returned to Tokyo. The external consultant for Renault—who had been the emissary to fly to Japan and approach Carlos Ghosn over his chairmanship the previous year—was now persona non grata at the French carmaker. The former prisoner at the Tokyo Detention Center may have been the world's best-known fugitive, but the woman who had worked alongside him since 2011 was warmly welcomed at the official residence of the prime minister. The dinner was small; two tables of eight people each. Claudine sat at the table of Prime Minister Shinzo Abe, who was accompanied by his official political advisor. As people got up to leave, the advisor approached her. "We very much regret the way this all took place," he said.

CHAPTER SEVEN

Dancing with the Dragon and the Bear

"**W**hen we looked at Nissan before, we liked the body but not the head," Zhu Rongji said to Kenneth Courtis, the Canadian economist who was vice chairman of Goldman Sachs Asia. It was Beijing at the dawn of the third millennium.

"Since Mr. Ghosn took over Nissan's management," Zhu, the Chinese premier, continued, "we now like the head too. Do you think he would be ready to try the same in China?"

As mayor of Shanghai in 1989, Zhu Rongji managed the turmoil that gripped China at the time with remarkable dexterity—not through a student massacre on Shanghai's Bund, but by exerting control over events and bringing about a return to order with an iron fist in a velvet glove. In the decade that followed the Tiananmen Square Massacre that crushed democratic aspirations in Beijing on June 4, 1989, Zhu Rongji embodied the decisive choice of the Communist Party of China, and even more so after he became prime minister in 1998. The choice was that the Tiananmen incident should not, and could not, mark an end to the economic reforms that had been launched by Deng Xiaoping a decade earlier.

Zhu Rongji, who would later serve as central bank governor, had mastered both English and economics, a rarity among Chinese leaders, as Deng himself observed. In the post-Tiananmen period, he was the face and guiding hand of economic reform after winning, with Deng's support, a standoff with Premier Li Peng, a conservative also known as the "Butcher of Tiananmen."

Among the priorities in Zhu Rongji's reform program was restructuring state-owned enterprises whose dominance and innate inefficiency weighed heavily on the Chinese economy. Restructuring had often been through conditional partnerships with foreign companies offering transfers of technology, know-how and management methods. Such investments would become easier as a result of China's entry into the World Trade Organization in 2001, the high point in Zhu's mandate as head of government. For U.S. investment banks, notably Goldman Sachs, which had invested much in China in terms of financial and human resources, the prospects were mouth-watering.

Nissan's Renaissance Noticed in Beijing

In Beijing, the spectacular recovery of Nissan had not gone unnoticed. Despite deep disputes and grudges inherited from the twentieth century, the two neighboring giants of Northeast Asia followed each other closely. In areas ranging from politics and trade to currency management, China paid close attention to the lessons it could learn from Japan, especially on how the first non-white power of the modern era handled its relations with the West, including its successes as well as its failures.

"At the very beginning of the millennium, the Chinese automobile market was still very small," recalled Carlos Ghosn. "But it seemed obvious to me that it was a natural market for Nissan." The automaker had barely recovered from near-bankruptcy and had just launched an offensive on the U.S. market when it took a huge gamble on China. Nissan had a modest presence in China dating back to 1993, when it partnered with Zhengzhou Light Automobile Works to produce pick-ups. And since 1997, its Bluebird sedan had been made and sold in China under a technical-support agreement with Ja Yun Bao Automobile Company. Sales reached 23,153 units in 2001.

When they welcomed Carlos Ghosn in Beijing, the reformist colleagues of Zhu Rongji had something else in mind. "I was received by Li Rongrong, head of the state assets commission, and Vice Premier Wu Bangguo, who oversaw all of China's industry. The message was clear: 'We don't want to allow you to establish a traditional joint venture. We want to license you to produce Nissan cars in China, but it has to be with Dongfeng." The company was a state-owned enterprise and the largest manufacturer of heavy vehicles in China.

Reforming China's State-Owned Enterprises

Li made reforming and reorganizing state-owned enterprise his life work and was named founding director of the State-owned Assets Supervision and Administration Commission when it was set up in 2003. Vice Premier Wu had overseen large enterprises and was a member of the Politburo Standing Committee of the Party, the center of power in China.

According to Carlos Ghosn, "their argument was well put together. 'We need to inject new blood into this sector. Despite the existence of your Nissan Diesel subsidiary, we know trucks aren't very important for you. What we want is for you to invest in the capital of Dongfeng's truck division and help them bring their standards up to international levels.' The Chinese put the market in my hands," Ghosn said, "and told me: 'If you help us sort out Dongfeng's activities in the heavy vehicle sector, you can enter the Chinese car market on a large scale'."

Dongfeng means "East Wind" in Chinese, and it was not just any old state-owned enterprise. Chairman Mao Zedong himself decided to set up the vehicle manufacturer in 1969. To protect it from the risk of a foreign invasion of coastal provinces, it was strategically located in Hubei in central China in the provincial capital of Wuhan, now world-famous as the home of the first recorded cases of Covid-19.

"On the Chinese side," said Carlos Ghosn, "the choice of Nissan for an undertaking of such scope was motivated by a single factor. Li Rongrong told me: 'There are other candidates but we're doing an agreement with you because you've shown that you're capable of respecting identities different from your own.' With Nissan, we showed we could respect the identity of a big Japanese company. 'You came from France, you respected the Japanese identity. We want you to do the same with Dongfeng. We won't do it with another manufacturer.' There was another aspect which should not be overlooked," said Ghosn, "although its importance is difficult to gauge. History is important for the Chinese and it turns out that Deng Xiaoping had been a worker at Renault for a few weeks in 1925." Moreover, when Deng visited Japan in 1978, the Chinese leader toured Nissan's plant at Zama, one of the most advanced in the world at the time.

Internal Resistance at Nissan

"Of course, I accepted it but I came up against a lot of resistance at Nissan," Ghosn said. "In fact, it was like that with all my initiatives. They had problems seeing three, five or ten years ahead. It was the success of the first few years that let me dare to come up with a strategy that shook up Japanese reluctance. I obviously had allies at the company who backed me, but it was personal support rather than a conviction that we had to go to China. None of it meant anything to them—the Communist Party, Dongfeng and trucks. The resistance also extended to whether our international expansion program should focus on China. Such a decision was not difficult in itself, but more so in what we would be giving up elsewhere. As soon as we decided to put priority on China, that meant other investments would have to be abandoned or delayed."

Ken Courtis, who took part in the negotiations for Goldman Sachs, was more direct. "I must have warned Carlos several times that the negotiators who came from Tokyo amounted to saboteurs. If it continued like this, we were heading straight towards failure and it would take another 20 years to enter China. A week later, he reorganized the negotiating team under Thierry Moulonguet and grounded the recalcitrant Japanese."

According to Carlos Ghosn, "my partner was really Li Rongrong because Dongfeng was among the state-owned enterprises under his responsibility. He was a remarkable man, very proud of his humble origins and technical experience. He used to say: 'I didn't get to be where I am by being the son of this person or that person but by rising through the ranks.' He was fascinated by management issues and was a genuine modernizer. He wanted state-owned enterprises to become as efficient and profitable as possible. The main topic of our talks was performance.

"Relations with Chinese leaders had to be cordial, even friendly, if we wanted to succeed, although personal relations outside official visits were limited. And we had to comply with the ritual governing relations with visiting foreigners, be they politicians or business people—the big dinners with several dozen people, our own colleagues and all the Chinese dignitaries who were more or less involved with the venture, with a parade of courses and much alcohol served by an army of hostesses. On such occasions, we went to the area where all the ministries are located in central Beijing. To keep him up to date on the progress of the project, I had dinner with Li Rongrong in Beijing on each of my visits. He'd mention possible concerns. The relationship was very close, for a very long time. After the venture started operating, we saw each other less often, especially as the responsibilities of Chinese leaders frequently change," said Ghosn.

On September 19, 2002, Nissan and Dongfeng announced a "large-scale strategic partnership" that involved transferring the bulk of the state-owned enterprises's auto activities to a new venture called Dongfeng Motor Company that was equally owned by the two partners. For Nissan, which had only just been resuscitated by Carlos Ghosn, the investment was substantial, at 8.55 billion yuan, more than 1 billion dollars at the time. Nissan secured the post of chief executive at Dongfeng Motor and the chairmanship went to Miao Wei, who headed the Chinese parent company and later served as provincial party chief in Hubei and eventually Minister of Industry and Information Technology.

Top Japanese Carmaker in China

Dongfeng Motor had ambitious plans to raise annual production to 550,000 units by 2006, twice the level of the Chinese partner in 2001. The forecast was comprised of 330,000 commercial vehicles, the traditional business of Dongfeng, and 220,000 cars under the Nissan brand. For 2012, the forecast was for 900,000 units, a target that was largely exceeded. At the end of 2010, chief executive Kimiyasu Nakamura announced that the forecast for 2012 had been raised by two thirds to 1.5 million units. That made Nissan the largest Japanese automaker in the Chinese market, on its way to becoming the biggest in the world. Toyota and Honda were in second and third places.

The manufacturing facilities of Dongfeng Motor were not in Wuhan, which had been reserved for French automaker PSA Peugeot-Citroën and later Renault as well. The first of five plants were built near Guangzhou, capital of the southern coastal province of Guangdong which included the Pearl River Delta.

"In the factory area in the Guangzhou region, the concentration of Japanese companies is very high," Carlos Ghosn said. "There are Japanese schools, Japanese restaurants—a complete social environment favorable to expatriates from Japan. By contrast, the French went to Wuhan, where PSA was located. Much later, when we wanted to build a Renault plant in Guangzhou near Nissan and its suppliers, the Chinese authorities refused. It was Wuhan or nothing.

"The design, architecture and organization of the Nissan plants came from Japan," Ghosn continued. "By 2018, Chinese plants were outperforming Nissan's plants in Japan. One reason was that they were newer. It was the same for the Renault plant in China. But it was especially because the Chinese workforce was trained, supervised and equipped so well that it was capable of world-class performance. It wasn't just the cost of wages. In China, there's ambition and the will to succeed that's much more superior to what you see in Japan or France today. China also has the capacity to train its manpower quite satisfactorily at all levels, from workers to engineers. The training of Chinese employees mostly took place on the spot, although Chinese engineers and technicians came to Japan, of course."

People Over Capital

"In an operation so big, it's important to understand that finance is not the most important aspect," said Ghosn. "What really makes the difference is being able to send engineers, technicians and managers who can ensure the launch and success. Human resources and skills are decisive. It turns out that in Japanese culture, the employee serves the company first. The question of volunteering to go to China didn't really come up. A designated employee would go and, if need be, the family would stay in Japan.

"Japanese distrust of the Chinese was a potential stumbling block, but it was overcome. On the ground, there was never any friction significant enough to come to the attention of senior management. As soon as you fix clear objectives for the Japanese, their commitment is guaranteed. On the other hand, I personally intervened a lot to ease management tensions between the Japanese and Chinese. At the beginning, there were quite a few conflicts.

"I used to go to China at least four times a year. Given the importance of the market, the scale of our investment and especially the need to maintain good relations with the Chinese government, it was important to explain to them what we were doing and to listen if they had any questions or complaints about quality, technology transfers and other things. This was all the more important as we didn't set out with a clean slate but with an existing asset in which we'd become partners with the Chinese government. The Communist Party is present in all companies and exercises de facto control in certain areas such as human resources and trade unions. In a joint venture, there's also a sharing of management responsibilities," Ghosn explained.

In December 2018—a month after Carlos Ghosn was thrown into his cell at the Tokyo Detention House—it was reported that the Nissan Old Guard was about to withdraw 1.1 billion dollars (7.5 billion yuan) in cash from Dongfeng Motor. The disclosure of such confidential information forced the Japanese manufacturer to deny it was preparing a war chest for a showdown with Renault, its main shareholder.

"Nissan is not preparing or executing any transfer that does not conform to the normal course of our business," a Nissan spokesperson said.

Ken Courtis—still well connected in China, including Wuhan—noted that 1.1 billion dollars was "roughly the amount Carlos Ghosn invested in China in 2005," to acquire 50 percent of Dongfeng Motor. He said the Japanese-Chinese venture "had established itself as the main source of growth and earnings for Nissan in an unbalanced relationship that benefited the Japanese manufacturer." And this was achieved even though "Japanese managers sent to China were mediocre at best."

Chinese Management Test

In 2003, as *Shift* was being written, Carlos Ghosn admitted that he intended to conquer the Chinese market, which had only just started to expand. This ordeal by fire would let him see if a Nissan executive with strong potential had the makings of a future successor.

"We sent those with the best potential to China to test them," Carlos Ghosn said fifteen years later. "But the experience was not very conclusive. It was effectively a battlefield where people could prove themselves. It was normal for someone from Japan to head a Japanese company in China. The Chinese would have found it hard to understand if we sent a Frenchman, a Brazilian or an American.

"Nakamura was a good boss in China, but he was a bit old," said Carlos Ghosn, referring to Katsumi Nakamura, the venture's first chief executive. Jun Seki, the senior vice president who was named Nissan's vice chief operating officer in October 2019, was a "fairly average Chinese operations manager" who "did not, in my opinion, pass the test that would have allowed him to become chief executive one day. Makoto Uchida, who succeeded him in China, has just been named chief executive but has not proven anything to date."

Uchida and Seki were part of the triumvirate that succeeded chief executive Hiroto Saikawa, whose "strategic" decisions after Carlos Ghosn's arrest were to reduce the focus on China and divest from electric vehicles. The third part of the trio was Ashwani Gupta, the former chief operating officer of Mitsubishi Motors who became chief operating officer at Nissan. The triumvirate unraveled in February 2020, when Seki—who had spent his entire career at Nissan—suddenly resigned to join Sidec Corporation, the world leader in small electric motors.

BRIC by BRIC

Nissan's expansion into China was "through the front door," Carlos Ghosn told Agence France-Presse in 2002. But if this faced internal resistance with the Japanese, what would be made of Renault's wish to take up a dominant position in the Russian automobile market after the Nissan chairman concurrently assumed the reins of the French automaker in 2005?

"When I arrived as Renault chief executive," said Carlos Ghosn, "I was convinced that development was going to take place in emerging countries. BRICS—Brazil, Russia, India, China and South Africa—were fashionable. The first priority was to increase Renault's capacity in Brazil in Curitiba while waiting for Nissan to take its turn in establishing itself in the country. No member of the

Alliance would enjoy an exclusive right to operate in a specific country. Everybody wants to go everywhere but you have to follow a schedule based on a long-term plan—BRICS first, the Middle East and Africa later.

"Yet Renault had a long history of big ambitions on paper with mediocre results. It's an issue we raised in *Shift* and I wanted to halt such practices. We would do only what we were capable of implementing properly. That's why it was completely unfounded to criticize me—as occurred in France—for favoring Nissan over Renault in opening China to one and not the other. When we decided that Nissan would enter China, I was running that company alone. It's true that Renault didn't really come to China until 2016, but in the meantime we increased capacity in Brazil, acquired the Russian company AvtoVAZ, and built the Renault-Dacia plant in Tangiers, the first since Brazil. We arrived in China when we were ready and the time was right.

"Acquiring, controlling and modernizing AvtoVAZ was an enormous challenge," Carlos Ghosn said. The huge, sprawling industrial complex on the Volga River was best known for its Lada vehicles. Lada was Russia's top brand—which had its moment of glory in the West in the 1980s with the Niva, a small and bracingly rustic all-terrain model that preceded the popularity of SUV vehicles. The Russian company is also a chapter in the world history of automobiles.

Vast Factories in Togliatti

Volzhsky Avtomobilny Zavod ("Volga Automobile Plant" or VAZ) was set up in 1966 under a cooperation agreement between the Soviet Union of Leonid Brezhnev and Italy, then dominated by the Christian Democratic Party and the most powerful communist party east of the Iron Curtain. Italy may have been a republic, but it was endowed with a reigning family, the Agnelli dynasty. The family founded the Fiat empire, which accounted for 10 percent of the country's gross domestic product. To make cars based on Fiat models, a gigantic industrial site was built more than 600 miles from Moscow. Covering almost 1,500 acres, the site included Togliatti, a new city named after Palmiro Togliatti, the veteran leader of the Communist Party of Italy. The first cars rolled off the production line on April 22, 1970, the 100th anniversary of Lenin's birth.

By 1975, VAZ could produce 700,000 units a year, making it one of the biggest auto plants in the world. But it was soon plagued by all the ills of planned economies that led to the implosion of the Soviet Union. There was too much vertical integration with the industrial complex producing its own steel and tires. It also suffered from over-employment, under-investment, technological obsolescence and demotivated employees. And then it sank into the organized crime that accompanied the collapse of Russian state structures and their anarchic privatization during the democratic but chaotic rule of Boris Yeltsin.

Renault already had a presence in Russia through a venture with the Government of Moscow. Known as Avtoframos ("France Moscow Automobiles"), it inherited the old Moskvitch brand dating back to the Stalin era. Avtoframos assembled Renault vehicles and Dacia models, the French carmaker's low-cost brand, giving the French automaker a real yet modest presence in a market of largely untapped potential.

"Russia was a natural market for Renault, much more than for a Japanese manufacturer," said Carlos Ghosn. "AvtoVAZ, which was wholly owned by the Russian government, needed help. Vladimir Putin wasn't happy with the company's performance or product quality. From this came the search for a foreign partner taking up to 20 percent equity.

"We were competing with General Motors and Fiat. I essentially negotiated with Ruben Vardanyan, the investment banker who was in charge of selling the 20 percent stake, and Sergey Chemezov, who had overseen the partial privatization from the beginning. He was a friend of Putin and a defense industry executive who Putin trusted."

Ruben Vardanyan, who frequently appeared at the World Economic Forum in Davos, was a philanthropist and advocate for the Armenian cause, responsible for making Troika Dialog the country's leading investment bank in Russia. In 2012, the bank was acquired by Sberbank, the largest universal bank in Russia which was also close to the Kremlin. Sergey Viktorovitch Chemezov was an engineer with multiple degrees—as is often the case with members of the post-Soviet nomenklatura. He met Vladimir Putin in Dresden in East Germany where the future Kremlin leader was working for the KGB. In 2007, Chemezov became chief executive of Russian Technologies Corporation. Renamed Rostec in 2012, it was Renault's partner in the AvtoVAZ venture.

Face to Face with Putin

"In 2008, I received an invitation to go to the Kremlin to meet Vladimir Putin," Carlos Ghosn recalled. "He greeted me and said: 'Mr. Ghosn, we're going to allocate the 20 percent of AvtoVAZ to you. We regard industrial projects to be worth the same. The reason you've won is because we trust you personally to respect the Russian identity of the company. You have already demonstrated this in France and Japan.' He added that we had to be satisfied with 20 percent and that anything higher was out of the question.

"You speak to him in English, you understand that he understands but he lets the interpreter do it. I met him at least twice at the Kremlin but also two or three times at his dacha near Moscow. He was neither warm nor cold in our exchanges, but he was friendly. His words were always very clear without ambiguity. During negotiations about acquiring equity in AvtoVAZ, he was categorical: 'You'll get 20 percent, don't ask for more.' He had a deadpan humor.

"Much later, when we were considering an increased Renault stake in AvtoVAZ, Chemezov raised the question of a Russian shareholding in Renault. I replied that it would surprise me if that would be accepted in Paris, but that it was a decision for shareholders. François Fillon, who was the French prime minister at the time, called one day and asked: 'Carlos, what's this story with the Renault shares? I've just had Putin on the phone saying you'd agree to a share exchange.' I replied: 'Mr. Prime Minister, I'm flabbergasted. You don't need my agreement. It's got nothing to do with me.' Nothing happened, of course. But at a Kremlin meeting three or four months later to take stock of AvtoVAZ, Putin said: 'By the way, regarding the Renault shares, I always wondered why the French government refused my offer. I thought they must have been afraid of me. But, in fact, I was wrong. They're afraid of you.' And he burst out laughing.

"I was perfectly aware of the scale of the strategic and operational challenge from this investment. It was just before the financial crisis and I was criticized a lot at the time, and even now. The recovery began after the financial crisis and Putin was happy with the product improvement—resulting from a huge effort to upgrade the workforce, promote Russian managers and other things—and he suggested we raise our stake to more than 20 percent. The entire venture was based on the transfer of best practices, the respect for identity, the continued existence of AvtoVAZ and Lada, and fighting to keep it as the top auto brand in Russia. We honored the agreement.

"The industrial equipment was largely obsolete and there was huge over-employment. Step by step, in cooperation with local authorities and trade unions, we cut the workforce. The approach was patient, spanning several years. We couldn't transform the company without reducing the workforce or investing in industrial equipment. The Russians didn't want a head-on collision. A number of deadlines had to be met. They never opposed our initiatives but they always wanted to influence the timing to ensure social acceptance. It was a long-term policy which was very well led overall."

Transforming a Bloated Operation

Of course, the activities in Russia were no walk in the park for Renault. The project was started when the Russian market seemed very promising (and still is, in the long term). But the French automaker had to face the challenge of massively restructuring the vastest auto manufacturing facility in the world at a time of growing tensions between Vladimir Putin's Russia and the West.

The challenge was to turn an obese and anemic enterprise into a top athlete that could rival the best in the world in terms of performance. Carlos Ghosn hired Bo Andersson, a graduate of a Swedish army academy with the rank of major who had worked in purchasing at Saab, the Swedish automaker that has since been liquidated. He was working in senior management at General Motors in 2006, when Carlos Ghosn negotiated a strategic agreement between the Renault-Nissan Alliance and the struggling U.S. automaker.

When he arrived at AvtoVAZ, Bo Andersson had just spent five years turning around the GAZ group, Russia's top manufacturer of light utility vehicles, buses and all-terrain trucks. GAZ was owned by Oleg Deripaska, an oligarch close to the Kremlin. Before seeking Andersson's help in 2009, Deripaska had tried to get GAZ to join the Renault-Nissan Alliance, but Carlos Ghosn thought the financial requirements were excessive. At AvtoVAZ, Andersson followed the paradigm of the Nissan Revival Plan, immortalized as, "Save the Business Without Losing the Company," at a classic lecture Carlos Ghosn once gave at Harvard University.

Employee numbers were slashed from 77,000 to 44,000, affecting white-collar workers more than blue-collar employees. The number of employee grades was cut from nine to five, unprofitable subsidiaries were eliminated and suppliers were rationalized. The Lada brand was relaunched with five new models at the same time as the Volga plant was making eight other vehicles under the Renault, Dacia and Nissan brands.

"AvtoVAZ today is nothing like it was before," said Carlos Ghosn. "The plant is much more efficient and the huge productivity gap with other Alliance sites has been continuously narrowing. It's not yet at the Chinese level but it's getting close. Nothing's impossible in Russia. With time and investment, I'm convinced it's going to be a high-performing company. The plant has enormous potential." Today, the Alliance brands control more than a third of the Russian market. Rivals like Germany's Volkswagen, or Hyundai and Kia from South Korea, have only about 10 percent each.

"The real challenge was to achieve such results without invading AvtoVAZ. The number of Renault executives sent to Togliatti didn't exceed thirty, about the same with Nissan in 1999. To succeed, we absolutely had to create Russian managers, either internally or by hiring externally. And management remained completely independent from Moskvitch management."

After several recapitalizations and other changes in equity, Renault now controls AvtoVAZ through its 67 percent stake in Alliance Rostec Auto B.V. Following steep losses and conflicts with suppliers, Bo Andersson lost his position running AvtoVAZ in 2016. The man who spent his civilian career confronting suppliers ended up getting hired by Yazaki Corporation chairman Shinji

Yazaki to head the European and North American operations of the Japanese company, the world's largest manufacturer of automotive wire harnesses.

A Judgement on Russia

Assessing the opportunity to invest in AvtoVAZ was ultimately a judgement on Russia itself, a judgement often obscured by politics. The Russian economy may be dominated by the oil and gas sector but it withstood Western sanctions after Moscow annexed Crimea and amid the vicissitudes of the world economy. Some indicators improved, notably demographics which were disastrous in the decade after the collapse of the Soviet Union. Russia is meanwhile a key entry point to access former Soviet republics in the Commonwealth of Independent States with its combined market of 240 million people where automobile ownership is far from European rates.

"This type of strategic decision comes not from consensus but a strong choice based on a shared vision," Carlos Ghosn said. "You have to convince those who are hesitant or reticent, but then you need to be decisive. If I waited for a consensus on Russia, I would've never done it. Same for China. Same for electric vehicles. Or the building of a new Dacia factory in Morocco. Leadership is not the capacity to ignore the opinions of others, but building a vision based on analyzing facts, listening to different opinions and taking responsibility. If the medium and long-term wellbeing of the company is at stake, I'll do it—even if there's hesitation and opposition."

Danger in Brazil

In 2012, Brazilian mining, oil and gas magnate Eike Batista sat atop a fortune of more than 12 billion dollars—the country's largest—which he hoped would one day surpass the wealth of Mexican businessman Carlos Slim, the world's richest man at the time. Like the parent holding company EBX Group, companies within his conglomerate all had abbreviated names ending in "X" as a synonym for growth. Batista was the son of a former president of mining giant Companhia Vale do Rio Doce, now known as Vale, who had also served as mines and energy minister during Brazil's military dictatorship. Batista's fortune was, however, a house of cards built on debt, which would collapse as Brazil's oil mania faded.

In 2010, Nissan was seeking a site for a plant Carlos Ghosn wanted to build to strengthen the Alliance's presence in Brazil, the country where he was born. Eike Batista made an offer that was well received at Nissan headquarters in Yokohama.

"Hari Nada, to whom Carlos Ghosn had entrusted the monitoring of the project at headquarters, was very enthusiastic," recalled an executive closely involved with the project. He thought Batista was great. Batista wanted Nissan to locate the site at Açu Port." Located north of Rio de Janeiro, this pharaonic project would be the cause of Batista's financial ruin.

"It was Claudine Bichara de Oliveira, the sister of Carlos Ghosn, who sounded the alarm, saying 'be careful, this could be dangerous'," the executive said. "She was her brother's eyes and ears in Brazil, and in this case saved Nissan from a potentially disastrous mistake. Moreover, numerous Brazilian officials we had to deal with ended up in prison, starting with the former Rio state governor. But Nissan was never the subject of any questioning."

To survive in the real world, risks are taken, investments made, market shares gained, political hurdles bypassed, traps avoided and partners well chosen. Country risk assessment is indispensable work, invaluable. In the auto industry, the sums at stake are considerable, projects are undertaken for years and the results—either positive or negative—last for decades.

"Brazil was among the BRICS and therefore a target," Carlos Ghosn said. "Renault had an advantage since the Curitiba plant already existed when I joined the company in 1996. But performance was very poor. This resulted from a practice that's unfortunately too widespread at Renault—we launch a project, get it running and then go back to Paris, leaving the people behind to cope as best they can. Headquarter plans take little or no account of new operations. Brazil has been the source of colossal losses for years. It's true that it's a very difficult market and also cyclical but—as in all markets like this—it's very profitable when things go well.

"There was also a Renault plant in Argentina, a significant industrial operation. It had only to be made to work a lot more efficiently with better integration with the Renault group and better control from headquarters. That's what we did. The results were so rapid that we had to increase capacity. At the Curitiba plant, I doubled capacity. A production unit in the car industry is equivalent to 150,000 to 200,000 vehicles a year. We also improved the sharing of responsibilities between Curitiba and Santa Isabel in Argentina."

Billion-Dollar Stake

"I finally launched Nissan in Brazil in 2011 by deciding to set up a plant in Rio. But, again, I came up against strong internal opposition. That was routine," Carlos Ghosn said. But "the Brazilian market was between 3.4 and 4 million units a year and was forecast to soon reach 6 million, making it the world's third-largest market after China and the United States." The project was ambitious—a "complete plant" producing 200,000 vehicles and engines a year, a one-billion-dollar investment creating 4,000 jobs at Nissan and the six Japanese parts makers that would be located on the site.

"I negotiated the agreement to set up the plant with Sérgio Cabral, the Governor of the State of Rio, who offered us attractive incentives," Carlos Ghosn said. "We chose Resende, near the border with the State of São Paulo. It was a time when the State of Rio was starting to generate deep-offshore petroleum revenues and was able to invest. São Paulo already had too many major industrial facilities. Minas Gerais was another possibility, but the Rio people were more aggressive and had significant backing from the federal government."

Visiting the Presidential Palace

Carlos Ghosn was a son of Brazil. He had to leave the country for health reasons when he was five years old, but he never stopped maintaining his links to Brazil, where some of his family still lived. The links were also professional—his first experience as an expatriate was with Michelin in Brazil, where he was sent to clean up the company's local operations. The success of this high-risk mission led to his meteoric rise at the French tiremaker. At the Planalto Palace, which houses the offices of the Brazilian president, the kid from Porto Velho was a visitor not quite like the others.

"There was always a kind of austerity there that wasn't at all in keeping with the country's image abroad," Carlos Ghosn said. "There were uniformed guards everywhere. It was quite ceremonial. In the waiting room, people were impeccably dressed, quite stiffly even. Very much according to protocol. But with Lula, the atmosphere was radically different. I arrived at Planalto and there were kids running around everywhere. Whole classes were visiting. There were balloons, popcorn, children eating ice cream. The ambiance was informal, *bonzinho* ("nice") as we say in Portuguese. When I entered Lula's office, he approached, put a hand on my shoulder and said: 'It seems you're from Porto Velho.' I replied: 'Yes, Mr. President.' He led me to a large map of Brazil and said: 'You see, my next big project is opening a road between Porto Velho and São Paulo to create a development zone for the whole of this part of the country.' We then sat down. 'Good. To you, now. What have you got to tell me?' He was very friendly, completely relaxed—not at all like his predecessors. On one of these visits, I told him I'd come with the son of Nelson Piquet, who was racing for Renault at the time. He got up and said: 'Come. Let's go and see him.' What struck me about him was that he was authentic and capable of making visitors feel relaxed whoever they were, be they heads of state or simple workers. He was completely indifferent to protocol."

From Lula to Dilma

The atmosphere changed with Lula's successor Dilma Roussef. "I came to show her the Resende project, quite a normal thing to do. But she's a schoolteacher. We were all there—several ministers, the representative of the State of Rio and others. Nobody dared say anything. She alone spoke. A technocrat. She lectured me about electric cars and how they wouldn't work even though we were in the process of investing 4 billion dollars in this promising new sector. I stopped her and said I hadn't come to sell her electric cars, but to announce to her some very good news for Brazil—we were going to build a new plant in the country.

"When we inaugurated the site, she didn't come. 'I don't understand at all,' the Rio governor told me. 'She needs to take care of her popularity. This is an important event for the country. She could have associated her name with an enormous investment, and she didn't come'."

In 2011, Nissan decided to double its stake in Brazil. According to a remark attributed to early twentieth century French statesman Georges Clemenceau, Brazil was "the country of the future and will remain so forever." Carlos Ghosn could not have predicted Brazil's deep recession or that Dilma's second mandate would end with her dismissal in 2014.

"Brazil was in the spotlight in 2011 and Carlos Ghosn had his eyes on the Olympic Games of 2016," said a key participant in the venture. "Nissan had to be ready for this, and we spent 230 million dollars as principal sponsor—as provided for in the agreement to build the plant and the various supports pledged by the State of Rio. But the brand awareness and gains in market share we achieved would require a decade, even more, in normal times. That was management according to Carlos Ghosn."

CHAPTER EIGHT

American Dream

In March 2020, United States Senator Lamar Alexander, and two other Republican senators, publicly denounced the "hostage justice" of Japan, describing Nissan's former board member, Greg Kelly, as the "leading example" of the system. The three senators had finally broken the deafening silence of American officials on the Japanese judicial system's discriminatory treatment of an American citizen—a loyal servant of Nissan for over three decades—under a plot hatched by the company's Old Guard. In a commentary published by the online news service *Real Clear Politics*, the senators noted how Mike Mansfield, former U.S. ambassador to Japan, had described the ties between the two countries as "the most important bilateral relationship in the world, bar none." Their conclusion: "If Americans and other non-Japanese executives question their ability to be treated fairly in Japan, then that most important bilateral relationship in the world is at risk."

Greg Kelly joined the headquarters of Nissan North America near Nashville in 1988. He worked and lived there until in 2008, when he left for Japan. By 2018, semi-retired for health reasons, he passed his time between Tennessee and Florida when he was not in Japan.

Kelly—the first American to sit on Nissan's board of directors—was arrested around the same time as chairman Carlos Ghosn on November 19, 2018. He was suffering from chronic neck pain and had to undergo back surgery two weeks later. Falling into a trap set by his "friend" and protégé Hari Nada, he joined the Nissan chairman at the Tokyo Detention House where he remained incarcerated for five weeks. Following discreet pressure by U.S. senators and diplomats, Kelly was released on bail on Christmas Day but was prohibited from leaving Japan. According to his wife Dee, the back surgery he had in Japan was not successful.

On September 15, 2020, Greg Kelly pleaded not guilty to conspiring to understate the remuneration of Carlos Ghosn as his trial opened at the Tokyo District Court. The trial was expected to last as long as a year. Confined to a small apartment, he was now the sole defendant in the Nissan Old Guard conspiracy. Carlos Ghosn had fled the hostage justice system the previous December, after deciding he was not going to spend the rest of his days in Japan. His successor, Hiroto Saikawa, and other Japanese executives who were accused of misappropriating funds as Ghosn and Kelly allegedly did, were not in the least bit worried. In an affair where the traitors were tightly knit, Carlos Ghosn had no doubt that Greg Kelly was paying the price for his honesty, loyalty and courage.

"My plight made big headlines, but you can't forget the ordeal imposed on Greg," he said from Beirut, describing his former colleague as "an honorable man, husband and father who was brutally taken from his family."

Tennessee Hosts First Japanese Transplant to U.S.

When Nissan was seeking a site for its first plant in the United States in the early 1980s, Tennessee Governor Lamar Alexander rolled out the red carpet to attract the unprecedented industrial investment of 500 million dollars to Smyrna, a town in Rutherford County near Nashville. The young governor won the confidence, and eventually the friendship, of Mitsuya Goto, the English-speaking executive who represented Nissan President Takeshi Ishihara.

According to American writer David Halberstam, the decision to create a "transplant" in the United States was the subject of a fierce internal battle at Nissan, where the formidable in-house union leader Ishiro Shioji had a strong influence on management. Nissan in the 1980s was not unlike Renault after it was nationalized in 1945. Under chairman Pierre Dreyfus and his successors, nothing important would get done without the backing of the CGT, the pro-communist trade union. In trying to attract Nissan's invest-ment, Tennessee faced intense competition from the rival states of Illinois and Ohio.

In April 2015, Lamar Alexander—then the Senior Senator from Tennessee—returned to Smyrna for one of his numerous visits to the town which had become the site of the largest automobile plant in North America.

"When Nissan came to Tennessee more than thirty years ago, there was hardly any employment linked to the auto industry in the state," Alexander said. "Today, three decades later, a third of industrial workers are in the auto sector, suppliers have set up shop up in 80 counties and average family incomes are a lot higher."

But the Nissan site in Smyrna transformed more than the local economy in Tennessee. It also upended the geography of the U.S. auto industry. Until construction of the Smyrna plant began in 1981, the industry was concentrated in the Great Lakes region around Detroit, on both sides of the Canadian border. Nissan's new plant was the first of a wave of Japanese "transplants," and others by German and South Korea carmakers. Factory labor moved from the north to the south, reversing the trend that saw massive migration of the African-American descendants of slaves on the plantations of *Gone with the Wind* to the industrial suburbs of the north. The historic rupture ended the monopoly of the Detroit-based UAW (now known as the United Autoworkers, Aerospace and Agriculture Implement Workers of America). It also led to legislation in the Southern states that provided for non-union factories.

Lamar Alexander urged the Big Three automakers in Detroit to seize the moment and managed to get General Motors to locate its Saturn subsidiary in the Tennessee town of Spring Hill, part of the Nashville Metropolitan Area, with a major investment and 27,000 jobs. It was not surprising that Alexander, first elected as governor in 1978, was still the state's most influential politician in 2020.

One Plant, Two Senators

Nissan's leap into the dark was not spontaneous. In the early 1980s, trade tensions between Washington and Tokyo were growing, and Japanese leaders were obsessed by the threat of American protectionism. Japan dreamed of becoming a superpower and American academic Ezra Vogel already saw "Japan as Number One," the title of his best-seller book published in 1979. In the corridors of power in the United States, the re-emergence of the nation defeated in 1945 was an economic and even existential challenge. Four decades later, America's "yellow peril" phobia is no longer towards Japan but China.

In Detroit, UAW unionists invited television cameras to watch them trashing a "Made in Japan" car. To maintain their lucrative market, Japanese automakers imposed "voluntary" quotas on exports to America, with support from the then Ministry of International Trade and Industry (MITI), which preceded the Ministry of Economy, Trade and Industry (METI). But the best defense against tariffs was to go and build cars where the customers were, and that meant making friends. "One plant, two senators" was the motto going around the Japanese auto industry in the 1980s. For Japan's mercantilists, globalization was a calculation, not a passion. It was based on need, not desire.

Like a Fish in Water

Carlos Ghosn's relations with the United States were different. They were not only rational, professionally and informally, but they were also shaped by his American sojourn with Michelin.

"If you associate the American management style with pragmatism, I learned a lot in the United States," Ghosn said. "I also appreciated the quantifiable approach to management. In France, there's an unfortunate tendency towards theories and grand speeches. When you arrive from France, you're surprised—and pleasantly so—by the pragmatism of Americans and their concern with quantifying things. Another important aspect of the business environment is the self-assured relationship to money—the more, the better. It's a successful criterion. Earnings are an essential indicator of good management and good health of a company—in a competitive system, of course. It pleased me a lot, all this pragmatism, absence of complexes and resorting to quantifiable data. My American experience enriched my way of managing. It was very pleasant for someone from an essentially French environment, where talk is too often dominated by ideology."

In September 1989, Michelin announced—discreetly, as the company usually did—the acquisition of Uniroyal-Goodrich, the second-largest tiremaker in North America. The 1.5 billion dollar deal made the tiremaker based in Clermont-Ferrand the world's biggest, ahead of the American leader Goodyear. Michelin already had significant operations across America, and François Michelin decided to put Carlos Ghosn in charge of integrating the two companies. He may have been barely thirty-five years old, but he had successfully just turned around Michelin's operations in Brazil—a very difficult market.

"For it to make sense, a merger must involve productivity gains," Carlos Ghosn said. "That means doing more with fewer means. In this area, Americans throw down their cards. On the other hand, Europeans have an excessive tendency to dither, delay and hide, often resulting in wishful thinking. In the United States, it's certainly more brutal. But it's more transparent.

"If you bring two companies together like Michelin and Uniroyal-Goodrich, there are obviously redundancies and job losses when duplication is eliminated. But that doesn't necessarily mean firing people. There's quite a range of means available to avoid outright dismissals such as early retirements, reductions in working hours and by freezing new hires.

"Michelin's headquarters were in Greenville, South Carolina, and Uniroyal-Goodrich's were in the rubber capital of Akron, Ohio—the South and the industrial Midwest, the same country but with markedly different mentalities. The headquarters of both companies were maintained. Akron remained the decision center for Uniroyal and Goodrich. We separated profit centers—tires for heavy-duty vehicles came under Greenville as a first step, and then tires for passengers and light-utility vehicles were put under Akron's responsibility."

America, America

Michelin's experience in North America inspired numerous principles that Carlos Ghosn used in the Nissan Revival Plan and Renault's "Twenty Billion Plan" before that. Why could success with an auto supplier not be taken higher, to the level of making cars? This explains why bringing the Alliance to the United States never left his mind.

"Today, the American market is still the first in the world in terms of profitability. That's because the product mix for sales is rich and the market is more homogenous than Europe. In the United States, sales of high-end cars, luxury brands, SUVs and pick-ups are high. In the 2000s, classic sedans were still the most important market segment. Today, vehicles built on small-truck platforms— SUVs, four-wheel drives and pick-ups—are the majority. For classic sedans, the Chinese market is now more profitable than the United States because of the ferocious competition in America. But the broader mix means global profitability is still higher in the United States. China is progressing in terms of volumes. Annual sales in the Chinese market are approaching thirty million vehicles, if you combine personal cars and light utility vehicles, while the American market is oscillating at around seventeen million if small trucks are included."

Ten Percent Target

"When we arrived in 1999, the Nissan share of the North American market was about 3.5 percent, with local production at plants in Smyrna and Mexico combined with imports from Japan," Carlos Ghosn said. "In the Nissan Revival Plan, I very quickly set a profitability target for the entire American market which was achieved. I had in mind a market share of 10 percent over the medium term for the simple reason that Toyota was not so far from that, and I couldn't see why Nissan couldn't do as well in the North American market. When I took over, the situation was clear cut. Toyota and Honda were ahead of Nissan, whose profitability was mediocre.

"Nissan's commercial management was not efficient, with steep discounts, no margins for dealers and marketing campaigns that weren't very successful. And then, secondly, the range could not meet American customer demands in terms of equipment and safety. Profitability is a function of product suitability to the market and Nissan had a big problem adapting products to American demand. Initially, there was essentially not enough dialogue between the people there and headquarters in Tokyo, with some very strange choices.

"It's true that marketing in the United States was still dominated by dealers, mostly multi-brand dealers. But their demands weren't all the same. The absence of a precise product plan at the center led to disorganized communications with the sales people. Toyota and Honda products were undoubtedly better targeted.

"I was in the field all the time during this period," Ghosn recalled. "And I spent a lot of time in the United States—not to make decisions for those involved, but to make sure those who had to make decisions had the right tools. Above all, ambition had to be restored. And comparisons had to be made, notably with Toyota, which was the benchmark.

"Nissan's technical center in the United States was in Detroit. Why? Because the Big Three automakers were still there. Most suppliers were also there. And many laboratories that work for the industry have operations there too. The technical center was dedicated to products destined for the American market. They could be global cars that needed to be adapted to American consumers, or cars conceived for the United States from platforms within the group.

"In the 1990s, there was almost no foreign expansion by Nissan. What existed had been done before. It was stagnant, still trying to exploit initiatives taken well in the past. Even more seriously, those expansion initiatives had led to no changes at the company level. There was no feedback that could have had an impact on how headquarters was operating. On paper, you could say the company was more internationalized than Renault when I arrived in 1999. But the mentality in Ginza was pretty similar to what I'd seen in Billancourt. It was heavily focused on what was going on in Japan with priority accorded to the Japanese market and delegations of Japanese emissaries to the United States or Europe. There was an appearance of internationalization," Ghosn said.

The early decision by Carlos Ghosn to invest massively in the United States was a rebuttal to those who were clinging stubbornly—as some still do today—to criticizing his policy of cutting costs. It was also a sign that Nissan was on the road to recovery.

Mississippi Plant Doubles U.S. Investment

"The first new expansion was in the United States," recalled Carlos Ghosn. "Right after the success of the Nissan Revival Plan was confirmed, I decided to build a new plant in Mississippi. This was the signal for an offensive on the American market, which saw Nissan's market share triple from 3 to 10 percent. Canton was the site of the first automobile plant in the state of Mississippi. I received precious assistance from Senator Trent Lott, who was the Senate Majority Leader at the time. We negotiated a good package with incentives and subsidies."

Trent Lott followed in the footsteps of Lamar Alexander, announcing to voters that Nissan would "revolutionize" the state's economy. Like the Smyrna plant near Nashville, the Japanese manufacturer set up the new plant near the Mississippi state capital in Jackson. The major suppliers followed. The project created 3,700 direct jobs and 6,400 jobs overall. With an annual production capacity of 450,000 units, the Canton plant was a huge investment—not far from one billion dollars, Carlos Ghosn's standard measure for achieving his American dream.

In her book, *The End of Detroit: How the Big Three Lost Their Grip on the American Car Market*, Micheline Maynard—who covered the auto industry for the *New York Times*—noted that Nissan built the Canton plant for one model, the Titan. In two decades, Japanese automakers, followed by their Korean rivals, had succeeded in overturning the Big Three of Detroit in the traditional market segment of family sedans. German automakers were meanwhile staking their bets on high-end brands like Mercedes, BMW and Audi.

Having largely lost the east and west coasts of the United States, the Big Three, which dominated the market for trucks and SUVs made on the same platforms, put up resistance to the foreign invaders in a vast zone spanning the Great Lakes region and the Midwest.

In terms of American auto fashion, trucks with supercharged engines like the Ford F-150 and its rivals had replaced the beautiful chrome-plated gas guzzlers of the 1950s and 1960s. Washington took care to protect these cash cows with tariffs of 25 percent on imports of trucks. In the early 2000s, the Big Three were producing 2.3 million pick-ups a year. Foreign manufacturers got around protectionist barriers by localizing production of both vehicles and parts.

"The content of vehicles manufactured in the United States was originated essentially within NAFTA," Carlos Ghosn said, referring to the North America Free Trade Agreement between the

United States, Canada and Mexico. "It was a question of costs, availability and avoiding excessively long supply chains for parts, but also a protection against fluctuating exchange rates. Localization was industrial common sense. The big Japanese suppliers were already in the United States and some of them accompanied us to Canton."

With the Titan, a big pick-up with an aggressive look designed by Shiro Nakamura—who Carlos Ghosn poached from Isuzu, much to the chagrin of Nissan veterans—Japan's number two automaker launched an assault on the ultimate bastion of its American rivals. On his numerous field trips, the Nissan chairman discovered that's what dealers wanted.

"The Canton plant was built to significantly increase capacity with priority on light utility vehicles, big pick-ups and large four-wheel drive vehicles like the Titan or Pathfinder. Canton's platforms were designed to handle large engines, whereas Smyrna was for everyday vehicles," Ghosn said. With its Intelligent Body Assembly System, Nissan was the Japanese pioneer in versatile assembly lines that could easily build very different models. "Smyrna is today the largest auto plant in both North and South America. But in terms of the best plants the Alliance has around the world, it's not in the top 25 percent. Nissan's best plants in terms of competitiveness are in China and Mexico."

Detroit Takes Note

If Carlos Ghosn never stopped looking at the United States, the interest was not just one way. Nissan's rapid and spectacular renaissance did not go unnoticed in Detroit, where the Big Three were in historic decline. The Nissan chairman wanted to find an American partner for the Franco-Japanese Alliance. But the shareholders of U.S. automakers were seeking to save their failed business model. Developed by Alfred Sloan, the founder and long-time president of General Motors who was the father of market segmentation, that model asserted that a generalist automaker should target all customers, or at least most of them. On the eve of the Global Financial Crisis that erupted in 2008, that meant eight different brands for General Motors and dozens of models, some of which sold only a few thousand units a month. The automaker was over-stretched. And the cavalier practices of the industry's financial arms—such as General Motors Acceptance Corporation—were not a clarion call but a blind rush towards a cliff. It was more like Daffy Duck and the Road Runner than John Ford. Detroit was living in denial, especially the affluent suburb of Grosse Pointe where huge auto industry fortunes flaunted themselves in fancy houses. The harshest and most lucid critics equated the white-collar bureaucracy of General Motors with that of a decaying Soviet Union under Leonid Brezhnev.

Moreover, American automakers were weighed down by trade union legacy costs related to retirement and health benefits, largely covered by the private sector in the United States. For General Motors, this financial burden was estimated at between 1,500 and 2,000 dollars for each vehicle. Little wonder the company was described as "a pension and health insurance fund that just happens to make cars." In December 2008, a commentary[8] published by the French online journal, *Mediapart*, highlighted how Sloan's way of doing business had become outdated:

"Viable forty years ago, when GM had more than half the American market, the model invented by Sloan has become impractical with its market share falling to 20 percent."

Industry insiders seemed incapable of such observations. On the sidelines of the Beijing International Automotive Exhibition in October 2006, Ford chairman Bill Ford—great-grandson of the company's founder Henry Ford—was offended when a television interviewer suggested that the family could lose control of the automaker.

"I don't understand how this could ever happen," Ford said. "There's no reason to think the way corporate ownership is structured should change." Although it held only 3.75 percent of the shares outstanding, the Ford family controlled 40 percent of the voting rights—which is why contacts between Ford and Carlos Ghosn were so short-lived. In August 2005, Bill Ford tried to poach him from Nissan to become chief executive of the U.S. automaker. Carlos Ghosn refused, having little interest in reliving his Michelin

---

8. Commentary by Philippe Riès.

experience in another family-controlled company where lineage and competence rarely go hand in hand, and where the former usually has more influence than the latter.

"Bill Ford told the press he wanted to hire me," Carlos Ghosn said. "I contacted him but it didn't work out. First, because I had a bias against family companies since my time at Michelin. Second, Bill Ford wanted to stay on as chairman of the board. At GM, it was clear—when you were chairman, you were in command."

Kirk Kerkorian Seeks to Clean up General Motors

In the absence of Carlos Ghosn, Bill Ford finally set his sights on Alan Mulally, who was hired from Boeing with a golden parachute of 15.4 million dollars if the Ford family lost control of the empire over the next five years. His plan was nothing like the Nissan Revival Plan or the "Nissan 180" recovery for growth deployed by Carlos Ghosn from Tokyo. Mulally negotiated 23.4 billion dollars in credit lines from banks and long-term loans to finance a brutal downsizing, with 16 plants closed and 40,000 jobs lost across North America.

Like Ford and Chrysler, General Motors was suffering from accumulated losses—10.5 billion dollars in 2005 alone. Shareholders were growing impatient, including Kirk Kerkorian. Having made a fortune in Las Vegas, the Armenian-American investor had accumulated 10 percent of the company's shares. He was determined to clean up the Augean stables at the seven towers comprising the global GM headquarters in Detroit, the unfortunately named Renaissance Center. For Carlos Ghosn, it was an opportunity to seize—bringing a third pillar into the Alliance, one that was firmly anchored in the North American market.

"It was an important market where our position was still weak," Ghosn said. "I always considered the Alliance as a cooperative platform between manufacturers which did not directly compete against each other on a global scale. The contacts with General Motors began in 2005. The company was not in a good state. The initiative was taken by Kirk Kerkorian, a large GM shareholder who was not at all happy about the way the company was being managed—and not without reason."

It was not only bureaucracy that recalled the Soviet Union at General Motors, but also the company's social policies. Back in 1984, an agreement between the UAW and the Big Three led to the creation of Jobs Bank, a mechanism to pay workers who were idled by automation to do nothing. This amounted to unemployment benefits for an indefinite period. When the system was at its peak in 2006, some 15,000 retrenched employees at the Big Three were getting 90 percent of their salaries plus contributions to their retirement and health benefits. The bill was astronomical for the three companies, and the system was damaging worker morale. What's astonishing is that Jobs Bank was proposed not by the trade unions but by GM management—the same management that included Bob Lutz, the man who questioned the prospects of the Alliance back in 1999. With its customary arrogance, the management was convinced that the mechanism would never come into play because GM would always work at full capacity.

The management of General Motors—immortalized in the documentary *Roger & Me* by American filmmaker Michael Moore—had another brilliant idea in the mid-1980s. This was to entrust its Japanese competitor, Toyota, with modernizing and managing its Fremont plant in Alameda County in California, the worst of all the company's plants in the United States. Renamed as New United Motor Manufacturing, the new jointly-operated plant made Japanese and American models on the same production lines. The Americans had to relearn how to make cars, especially small ones, and the Japanese desperately needed allies against the rampant protectionism in the corridors of Washington.

New United Motor Manufacturing quickly became the best GM plant in North America, as Chevrolet-badged vehicles were actually Toyotas. But General Motors proved incapable of transplanting to the rest of the company the management know-how and equipment brought by Toyota. For the incompetent barons who considered their plants as personal fiefdoms, it was always my way or the highway. The Global Financial Crisis sealed the fate of this particular venture—but not the Fremont plant itself, where an even greater revolution later took place. Under Elon Musk, the facility housed the first assembly lines for the Tesla.

Case of the Purloined GM Study

"I didn't know Kirk Kerkorian," said Carlos Ghosn. "He asked to meet me. 'GM's losing its leadership position,' he said. He found chief executive Rick Wagoner both 'soft and quite arrogant.' I replied that I saw the possibility of doing something together within the Alliance. GM would remain GM, but we could work on synergies. A study was launched and a team was put together with representatives of GM, Renault and Nissan.

"This study was confidential, but showed huge synergies. It was stolen from me when prosecutors raided my apartment in Tokyo. They took all my archives. I asked for them back, but I'm still waiting. The only thing they didn't take from the apartment was cash. They stole—because there is no other word to describe it—a very large number of personal documents which had nothing to do with their inquiry. I was the only one to have this study because its distribution was forbidden to avoid any charge of insider trading. The GM lawyers weren't so easy going—they ordered all copies destroyed to avoid leaks to the press.

"The study group notably included Bo Andersson, the head of purchasing at GM who we'd see in Russia a few years later as head of AvtoVAZ," said Ghosn. "There was also Fritz Henderson, who succeeded Wagoner when GM was taken over by the government. Wagoner's right-hand people took part actively in the talks and were not at all opposed to joining the Alliance. But he was hostile. He told me clearly that the only reason he accepted the study was because it had been ordered by the board.

"I was also direct: 'Look, Rick, I never do hostile bids. If you don't agree, let's leave it at that.' I never submitted an offer to the GM board as that would have required a management agreement," Ghosn said. "To Kerkorian, I said: 'If you want us to move forward, GM has to be headed by a chief executive who has faith. I won't do anything without a supportive chief executive. I don't know how to do a hostile bid and I don't think one would succeed.' Kerkorian did not have a majority on the GM board to get rid of Wagoner, which was needed to move ahead. I can still hear him saying: 'I have my own plan to rescue GM and I don't need you.' The company later collapsed and Wagoner was fired.

"As we were doing this work," continued Ghosn, "the finance minister in France was Thierry Breton. He wanted to take part in the talks. He wanted to know everything." Before becoming minister, Breton was a businessman who gained a reputation in France for turning around several troubled companies. "After I was arrested, he was the sole French business leader to publicly come to my defense," Carlos Ghosn said. "But relations with Minister Thierry Breton were not easy. It was a complicated deal. If GM management was hostile and the French government wanted to get involved as a Renault shareholder, it would be impossible. I decided to drop it."

"It Would Have Been Magnificent"

The Global Financial Crisis halted the death of General Motors under Rick Wagoner. On June 1, 2009, GM filed for bankruptcy in a New York court. It had assets of eighty-two billion dollars to meet commitments of 173 billion dollars, making it the biggest industrial bankruptcy in history. General Motors chairman Jack Smith had promoted Rick Wagoner, whose background was in finance, to run GM's automobile operations in North America in 2000, when the company had 33 percent of the market. By the time of Wagoner's downfall in 2009, the GM market share had plunged to 18 percent. During the last four years of his mandate, GM suffered accumulated losses of some eighty billion dollars. Having sat atop the podium of the world auto industry for decades, General Motors ceded its leading position to Toyota, which was on its way to becoming the American market leader as well. GM had just invested massively in China, which was now its largest market. But its European operations were bleeding cash year after year. And in North America, it was incapable of exciting consumers with vehicles that lacked originality and quality, which was always below that of its Asian or European rivals.

"The contacts established during the talks in 2006 later led Barack Obama's car czar, Steven Rattner, to propose me as chief executive of GM," Carlos Ghosn said. "The people who took part in the talks found me reasonable and not aggressive, but knowing what I wanted. The feeling was that we could find common ground.

"When Rattner contacted me, I took up the same idea as before: 'Why not join the Alliance?' But he had no faith in the Alliance.

Obama administration officials were more interested in my approach than the Alliance, which they did not fully understand. They found it too complicated.

"The synergies would have mainly come from purchasing and sharing platforms and engines. The savings would have been enormous. We could have taken the GM engines for large pick-ups and reduced our investment in that area. At the same time, we would have brought a workload management schedule to GM plants. It was a win-win.

"There were also places with great potential where we could cooperate locally—in Brazil with Renault, in Europe where GM was always in difficulty, in China and also South Korea, where they controlled Daewoo and we controlled Samsung. There were synergies all over the place. It would have been magnificent," Ghosn remarked.

The social bill at General Motors was extremely high, both before and after the Obama administration took the company over with an injection of fifty billion dollars. By this stage GM had 243,000 employees, down by 143,000 from when Wagoner took over in 2000.

GM Files for Bankruptcy

The rapid move to Chapter 11 bankruptcy proceedings led to further bleeding in terms of production capacity and jobs, many in North America. Similar to bank failures, the proceedings led to the creation of two new companies—the "good" one which inherited the viable GM assets and the "bad" company with the debt and bad assets, known as Motors Liquidation Company. Four out of eight automobile brands disappeared as the "new GM" aimed to cut the workforce to 168,000 by the end of 2009.

For GM operations in Europe, the bankruptcy proceedings in the U.S. were a partial postponement. For two decades, Detroit was unable to make money from Vauxhall, the British automaker acquired in 1926, and Opel, the German manufacturer bought in 1931. Europe was a source of recurring losses. After a failed attempt to spin off GM Europe to Canadian automotive supplier Magna, the European operations were acquired by French automaker PSA

164

BROKEN ALLIANCES

Peugeot-Citroën in August 2017. Applying lessons learned from Carlos Ghosn, PSA chief executive Carlos Tavares transformed Opel and Vauxhall into profitable operations in less than a year—without any special drama.

"When it comes to synergies, why do some people automatically conclude that it's a bloodbath for jobs?" Carlos Ghosn asked. "In a merger, a bloodbath is when there's too much duplication. That wasn't the case here, there was very little. The main advantage of synergies is not eliminating but sharing. We can avoid new investment by profiting from what the partner puts into the communal pot. If we'd decided to put Renault and Peugeot together, there would have been a social bloodbath because you can find duplication everywhere. By contrast, bringing Renault and Daimler together would not result in a bloodbath, as they complement each other in numerous areas. GM joining the Alliance would have responded to the same logic.

"What happened next resulted from bankruptcy for which management bore responsibility," said Ghosn. "GM was dysfunctional for years and this was visible to the naked eye. Joining the Alliance would have let it recover rapidly through benchmarking and transfers of best practices, with synergies emerging despite all the inefficiencies. We would have put figures on all this, of course.

"If the deal had been closed in 2006, GM would have kept its board of directors," Carlos Ghosn said. "We'd thought about an exchange of shares." And the Renault-Nissan venture in the Netherlands, which oversaw the Alliance, "would have adapted to accommodate the new partner. I would have joined the GM board, not necessarily as chairman because the steering would have been done at the Alliance level.

"Obviously, it would have been impossible to bring the world's top automaker into the Alliance without changing it. How would we have organized the work to effectively bring out the synergies? It would have been organized with Nissan and Renault under a centralized framework. But this idea was never pushed to its conclusion as I gave up after Wagoner's opposition. There were constant reflections and speculation about how the Alliance would evolve. The central question always is to know why two parties are being brought together. Do the potential gains justify the undertaking? You have to answer yes or no. And then implement."

"Biggest Mistake of My Life"

For the Obama administration, the government takeover of two of the Big Three was strictly pragmatic—a temporary measure designed to avoid the liquidation of an industrial empire employing hundreds of thousands of people across the world. The draconian conditions attached aimed for the government to withdraw as soon as possible once viability had been restored and the patients were able to walk without the crutches provided by federal funds. No American administration, even the most progressive, had ever considered that the federal government would get involved in making cars. So whoever headed the "new GM" had to be able to guarantee the government's withdrawal as quickly as possible.

"Rattner called me and we even had meetings at his home in New York," Carlos Ghosn said. "With Americans, the dialogue is always very direct: 'Carlos, we'd like to meet you as soon as possible. I've just spoken to the president and we'd like you to become the new GM boss'."

A former reporter for the *New York Times*, notably in Washington, Steven Rattner decided in the early 1980s to stop writing about the "masters of the universe" to try and become one of them instead. His investment banking career spanned Lehman Brothers, Morgan Stanley and Lazard Frères. In 2008, by which stage he was number two at Lazard in charge of mergers and acquisitions, he left the investment bank to form a private equity venture with colleagues. After the election of Barack Obama, Treasury Secretary Timothy Geithner hired Rattner—part of the Democratic elite of Wall Street—to run the Presidential Task Force on the Auto Industry. He was soon known as the "car czar" among media.

"At the first interview, I once again raised the Alliance," said Carlos Ghosn. "But the reply was: 'We're interested in you and we're offering the job to you.' It was as simple as that. I replied that it would be complicated to leave my two companies in the middle of the crisis. But taking into account the way I've since been treated . . .

I should have selfishly considered my own interests. History would have been very different."

Steven Rattner recounted this meeting in his book *Overhaul: An Insider's Account of the Obama Administration's Emergency Rescue of the Auto Industry*. But he did not reveal the package, reportedly fifty-four million dollars a year. This has not been confirmed by Carlos Ghosn.

"It was 2009, at the worst point of the financial crisis. Renault and Nissan were not doing well, and I was going to leave the mothership and go to GM? He gave me time to think, but it was not going to happen. Yet three of my four children are American citizens. From a professional point of view, it was probably the biggest mistake of my life. Moreover, it would have been fun, a piece of cake . . . GM's weaknesses were glaringly obvious—the lack of decisions and lack of clarity when they were finally made, the choices not made, contradictions everywhere, a company given over to the auto barons. The application would have been difficult, but that's my cup of tea—putting changes into place and getting them accepted. With all the work accomplished in 2006, I was well prepared."

Golden Eggs at Chrysler

After Ford and General Motors, there was still Chrysler, the smallest of the Big Three—or whatever was left of them. Chrysler had a troubled past, having already sought federal government assistance. It was turned around by Lee Iaccoca, who became an industry icon and household name at Chrysler after being fired as Ford chief executive by chairman Henry Ford II.

When the Global Financial Crisis pulled the rug out from under the feet of Detroit, Chrysler was controlled by Cerberus Capital Management, a private equity fund in New York. Two years earlier, Cerberus liberated German automaker Daimler from the burden its American subsidiary had become. The "merger of equals," sought by Daimler chief executive Jürgen Schrempp to become a global company, ended up as a costly mistake for the Mercedes manufacturer.

Cerberus was headed by Michael Feinberg who used to work at Drexel Burnham Lambert, a failed U.S. investment bank that was legendary for both good and bad reasons. Cerberus had no experience in the automobile industry. But the financial arm of Chrysler was seen as a goose that laid golden eggs, whose earnings far outweighed the risks of acquiring the company. Chrysler itself faced problems, as customers were increasingly turning away from its narrow range of models. At the same time, its production costs were too high and the company lacked a pipeline of new products. Yet financing loans to feed the earnings of automakers required customers. Chrysler started burning cash at an alarming rate, a situation exacerbated by a ten-billion-dollar charge that Cerberus imposed on Chrysler as the price for taking control, a common practice among private equity funds. Cleaning up the automobile operations to support the financial arm was therefore a matter of urgency.

"Cerberus called me," Carlos Ghosn recalled. "They wanted Chrysler to join the Alliance and negotiations effectively began. I entrusted Alain Dassas and Carlos Tavares, both originally from Renault, who now had senior positions at Nissan. It was just before the crisis of 2008. We made a lot of progress and also found many synergies. What stopped everything was the financial crisis. We now had priorities other than a merger. Dassas and Tavares had been extremely keen for an agreement and were very disappointed that it didn't go ahead."

On April 30, 2009, Chrysler was put under Chapter 11 bankruptcy protection. Thanks to intervention by the federal government, which briefly took over the company, Cerberus managed to save 19 percent of its investment. Nobody mourned the fate of the dozens of speculative funds that Michael Feinberg convinced to join the Cerberus venture. Those who refused to accept Chrysler's debt restructuring were publicly denounced by Barack Obama.

The main shareholders in the "new Chrysler" were trade union members through the UAW pension fund. But after the brief "patriotic" period with Cerberus, everyone knew that a foreign shareholder was only a matter of time. Fiat acquired an initial 20 percent, which progressively rose to 100 percent in 2014. The Turin-based automaker had invested four billion dollars to take control of America's third-largest manufacturer. That compared with thirty-six billion dollars invested by Daimler in Chrysler in 1998, and seven billion dollars spent by Cerberus to acquire its 80 percent stake. The Agnelli family who controlled Fiat had Sergio Marchionne to thank. In 2004, the Italian-Canadian businessman was appointed chief executive of the auto division of the family empire.

"For the Agnelli family, it was an unexpected lifebuoy," Carlos Ghosn said. "Fiat was in a precarious situation, but got Chrysler financed by the Americans and rode the recovery. They did very well." Indeed, John Elkann—the grandson who Gianni Agnelli had left in charge of the family's destiny—did not have to get a green light from a government shareholder by pleading his case before a finance ministry, as would have happened in France.

"I never stopped looking closely at market opportunities but without abandoning organic growth which was our center of gravity." Nissan and Renault resumed their expansion after the financial crisis, which resulted in losses for both companies in 2009, the only time they fell into the red during the mandate of Carlos Ghosn. "Nissan flirted with 10 percent of the North American market in 2017," he said. "Businesses cannot have a fallback strategy, there's no such thing. When your mission is to be the number one generalist manufacturer in the world, you cannot withdraw from a major market, even if it's difficult and you're not making a lot of money."

Saikawa Interferes in North American Market

The alleged failure of Carlos Ghosn's growth strategy in the United States featured prominently in the Nissan Old Guard's invented stories to destroy the image and reputation of the former chairman after his arrest. Spoon-fed by an army of communications people mobilized by Nissan, a complacent international media picked up the chant without even contacting the people brought into question or—as the *New York Times* did—completely ignoring their version of events.

"Results were very good until 2017," Carlos Ghosn said. "The downturn took place in 2018 when Saikawa started directly interfering in management on the ground. He made things worse by demanding a reduction in discounts. Reduced volumes increased unit costs and we fell into a very dangerous spiral."

According to José Muñoz, the executive committee member who resigned less than two months after Carlos Ghosn's arrest, "Nissan's biggest market was North America and we've seen a disaster since Mr. Ghosn and I were forced to leave the company. When I was presiding over North American operations, they contributed to half of global earnings compared to about a third for other Japanese manufacturers." The difficulties started when Hiroto Saikawa was promoted to the position of chief executive at Nissan. At this point, José Muñoz was no longer on the ground in the United States but at Nissan headquarters in Yokohama, where he was chief performance officer.

"Saikawa wanted to directly manage the North American operations, going against my directions," said Muñoz. "His policy was to ease the pressure on China and increase it in North America. The region was supposed to report to me. He was speaking directly to Denis Le Vot, the chief executive of Nissan North America who came from Renault and didn't know the brand or the American market. It's an extremely competitive market—a decision taken today will have immediate impact. You cannot follow decisions taken two years earlier. Unlike Europe, the market's based on stocks, not orders."

José Muñoz gave an example of how the Nissan Old Guard manipulated facts with sales to car-rental fleets. "The United States was hit by two hurricanes during this period which led Nissan, like other automakers, to write off the value of numerous destroyed or damaged vehicles. Victims were compensated in kind, not in cash but with cars. These vehicles were included in sales to the fleets. But they then fell back to their normal level," Muñoz said. "And here. By that time, Mr. Ghosn nor I could be held responsible.

"For quite some time, my impression is that Saikawa sabotaged the North American operations by taking advantage of Denis Le Vot's inexperience. I even called Greg Kelly, who was a member of the board, to ask if he could intervene with Saikawa and Le Vot: 'Please ask Saikawa to stop interfering. He doesn't know the situation and this will turn out badly. Tell Denis he should report only to me.' I contacted Le Vot to warn him: 'Saikawa is giving you instructions, but if things turn out badly, I know him well enough that he'll blame you'."

"It's true that the product range was aging and there were problems with CVT, a very serious issue in the United States," Muñoz said, referring to Nissan's Continuously Variable Transmission system. A source of pride among Nissan engineers, the system was the source of numerous legal cases in the United States involving angry customers encouraged by specialized law firms. "When John Martin and I took over manufacturing, the quality issues progressively decreased. Nevertheless, CVTs and all the legal actions launched against Nissan remained a weak point. But we reduced discounts and the volume of sales to the fleets were excellent in 2016 and 2017."

How do you make a bad situation worse? After Carlos Ghosn, José Muñoz and others were purged, the Nissan Old guard appointed José Luis Valls to head the crucial North American operations. Valls was an Argentinian who was the deputy and successor of Muñoz in Mexico, where Nissan had a significant presence. According to Muñoz, "they rewarded him because he contributed to the Carlos Ghosn inquiry when he headed South America by giving information to Hari Nada about Brazil, notably the role of Mr. Ghosn's sister Claudine. But he had no experience with the North American market." Fifteen months later, in May 2020, Valls was kicked out, as a considerably weakened Nissan—like the rest of the auto industry—faced the disastrous impacts of the Covid-19 pandemic.

Fiat Merges with Chrysler

On Carlos Ghosn's desk, the Chrysler file was not closed. "After Sergio Marchionne died in 2018, I was in regular contact with John Elkann about possible cooperation," he said. "So they wouldn't be surprised if this leaked to the press, certain Renault board members were informed of these contacts.

"The circumstances were obviously very different to those created by the coup d'état of November 19, 2018. Nissan was strong, Renault had just posted the best results in its history and Mitsubishi was in full recovery mode. For the second year in a row, the Alliance was number one in the world. We had the platforms and the technologies, we were on course and had a performing leadership team. By contrast, Fiat-Chrysler lacked platforms and technologies—it was way behind in electric cars—and did not have a real presence in

China, the world's biggest market. But at the end of the day, they were the ones needing a deal. Their strong point was the United States, where only Nissan had a significant presence, which was obviously a plus." Fiat-Chrysler Automobiles would have brought to the Alliance "brands with strong international potential that were still underexploited, like Jeep, and very profitable operations in the United States with Dodge's Ram pick-ups. That would have allowed for concentrating and rationalizing investments in large pick-ups to the benefit of both Ram and Nissan. The synergies would have been immediate." Moreover, Fiat-Chrysler had luxury brands like Alfa Romeo and Maserati that the Alliance lacked.

"In addition, there was an important element for me—John Elkann was young," Carlos Ghosn said, referring to the grandson of Gianni Agnelli who was barely more than forty years old. "The bonus was that the group was financially healthy and could have bought out the French government's stake in Renault." For the chairman of both Renault and Nissan, it would have been "out of the question" for the French government to be present in an alliance with Fiat-Chrysler. "But to get rid of the French government, we had to bring in a European investor considered admissible. An Italian company as reference shareholder for the group would have been—in principle—acceptable to the French government, more so than a Japanese or any other non-European company. We were at the beginning of this process, and scheduled a detailed working meeting for January 11, 2019." By that time, however, Carlos Ghosn was in prison.

CHAPTER NINE

Globalization After All

February 9, 2012, was a big day in the history of Morocco. In an industrial zone next to the new port in Tangiers, the largest automobile plant in the southern Mediterranean region was inaugurated. King Mohammed VI took the journey from Rabat, accompanied by his government. The delegation was received by Renault chairman and chief executive Carlos Ghosn. France was represented by its ambassador.

During the campaign for French presidential elections in 2012, both the extreme right and the extreme left were unanimous in their outrage over this latest example of "delocalization." In fact, the new Renault-Nissan plant in Tangiers was mostly dedicated to building cars under the Dacia brand, whose historical production base was in Romania. It was not clear if the Romanians protested, but there was no need to protest—the factory in Pitești was running at full capacity, producing 400,000 vehicles a year. The Tangiers plant was creating new capacity.

Renault's move into the market for low-cost cars or "entry-level" models was a remarkable success. In the European Union, it was not only customers in middle-income countries and new members in Eastern Europe that were condemned to the market for second-hand cars. Customers in the more advanced countries were too, including France. And so were those in emerging economies like Morocco. It was not long before police could be seen driving in Logans, the new Dacia model launched by Renault, in a dramatic car chase in *The Bourne Ultimatum*, the third installment of an American action thriller.

"Prime Minister Driss Jettou came looking for the plant," recalled Carlos Ghosn. "There'd been rumors in the press indicating that Renault needed a new plant, basically for the Dacia brand. There was nothing official. I simply confirmed that we lacked capacity in the entry-level segment. Schweitzer had launched low-cost vehicles but when I came back to Renault in 2005, Dacia had one model only—the Logan. We developed a complete range from family sedans to SUVs and vans. The market was no longer just Romania and Eastern Europe. Dacia vehicles were widely distributed, and we couldn't meet demand."

In the fifteen years from 2005, Dacia sold 6.4 million vehicles in Europe and was one of Renault's main profit centers. Prices were well above the initial target of five thousand euros. The brand attracted a loyal customer base that was much larger than expected. In rural or peri-urban areas in Europe, the Duster SUV recalled Renault's success with its legendary 4L model, of which eight million units were distributed. Contrary to the fears expressed, especially by the French automaker's trade unions, Dacia did not cannibalize Renault sales, or, if so, only marginally.

Good Business in Morocco

"My assistant, Anja Wernersbach, told me one day that the Moroccan prime minister was in Paris and wanted to see me," Carlos Ghosn said. "The next day, I saw Driss Jettou arriving alone. He said: 'I read in the press that you're looking to set up a new plant. I have the King's approval to ask you what we should do for it to be set up in Morocco, especially in Tangiers where we're building a deepwater port'."

Renault already had a small industrial presence in Morocco— Somaca, an assembly plant in Casablanca. Established under an agreement between Renault and the newly independent state in 1959, it relied on parts and components from France, but capacity was limited. Between 1959 and 2016, its single production line had assembled only 500,000 units.

The new project was on a much larger scale, aiming to double Dacia's capacity. A plant in Romania was possible. Another option was Turkey, where the Renault venture with Oyak was one of the company's most important and most profitable factories. Morocco was not on the radar screen.

"Establishing a Dacia plant in a very advanced country was out of the question," Carlos Ghosn said. "When it comes to competitiveness, salaries aren't the only competitive factor, although they do count just the same. Lots of other things come into play, like the fiscal environment, energy costs, infrastructure, and the training and quality of the workforce.

"Driss Jettou said: 'If you're ready to launch a feasibility study, I'll personally supervise it and I'll put the industry minister, the finance minister and all resources necessary on to the case.' They formed a high-level team that was very professional and we completed the work in four months. They offered all the right conditions."

The Tangiers plant was a model industrial facility of the twenty-first century, located next to the port with a pier dedicated to exports. Production processes benefited from the experiences accumulated by the Renault-Nissan Alliance. It was also a clean plant, with carbon dioxide emissions reduced by 98 percent compared to old factories with the same capacity. Water consumption was 70 percent lower than comparable plants, meaning zero water waste thanks to Veolia Environnement, a major French water treatment company.

"I met the King several times," Carlos Ghosn said. "He was very courteous and took great care to make sure the government did everything necessary for the project's success. Relations with Moroccan authorities were excellent during this period. At the inauguration, the King and the Moroccan government were obviously there in force with the new prime minister, an Islamist. Apart from the French ambassador to Morocco, who sought refuge in a corner, not a single representative of the government in France was there. An investment of more than one billion euros, the first foreign factory set up by Renault in ages, and nobody came to represent the French government? That tells it all."

Just like Nissan's plant in Canton, Mississippi, transformed the face of the local economy, the Renault-Dacia facility in Morocco did the same, but with a twist.

"They did a great job," said Carlos Ghosn. "Ten percent of the output was sold locally and the rest exported. Our presence encouraged suppliers to come. Then Ford and PSA arrived." In May 2015, Ford announced the establishment of an assembly line in Tangiers, taking into account the environmental, infrastructure, material and training precedents set by Renault. And in 2019, PSA inaugurated a full plant in Kenitra, not far from Tangiers, with a production capacity projected to reach two-hundred thousand units in 2021 for the group's four brands—Peugeot, Citroën, Opel and DS, a legendary Citroën sedan from the 1960s that was recreated as a luxury French brand in 2014.

It was a virtuous cycle for an emerging economy. In 2020, a regional United Nations agency cited Morocco as a country that had entered a new phase of development since the Renault-Dacia plant was set up. The agency said the country's integration into global supply chains was linked to social and educational progress.

Beyond Morocco was sub-Saharan Africa, with its dynamic demographics and a very enterprising private sector that was unrestrained from the failed post-colonial structures that had been all too common. In Africa, education levels had increased significantly and middle classes were slowly emerging in large urban centers. This was where French manufacturers finally turned the page on protected post-colonial markets to regain ground in the face of primarily Japanese and South Korean competitors with the Chinese and Indians waiting in the wings.

"It's not well known, but the Alliance is number one in the African market," said Carlos Ghosn. "For new cars, the markets are the countries of northern Africa and South Africa—the biggest market followed by Algeria, Morocco and Egypt. They account for 70 percent of the market. For the whole of Nigeria, 50,000 new cars. We're number one in Morocco, and Renault is the leading brand in Africa and if you take all three components of the Alliance together, it's by far the largest in Africa, ahead of Toyota and Hyundai. The African market is in the process of taking off, with Renault dominating two of the continent's four main markets."

Positive Fallout in France

The French political system is inward-looking and based on patronage with a short-sighted horizon focused on electoral calculations. Those who seek to block emigration from former colonies in northern Africa are the same people who criticize an investment creating more than 6,000 jobs in a country with acute unemployment among young people who, whether qualified or not, dream of a better life in

Europe. These critics include leftists who criticize "poverty wages" paid to Moroccan workers, even though they are much higher than those paid elsewhere in the country.

Carlos Tavares, who was Carlos Ghosn's deputy at the time, showed that the one-billion-euro investment in Morocco had a positive fallout for France in general, and Renault in particular. Yet the French political class, especially its upper echelons, had a lot to do with the country's inability to understand globalization. There's a widespread ignorance of private enterprise where most heads of state or government—largely from the inner circle of civil servants—have never held an ordinary job. These people distrust the outside world and have only a vague command of English, if any at all.

Take François Hollande. When he was elected French president in 2012, the former first secretary of the Socialist Party—a graduate of the HEC business school and the inevitable École Nationale d'Administration for civil servants—had never been employed by a company, not even for an internship. And he had never set foot in Asia, the most dynamic region in the world, apart from a few days on vacation on a beach in Thailand.

"When a company establishes itself in a foreign country, it should—if possible—measure the benefits to labor in the home country," Carlos Ghosn said. "For example, what are the positive fallouts for France if I build a factory in Morocco? What's the plan for the additional work for engineering, support functions in France and French trainers? These things can be measured and do get measured.

"The new operation does not reduce activities in the home country—on the contrary," Ghosn explained. "Even opening a plant in China is positive for company activities in France or Japan. Globalization is reflected in a range of localizations. At first, you attack a market by exporting to it, often marginally. If the exports take off, establishing a local presence quickly becomes inevitable. That's true everywhere.

"Lamenting the absence of new plants being set up in the country of origin is pointless. That goes against economic models. People have to understand that activities in a country that is an investment destination are reflected in additional activities for a wide range of functions in the home country. There have been studies. There have been estimates. But politicians don't want to listen.

"On the other hand," said Ghosn, "when we inaugurated a plant near Oran in Algeria in November 2014, Foreign Minister Laurent Fabius and Economy Minister Emmanuel Macron attended. It was Algeria, of course, but only a small plant with a maximum capacity of 50,000 cars a year." It was 51 percent-owned by the Algerian government and, as the French press highlighted, the outcome of an accord signed in December 2012, during a visit to Algiers by President François Hollande.

A French Presidential Ritual

The idea that political power is the key to economic growth and prosperity is anchored in French public opinion, perhaps best illustrated by the Great Presidential Visit Abroad. This monarchical ritual mobilizes business leaders, sometimes by the dozen, to accompany the head of state to foreign lands where brilliant agreements are signed, generating grand headlines back home.

Such agreements are obviously the product of months or even years of legwork by teams of professionals working in the trenches to boost French exports. At best, the government role in their conclusion is minimal, if anything, and sometimes disastrous in the case of "major agreements" where taxpayers end up footing the bills, a specialty of the French nuclear power industry.

Carlos Ghosn never played these games. "Firstly, politics doesn't interest me," he said. "The pace is too slow. There's more talk than action. I never envisaged a political career. In Paris, I became a member of the Le Siècle[9] but hardly went to any of their dinners. I wasn't a snob towards Medef[10], but their meetings bored me.

9. Founded in 1944, Le Siècle ("The Century") is an association that includes politicians, government officials, trade unionists, business leaders, journalists, cultural figures and scientists who meet for dinner in Paris every month. It had 566 members in 2020. Renault chairman Louis Schweitzer chaired the group from 2002 to 2004.
10. Medef is the Mouvement des Enterprises de France ("Movement of French Enterprises") and is the largest French employer association with 173,000 member companies, mostly small and medium-sized enterprises.

"There was another, more fundamental reason," Ghosn continued. "If I headed only Nissan or Renault, it would have been a mistake to refuse efforts to integrate into the local business community. Nobody in Paris or Tokyo would understand. But from the moment I was truly crucified by my schedule between Nissan, Renault, then Mitsubishi and the Alliance, I simply had no time. My days were long with no downtime, and I had a family. And family is important to me.

"Since Jacques Chirac, I was invited by all presidents on all official visits to countries where the Alliance had a presence. I didn't take part in any of them. None of them criticized me in the open, but it's very likely it didn't go down well. The reason was simple—if you agree to take part in one of these trips, you have to get involved. It's a huge waste of time. So, I was never part of any official delegations, be they French, European or Japanese." In France, it was tantamount to lèse-majesté.

"From the time I made the choice and accepted the assignment, I had no time for anything else," Ghosn said. "In fact, I asked Schweitzer to remain in Japan after 2005. 'I'm in no rush,' I told him. He was the one who demanded I go back to Renault, even though he could have had another mandate in Billancourt. But he insisted, saying: 'I want to leave and there's nobody else to run Renault but you.'

"Schweitzer suggested I find someone else to run Nissan. But I didn't see anyone and added that the people at Nissan wouldn't understand me leaving the mothership six years after I arrived when everything was going tremendously well. I was really happy where I was. And there would have been nothing exciting about going back to Paris and once again finding all the problems of co-existing with the French government—even if the president was Jacques Chirac, who was not an interventionist.

"As soon as I accepted the two jobs, I put an end to my social life. I was in Japan every month. Then France, America, China and later Brazil and Russia. My four children meant a lot to me. There was a tradeoff between time spent on the business and that on social functions representing the companies.

"The consequence was not being popular in business circles," Ghosn said. "But I had the satisfaction of having a very close family.

It's true that I undoubtedly didn't do what was necessary to integrate with influential networks or circles. But it was a choice from the start."

Japan's Kei Cars to the Rescue

According to Pascal Lamy, former director general of the World Trade Organization, markets were global, but politics remained national. Multilateralism failed to provide the planet with governance to manage differences or divergences in "collective preferences" of people under national frameworks. Even the European Union, the most ambitious project to address this central contradiction of globalization, had its limits.

When Hiroto Saikawa betrayed Carlos Ghosn on November 19, 2018, he accused the chairman of "neglecting" the Japanese market. "That's wrong," Carlos Ghosn said. "We gave it the priority it deserved, but the Japanese market was not neglected. There was a set of priorities that took into account company interests, not nationalism. The Japanese market's a profitable market, but it's stagnant."

Japanese sales had collapsed 70 percent from their peak of 7.8 million units in 1990, the beginning of the lost decade that followed the bursting of the country's bubble economy. The market was sluggish, hardly surprising in a country losing 350,000 people a year, leading to the extinction of the last Japanese to turn off the lights around the year 3000 if current demographic trends continue.

The Japanese market was also changing with a growing share occupied by microcars. These ultra-light vehicles, known as kei cars in Japan, accounted for a third of sales and were especially popular with women and the elderly. In exchange for tax benefits, kei car manufacturers had to limit engine sizes to 660 cm^3 for both personal and commercial vehicles. At the other extreme, the high-end market was dominated by German and other foreign manufacturers for three decades after the removal of non-tariff barriers, which had long made the market impenetrable.

"Our relationship with Mitsubishi Motors Corporation started after we observed the Japanese market evolving and realized that we could not compete without being in the kei car segment, the most dynamic," said Carlos Ghosn. "Nissan was absent, and investing in a product whose only market was Japan didn't seem too exciting, so we had to find a partner. We tried with Suzuki and Mitsubishi as original equipment manufacturers. They supplied us with cars meeting Nissan's specifications that were sold under its brand. That made everyone happy. When Suzuki decided to team up with Volkswagen, the relationship became more complicated and we transferred most of this production to Mitsubishi."

Mitsubishi Motors Corporation was the problem child of the Mitsubishi conglomerate broken up by the Americans after World War II. At the beginning of the third millennium, it teamed up with Daimler in a prestigious but unhappy marriage, which started to sour when the German manufacturer uncovered serious quality problems at the Japanese carmaker. Despite getting a rebate on its investment, Daimler threw in the towel in 2004, around the same time as things started going badly in its merger with Chrysler in the United States. Daimler progressively reduced its stake in Mitsubishi, from 37 percent to 12.4 percent, which it discreetly sold to U.S. investment bank Goldman Sachs in 2005. The bank made an offer to Carlos Ghosn, but he found the price too high. Mitsubishi's subsequent attempt to break into the American market was a financial disaster. Similar to the sub-prime mortgage fiasco that lit the fuse of the Global Financial Crisis, Mitsubishi started offering "Ninja" car loans to buyers with no incomes, no jobs and no assets—and no repayment for the first year. In short, the buyers got a free car for a year before discarding the loan. The bill for Japan's sixth-largest carmaker came to one billion dollars.

Mitsubishi Family's Problem Child

Yet another scandal tarnished the name of the conglomerate when Nissan found that certain fuel-consumption tests on kei cars had been falsified. Of the 600,000 vehicles affected, 468,000 had been sold under the Nissan brand. It later emerged that falsified tests had been occurring for a quarter of a century. Had Nissan not stepped in, the legal consequences of the scandal could have been fatal.

"Osamu Masuko, the head of Mitsubishi Motors, came to see me to talk about their difficulties," Carlos Ghosn said. "I was not interested in hostile takeovers and everyone knew it. I indicated that Nissan was ready to help, but that this required an alliance. We acquired 34 percent of the capital of MMC with several conditions concerning governance and the composition of the board of directors, which I would chair. Masuko would remain as chief executive as naming someone from Nissan was ruled out.

"The deal was closed very quickly. I contacted the heads of the three main (Mitsubishi family) shareholders—the industrial company, the bank and the trading house. They were fed up with their involvement with their automobile affiliate and seeing their image sullied. I reassured them of our intentions, drawing on Nissan as an example. The reputation I had in Japan facilitated the deal. For 237 billion yen, Nissan became the main shareholder with 37 percent. It was a good deal, also for Renault, the main shareholder in Nissan.

"I made a commitment to keep the brand and protect the company's autonomy as they feared being absorbed outright by Nissan," Ghosn said. "It all happened rapidly and the recovery was spectacular. It's dreadful that the MMC share price almost halved after my arrest. The culprits behaved like Barbarians in Rome. It was vandalism.

"The management flaws at MMC were obvious. And the problems of scale were enormous for a company that barely sold a million cars a year. They plugged into joint purchasing with enormous benefits. We benchmarked their plant with ours, which led to spectacular improvements, notably in quality, which was the weak point that caused their last scandal. Like Nissan before 1999, there was an intrusive bureaucracy, a crying lack of initiative and very little interest in earnings. All this was aggravated by too small a scale. We got them out into the field at Nissan and Renault plants to study how we worked and to broaden their horizons. There were also immediate savings in research no longer needed on technologies the Alliance had. The recovery was a walk in the park. With very high requirements, we put the company on to a growth path.

"The deal was very well received at Nissan, provoking a certain pride," recalled Ghosn. "Mitsubishi employees feared falling into Nissan's clutches. My job was to reassure them. My reputation as a dictator, which some are now trying to stick to me, did not correspond to reality at all. I've always been a peacemaker and that's how I was perceived at Mitsubishi. When it came to personnel, it was always the same approach. No invasion, just some crucial skills, often requested by Mitsubishi.

"In any case, there were so many projects going on at Nissan that managers were seeking to preserve their teams. I had to force some transfers from Nissan and also attract candidates from Renault, most of whom acquired experience in Japan through the Alliance. The best example was obviously Ashwani Gupta, who was in charge of all light vehicles for the Alliance. He succeeded so well that I named him chief operating officer at Mitsubishi to replace Trevor Mann, who wanted to go back to England."

Troubled Japanese automakers traditionally relied on foreign partners to help them get back on their feet—Mazda with Ford, for example, or Mitsubishi with Daimler and Suzuki with Volkswagen. Sanctioned by authorities, many such marriages ended in divorce, often acrimonious. The Alliance was an exception, at least until November 19, 2018. Japan's top automaker, Toyota, drew most of its domestic rivals into its orbit, with the notable exception of Honda. By bringing Mitsubishi into the alliance, Carlos Ghosn saved Nissan from being alone in its home market.

Leadership in Southeast Asia

"MMC was not well established in Europe or the United States," Carlos Ghosn said. "But the company gave us a much stronger presence in Southeast Asia with plants in Thailand, Indonesia and the Philippines. They became benchmarks for the Alliance in this part of the world, whereas Renault or Nissan were benchmarks elsewhere. It was a big success."

Nissan was able to rely on Mitsubishi to improve the performance of Siam Motors, its subsidiary in Thailand. Nissan held 90 percent of the company, the automobile division of a family conglomerate that distributed Nissan vehicles in Thailand, the Detroit of Southeast Asia. But it was slow to realize its full potential.

"Siam Motors was a family company we bought that had not been run very well in the past. The Nissan executives we sent there didn't really succeed. It was a culturally difficult environment for our Japanese colleagues. They had to compensate individual weaknesses with collective action—that's the great strength of Japan. But it's hard to get the same results abroad. The Japanese work hard, display great loyalty to their company and communicate very quickly and smoothly with each other. These qualities count enormously in industry. However, brilliant individuals are pretty rare, undoubtedly because the education system and society doesn't let people emerge and stand out," said Ghosn.

And when some take the risk, it can turn out badly. In *The Reckoning*, David Halberstam recounted the story of Yukata Katayama, a Nissan employee exiled to California in the early 1960s to market Datsun cars. Known as "Mr. K" among American dealers, sales were much higher than expected. But he was in constant conflict with headquarters in Tokyo for adapting products and services to American customers. He literally imposed the concept of the Datsun 510 model on headquarters, which changed the image of Japanese cars in North America. It was like the BMW 1600 model at a third of the price.

Rather than being grateful, Nissan executives back in Tokyo took umbrage at the popularity of "Mr. K" on the other side of the Pacific. Katayama fell in love with the American way of life and almost went native, at one stage buying a house for 25,000 dollars so he could entertain customers at home—a practice unheard of in Japan. In 1977, he was brutally recalled to Tokyo and banished to an obscure subsidiary.

"Mitsubishi was better than us in Thailand, including in manufacturing," Carlos Ghosn said. "We relied on them to turn Siam Motors around. Plants would not be transferred from one company to another but there are numerous ways to improve things like benchmarking, better distribution of roles and so on."

So it was old news when the Alliance announced in May 2020, that a new page had been turned, according Mitsubishi the role as leader in Southeast Asia. It was the same with Mitsubishi's rechargeable hybrid engines. Carlos Ghosn had decided not to follow Toyota, which had lost money for years in hybrid technology, considered too complicated and costly, given the modest mileage gains. Nissan had instead invested massively in all-electric engines from 2010. But since the plug-in hybrid technology had already been developed, and investments were made by Mitsubishi, all Alliance partners could reap the benefits.

"If we didn't use Mitsubishi's rechargeable hybrid technology in the Alliance, Nissan and Renault would have had to make their own investments," Carlos Ghosn said. "When MMC joined the Alliance, the pace of seeking synergies didn't slow down. I didn't cut back the program."

Japan's Only Choice: Globalize

Mitsubishi Motors dealt with the possibility of solving an unresolved internal problem that existed for many years by leveraging integration with the rest of the world. Globalization was not without difficulties, risks and dangers. At the same time, however, it was also a reservoir of solutions, a panoply of guarantees and a security factor.

Well before China, Japan certainly benefited the most from the multilateral framework put in place after World War II that resulted in strong and continuous growth in international trade. The paradox was that most Japanese tended to remain withdrawn from this framework, a tendency that seems to be growing. In 2019, some 24 percent of Japanese citizens held a passport, down from 27 percent in 2005, and the lowest proportion among advanced economies. Far from improving, the command of English seems to have declined in younger generations and fewer Japanese students are tempted to pursue their education at universities abroad.

"When I arrived, practically no-one at Nissan headquarters had a good command of English," said Carlos Ghosn. "To find an English-speaking secretary, I had to search through all the company's departments. My first assistant came from the international sales division. In fact, Nissan was an extremely traditional Japanese company—very narrow, very closed, very siloed and we had a hard time correcting the situation. Corporate life was corseted by a list of endless bureaucratic rules from allocating pencils to adjusting office temperature."

"Japan has nothing. Agriculture is weak, there are no significant oil or gas resources, no minerals. There's not enough arable land. The archipelago is rattled by earthquakes every day and regularly suffers from typhoons. In a hostile regional environment, Japan's only resource is the Japanese people. And it became an economic power only by conquering world markets. They can't be against globalization. Pulling back would signal their death warrant. Japan isn't in love with globalization. It became enthusiastic out of obvious necessity. The model of a Japan that's autonomous or economically self-sufficient is quite simply not viable," Ghosn said.

But if Japan's attitude towards globalization seems paradoxical, what about France? The latest figures show that 1.35 million Japanese were living abroad as long-term or permanent residents at the end of 2017—about 1 percent of the population. France, with less than half the population, had twice as many expatriates.

"The experience we had in the Alliance was that it was easier to get French people to come to Japan than Japanese to go to France. For the Japanese, the cultural gap with the rest of the world is much wider," Carlos Ghosn said.

Adaptation is inevitably more difficult, the disorientation stronger. The French community in Japan, however, is nothing compared to the big concentrations in Greater London or the San Francisco Bay Area.

Who Consigned France to Rust Belt Status?

As the case of the plant in Tangiers showed, globalization got bad press in France, where it was blamed for the country's deindustrialization. Without exaggerating, relocating abroad accounted for only 5 percent of industrial job losses. Most were from technology upheavals and productivity gains, along with the loss of French competitiveness in Europe. People forgot that direct foreign investment had created millions of industrial jobs in France and refused to admit that public policies, especially fiscal policy, had strongly contributed to undermining the country's industrial base. One example—a source of recurring controversy—was the famous "production taxes" levied on companies irrespective of whether they were profitable or not. These taxes amounted to 9.7 percent of the value added by French industry in 2018, compared with 4 percent in Germany. The taxes themselves were a fiscal cluster bomb, with more than 200 categories.

Another aberration was that France had predatory taxes to "make the rich pay" like the annual stamp duty that was punitive on the largest cars. The tax lasted for more than five decades and, as a result, French automakers dropped out of the top end of the market where they excelled before World War II. The Germans made more vehicles at home because profit margins on high-end cars were much better than for smaller cars, where European competition was much more intense.

Yet France was the same country where luxury goods manufacturers had taken over their Italian and even American rivals to conquer the planet, employing 140,000 people directly, and up to two million indirectly. The luxury goods industry generated a trade surplus of more than twenty billion euros, as much as the aeronautics sector. Thanks to luxury goods, and certainly not fiscal policy, France was arguably—and ironically—the only economy in the world where the trickle-down theory, popularized by American economist Arthur Laffer, actually worked.

"Despite everything, French industry has recently recovered," Carlos Ghosn said. "Production at Renault's plants in France increased between 2014 and 2018. The low point was after the Global Financial Crisis. Some of the most harmful mechanisms like the 35-hour work week have been addressed. France is a very profitable market for Renault, and we've worked hard to maintain a strong position there."

Two competitive agreements with trade unions in 2013 and 2017 allowed Renault to narrow the performance deficit at French plants compared with the best at Renault and across the Alliance.

Dizzy from Deglobalization

"Deglobalization?" asked Carlos Ghosn. "I don't believe it. Corrections are taking place, explanations are required, and tests are necessary. There's a temptation in Europe to question European development by blaming the E.U. for everything bad—with Brexit on the one hand and certain Eastern European countries on the other. My opinion is still that we're going through a mid-life crisis.

It's a matter of rectifying the excesses of globalization, especially in regard to respecting identities, and refocusing. Brexit is a test, but the European Union can emerge stronger."

Brexit perfectly illustrated the irrationality of crowds—a referendum campaign that brought to a climax decades of systematic work by much of the London press against Brussels; the gross lies spread by the harbingers of secession, notably Boris Johnson, described by *The Economist* as the "Clown Prince," and the evil role played by his henchman Dominique Cummings in manipulating public opinion through Cambridge Analytica using data acquired from Facebook.

Britain's membership of the European Union gave it unrestricted access to the single market, allowing it to rebuild an auto industry that almost died from lack of investment amid low productivity caused by political incompetence, social irresponsibility and the national malaise of inertia.

None of the six major automakers operating in the United Kingdom were British. Top ranked Jaguar Land Rover was owned by the Indian family conglomerate that controlled Tata. Nissan, the number two, was Japanese and third-ranked Mini belonged to German manufacturer BMW (which also owned Rolls Royce whereas Bentley was controlled by Volkswagen, also from Germany). Japan's Toyota and Honda were in fourth and fifth place. As for Vauxhall, it finally left the decaying empire of General Motors with its European operations bought by PSA Peugeot-Citroën.

Auto production in Britain peaked at 1.72 million units in 2016 before falling for three consecutive years, largely caused by uncertainties over Brexit. In 2016, Nissan produced 500,000 vehicles at its massive Sunderland plant in northeast England, which employed 7,000 people directly and generated jobs for another 40,000 across the country. Nissan exported more than 60 percent of the plant's output to the E.U. Yet in the referendum on Britain's future status in the European Union in May 2016, a majority of 61.3 percent in Sunderland voted to leave, while only 38.7 percent elected to stay. The outcome, which commentators described as being like "turkeys voting for Christmas," probably reflected a "secret" compensation deal that Carlos Ghosn negotiated with the British government, allowing people to vote how they pleased without paying the price.

Theresa May's Assurance on Brexit

"What I negotiated with the British government was an assurance that Nissan would be compensated for the negative impact if the United Kingdom left the European Union," said Carlos Ghosn. "They were fully aware that industries based in Britain had to remain competitive if they isolated themselves from the continent. I told Theresa May: 'We are committed to staying in Britain if you are committed to preserving our competitiveness.' They confirmed this in writing."

What did compensation mean? If Britain left the E.U. without an agreement when the transition period expired at the end of 2020, Nissan vehicles would automatically be taxed by 10 percent. But the depreciation of the pound compensated for this. At the same time, Nissan could gain British market share with equivalent taxes imposed on imports of vehicles from the European Union. In the event, Britain left the E.U. at midnight on December 31, 2020, with a last-minute agreement guaranteeing that British car exports were safe—for the time being.

"What would a written agreement be worth?" asked Carlos Ghosn. "The point was not to send an invoice. The British government knew perfectly well that industries could leave the country if they wanted or if it was necessary. It would obviously be a gradual departure—once a new model came along, it would not be produced in Sunderland. Employment would decline. It would be the same thing with the same consequences for the next few models. Everyone would lose, the country and the company, but the stage was set from the start. If a manufacturer ceased investing in the United Kingdom, unambiguous responsibilities would have to be taken. No-one can fight the reality of the market, no-one. But I would be able to say: 'I've been honest with this country. I've been very transparent and nobody can say they're surprised. We discussed it and you replied, but you don't live up to your commitment.' I don't know what our competitors did. On our side, it was very clear in our exchanges with the prime minister at the time. Nissan has the documents that confirm this agreement in principle."

The collapse of the Berlin Wall and the Soviet Union in 1989 led to a second wave of globalization. Were value chains overstretched, too complicated, and consuming excessive fossil fuel? Probably. But companies started to make corrections themselves.

China became the "factory of the world," but mass production increasingly faced competition from Asian neighbors such as Vietnam and Cambodia. Diversification was the right response, not turning inwards or closing borders. Will some manufacturing be relocated back to advanced economies after fears of shortages triggered by Covid-19? It's possible. But more often than not, without jobs.

Taiwan Semiconductor Manufacturing Company, the world's largest semiconductor foundry, plans to invest twelve billion dollars in Arizona between 2021 and 2029 with only 1,600 jobs created. That compares with 3,500 direct employees with an investment of one billion dollars in an automobile plant. Tesla, which partly hopes to revive the American auto industry, chose China for its second plant, and Germany for its third—highly robotized like its first plant in Fremont, California.

Trump and NAFTA: Much Ado About Nothing

Smart protectionism is an oxymoron. The protection of national players favors rent-seeking behavior, discourages innovation, maintains technological laziness and heavily penalizes the consumer— the main beneficiary of globalization.

"Even the most virulent protectionists know very well there are limits that can't be crossed because they know they'll lose if they go too far," said Carlos Ghosn. "Look at what happened with the United States and Mexico. NAFTA was two decades old. The forces involved weren't the same, so it wasn't abnormal to re-examine it. Mexico had evolved, and so had the United States. But the wall Donald Trump dreamed about was not built. Nor were tariff barriers raised. The treaty was renegotiated and goods are still flowing between Canada, the United States and Mexico." And Nissan's three plants in Mexico were still integrated with the Smyrna and Canton facilities north of the Rio Grande.

"We aren't witnessing and won't witness a halt to globalization, but a rebalancing, notably with regional and bilateral accords, none of which aim to end trade. We hear a lot of talk and threats. But in fact, globalization will keep progressing, searching for a better balance, which will perhaps make it more solid. The vitality of globalization can be measured by how it doesn't ignore problems, but resolves them as it moves ahead."

CHAPTER TEN

How to Become World's Number One

The wave came at 3:37 p.m. It was March 11, 2011 and it was almost fifty feet high at the Fukushima Daiichi power plant, whose six nuclear reactors overlooked the Pacific. The tsunami engulfed four reactors protected to withstand a wave of less than twenty feet. Located on ground that was more than forty feet higher, the fifth and sixth reactors were spared. But down below, the cooling systems were flooded and not working. Over the next four days, reactors one to three would melt down in what was the world's biggest nuclear accident since the Chernobyl meltdown in 1986.

The initial reaction of Masataka Shimizu, chief executive of Tokyo Electric Power Company Inc. (Tepco) which managed the facility, was to order a total evacuation of the site. Prime Minister Naoto Kan, from the Democratic Party of Japan, ordered him to keep fighting. Holed up in the company's headquarters, Shimizu avoided the media—and taking responsibility. He did not visit the site until a month later on April 11.

In Tokyo, almost 160 miles to the south, panic was in the air, especially among expatriates who stormed the last flights out of the Japanese capital before airports were shut down for several days. Some foreign and Japanese companies relocated to Osaka, 370 miles to the west of Tokyo. What would have happened if the megalopolis of thirty million people had to be evacuated?

Rushing to Fukushima

"I was in Paris when the earthquake hit and returned to Japan as soon as the reopening of airports allowed," Carlos Ghosn recalled. "I was among the first, to boost troop morale, go into the field and engage the company with people affected.

"The Nissan plant directly affected was making engines in Iwaki, a city near Fukushima. No staff had died but, when I visited the plant fifteen days after the earthquake, there were gaping faults in the ground and production lines that were partly destroyed. The damage to buildings was substantial, so we had to bring in companies to restore the plant. But they refused to come because of the radiation.

"That's why we went there to assert our presence, meeting the mayor and the prefectural governor—to send a message to the construction companies that it wasn't dangerous since we were there and they'd do best to come quickly if they wanted to keep working with us. I told local television stations that we were going to roll up our sleeves and rebuild the plant. But it took several months to restore.

"Faced with dangerous situations, company bosses in Japan are generally not very visible. It was a very busy period and Nissan was the first automaker to resume normal operations because of our ability to react, and because we were better organized. Nissan pulled well ahead of its rivals in the financial year that followed, undoubtedly because it was the most internationalized. In the disaster, it was the one that put up the best resistance.

"We made some interesting observations—the usefulness of electric cars when gasoline supplies are interrupted or disrupted, for example. Electricity sockets are everywhere. For emergency transport, cities requested the first generation of the Leaf that had been put on the market in December 2010. It took less time to restore electricity networks than to repair roads to get gasoline tankers through. And the e-NV200 van could be used as an emergency power source."

Tepco Executive Impunity

The Fukushima disaster had long-lasting negative impacts on Japanese industry, cutting power generation by 30 percent and inflating the import bill for fossil fuels. Only nine out of 54 reactors in service in March 2011, were running nine years later in March 2020. Twenty-one would never operate again. The Fukushima plant will continue producing millions of tons of contaminated water until on-site storage capacities peak in 2022. The government was considering the best time to let Tepco discharge it into the Pacific. And the three charged for criminal negligence were acquitted. Masataka Shimizu had never been concerned.

"Industry wanted reasonable electricity prices to return as quickly as possible," Carlos Ghosn said. "The decision to freeze nuclear power usage was obviously a mistake. The safety problem didn't come from nuclear power itself, but from the design of the plant, despite common sense and decades of warnings ignored. It was a management problem and those responsible for the disaster enjoyed total immunity."

Behind such impunity was the discriminatory and partial workings of the Japanese judicial system, notably public prosecutors. But the indulgence shown to the bosses of Tepco, Toshiba, Olympus, Kobe Steel and Takata—just to name a few Japanese companies involved in recent scandals—reflected two founding myths of the "Japanese model" that had been on people's minds since the 1970s and 1980s. That was when the model became a benchmark for high economic growth.

Myth number one was that Western business leaders were motivated by self-interest and greed, but Japanese business leaders involved in wrongdoing were always acting in the interests of their companies. They graduated from college, entered a company, worked their way up, sacrificing their family life and personal happiness. The businessman briefly occupied the top of the pyramid, but did not exist outside the group without the collective of which he was an indistinct part. Caught red-handed, a Japanese business leader would usually get off by exercising the ritual of contrition with apologies to all stakeholders, the general public, customers, colleagues and sometimes even shareholders with a 90-degree bow to the cameras. Resignations followed when necessary, and then a comfortable life in semi-retirement as a "senior advisor" with an office, a company car with a driver and a young secretary serving tea, all at the company's expense.

Japan's Consensus Fiction

The other myth was "Japanese" consensus. In 1984, a group of French researchers who passed through the Maison Franco-Japonaise in Tokyo examined this "consensus ideology" in a book entitled *Japon. Le consensus: mythe et réalités.* That mythical consensus was used by the Japanese but also by those in the West who were uneasy about Japan emerging as a top-ranking economic power. Under this myth, Japan was a harmonious non-confrontational society with a large middle class where corporate vocabulary was dominated by a few key words—*ringisho* (announcing a decision to staff), *hanashiai* (meetings, which are abundant) and *nemawashi* (the compromise, which is sacrosanct). Facing social tensions in the 1970s, when the period of strong post-war growth came to an end, Western employers—especially those in France—looked at Japan. Here was a land where strikes were almost unknown, where workers sang the company song before turning on their machines, where overtime was not claimed and leave not taken.

This traditional and naive image of social relations ignored the violent conflicts after Japan's defeat in World War II and the brutal oppression that followed, recalling the wiping out of all opposition by military police before 1945. The image also forgot that lifetime employment, a pillar of the "social model" of Japan, was rooted in gaining the loyalty of an unstable and rebellious workforce in the early days of the country's industrialization.

Above all, the consensus ideology ignored strong, imperious and even dictatorial personalities who were legendary leaders like Akio Morita at Sony, Kazuo Inamori at Kyocera and Konosuke Matsushita at the company that bore his name until it was changed to Panasonic.

In the auto industry, Honda Motor Company owed its independence to the strong will of Soichiro Honda, its founding president who defied the Ministry of International Trade and Industry to turn the motorcycle maker into a car giant rivaling Toyota and Nissan. Elsewhere in the industry, Eiji Toyoda, the "emperor" who was a cousin of Toyota's founder, transformed the company into a global giant over four decades. And Taiichi Ohno—an exacting master, prone to anger and sometimes even violence—was father of the Toyota Production System that changed the world.

In reality, power in Japanese companies was a lot more concentrated and exercised less consensually than legend would have people believe. Renault chairman Louis Schweitzer witnessed this firsthand during negotiations on forming the Alliance with Nissan chef executive Yoshikazu Hanawa in March 1999.

"The role of Hanawa, his personal power within Nissan, was much stronger than he said. After the agreement was announced, but before it was implemented, he slashed the number of executive committee members from 37 to ten," Schweitzer said. "Of course, he did it the Japanese way—those who were moved aside became advisors or were sent to subsidiaries. All the same, he moved two thirds of the directors over eight days by himself. We hadn't requested anything, although it made things easier for us. My belief is that he was the boss and that the choice of the Alliance was his decision at the end of the day."

Pushing People to Excel

"The art of management is pushing colleagues to surpass themselves while believing it's possible," said Carlos Ghosn. "If goals are pushed to a level that people don't believe in, you've lost. If, by contrast, they're not ambitious enough, they won't surpass themselves. You should always be in the area where success is unlikely but possible, so people can be creative, imaginative and take calculated risks. This approach is diametrically opposed to that taken by accountants who reduce forecasts and cut investment. Our mission is the growth of the company, its profitability and everything that goes with that. But if you're sure of meeting an objective, you don't have to go beyond it.

"In terms of management principles and convictions, it's all been written in *Shift*, even if they've evolved. First, work has to be associative to be efficient. Objectives must be understood and accepted by everyone, as it's not a decision itself but its implementation that's important. Decision making is just the start of a long process that lasts until the result is achieved. Should decision making be fast or take a long time? Should it be a collective or individual decision? The gauge is the measure of the result, which means changing reality—what's the best way to get it?

"I can cite big decisions ranging from whether or not to enter China or Russia, the strategy for electric vehicles or downsizing during the Global Financial Crisis. They weren't easy and they raised questions and even resistance. If you want to achieve a desired result, they have to be explained. It's not a matter of consensus, which is often just tarting things up. You need to get an agreement of convictions. And that's where national cultures differ. In Japan, France, China and the United States, approaches aren't the same. You sometimes have to delay a decision to ensure it is executed well. A rapid decision doesn't mean anything—it's rapid results that count."

Simplification

"A golden rule for my approach to management is simplification," Carlos Ghosn said. "A leader has to simplify issues and make them comprehensible. Those who complicate things are the opposite of leaders. A leader simplifies, sets priorities and justifies. The complex world around us requires a simple image. And if the message is simple, communication is a lot simpler."

Governing is choosing. Not choosing or choosing everything or making bad choices for bad reasons is the privilege of politicians. In democratic systems, incompetence is sanctioned by voters—in principle. In many cases, the impacts of bad decisions or failing to make choices won't be felt until after the departure of the person responsible. The explosion of public debt, for example, leaves a bill. But when bond market vigilantes are disarmed by central banks through financial repression, as Japan has shown for close to thirty years, the punishment is canceled or indefinitely delayed, a luxury not enjoyed by the private sector.

"A manager has to make sure decisions are taken at all levels, not only his own," Carlos Ghosn said. "The big danger for companies is not so much the one who decides badly, but the one who makes no decisions. People in a company who analyze, reflect, make decisions and take responsibility for them have to do their work. The manager is their guarantor.

"Whether many or only a few decisions are taken at the top depends on how mature the business is. But only the boss can make major strategic decisions. If not, some might appeal decisions like opening in China and doubling our production capacity there, especially those who are hostile or hesitant. That's the surest way to paralysis. If the decision is taken at the top, it can't be appealed. It's easy to say, but complicated to put into practice. You have people who never make decisions, and those who claim responsibility for all decisions. In both cases, there's a danger of the business being brought to a standstill."

Barely Consensual Decision

"There was no consensus on investing heavily in electric vehicles," said Carlos Ghosn. "The opponents had different views—ranging from waiting, to following Toyota and throwing everything into hybrid cars. It was considered too early for all-electric vehicles and too expensive. But in reality, every technological revolution—especially this one—inevitably costs a fortune.

"Allocating investments is essentially the manager's responsibility. The hardest decision isn't what to do, but working out what you can't do as a result of a decision. Choosing electric vehicles implied negative trade-offs on other projects and these were questioned. When you decide to invest one billion dollars a year over five years on electric vehicles, money is not available somewhere else. Resources are not unlimited.

"Opposing innovation head-on is very rare. What's rejected is the series of sacrifices. Today, the trade-offs are all the more complex as the investments required in this industry will be colossal. In an industry like automobiles, there are a lot of complex decisions to make. They must be subject to in-depth discussion by special committees, and the boss taking responsibility when a decision is made. At the end of the day, it's only one person who makes the decision—the boss—but the decision is determined by the quality of internal discussions.

"There's a new unprecedented side to this technology revolution in the decision-making responsibility of the boss—choosing partners. Since we don't have all the technology, with whom should we develop a self-driving vehicle? Nvidia? Google? Should we attempt such a venture ourselves? Or form an alliance with Daimler? These choices are crucial today as the auto industry is in a phase of technological upheaval. That wasn't the case twenty or even ten years ago. We've now reached that phase, and my own work evolved a lot as a result. The choice of a technology partner is not for engineers. It's a critical decision made at the top."

No Smooth Sailing

"There's never a period of sailing in calm waters in this industry," said Carlos Ghosn. "Take Nissan's journey from 1999 to 2018. We had the Nissan Revival Plan and the return to growth. Then we had to deal with the Global Financial Crisis. Then came the Tohoku earthquake and tsunami, which devastated a part of Japan's industry. Then Brexit, which destabilized European production, and the crisis between the United States and Mexico with the renegotiation of NAFTA. Add to those complications, the international repercussions of the trade war between the United States and China, as well as international sanctions against Russia and Iran. To this non-exhaustive list has been added the Covid-19 pandemic, whose medium and long-term fallout is still poorly measured. Companies don't need strong leaders when things are going well, but they do during bad weather, crises and revolutions. And that's what our industry faces more than ever before with self-driving vehicles. The upheaval is permanent. If a leader is good during a crisis, he is good, period.

"Until 2005, we went from strength to strength with the Nissan Revival Plan and Nissan 180," said Carlos Ghosn. "But it was in no way easy with the volume of work, my personal investment and the changes imposed on the company. Take the example of cross-functional teams, one of the most studied and most copied innovations. I used them in the United States in the merger of Michelin North America and Uniroyal-Goodrich. As part of the Twenty Billion Plan, Renault adopted them between 1997 and 1998. Then Nissan. Each one was an improvement based on past experience. They were of no use at all at Dongfeng at first, as we were starting with a clean slate. When are cross-functional teams useful? When you have to get people out of their silos to feel the reality of the company as a whole so they understand that its optimal functioning is not the sum of its parts operating optimally in each sector of activity."

Horizontal Teamwork

One area for cross-functional teams was purchasing, which amounted to about half of an automaker's turnover. "The aim was to purchase at better and best prices," said Carlos Ghosn. "But what's the best price? The lowest? What are the effects of this or that purchase on the final product, the car that comes off the line? As soon as you put a buyer and seller together, the former will understand that making concessions to the supplier is possibly good for the company from time to time, even if it's not good for his own game plan. Cross-functional teams share the interests and objectives of very different sectors. We collectively seek a smarter decision as different issues are taken into account."

"In practice, industrial costs are lowest when the product is identical. Recall Henry Ford's comment that customers could have a car in any color they liked as long as it was black. If a factory manager considers only optimizing costs, he's calling for the highest standardization possible. But the market won't accept that. He has to understand commercial aspects of the production process that are more complex, more diverse and consequently more costly.

"In companies with silos, there's little or no dialogue. Each optimizes its sector. The result is a shortfall in overall performance. You can—even must—be able to accept below optimum at the sectoral level to optimize business performance."

Reducing internal compartmentalization was a particular dynamic of the Alliance with the key words being synergy and calibration.

"The Alliance is an association," Carlos Ghosn said. "Results are achieved at the company level. Benchmarking was huge work. We could compare the performances of all plants in the Alliance in terms of production quality and so on. Rankings came out every year, and benchmarking affected other areas like sales.

"Why did we do this? Because without a ranking, each factory manager always has a good argument to explain why the results aren't better. A plant ranking 69 out of 70 would be a shock to the troops. But if you're number one, you feed the hunger to learn among the others as nobody wants to come last. Those who lagged asked to go to Mexico or China to learn.

"Benchmarking has always been one of my tools," Ghosn continued. "When I arrived at Nissan in 1999, one of my first initiatives was to compare Nissan's purchases with those of Renault. If I could prove that they were paying 100 for an identical product bought by Renault at 80, they could not reject the findings."

The drastic cuts to the number of Nissan's suppliers, and the rationalization of its purchasing system, were a celebrated model that was copied. But after Carlos Ghosn's arrest, there were voices criticizing the social consequences, including in the government.

"The group notion that Nissan had to protect its suppliers and that I should be criticized for cleaning things up is absurd," Carlos Ghosn said. "Nissan was bankrupt and would have dragged down everyone with it. There's no good management that leads to bad results."

Standardization and Synergies

"Our main indicator measured progress in synergies. Each company ran its own operating account but what we measured at the Alliance level was how far synergies had advanced. All elements could be found in the results of each company. That's what the Alliance dashboard was—synergies and benchmarking. From such assessments came diagnostics and the imperative for people on the ground to work towards recovery. If they were in difficulty, we could decide to send in a support team.

"When we developed the Nissan Revival Plan, I announced it would be the plan of Nissan, not the Boston Consulting Group or McKinsey. We didn't hire any consultants. Later on, they were used in new areas where we had little or no knowledge or when we had to move quickly and didn't have time to use our own internal resources—like artificial intelligence or self-driving vehicles, for example. Or when a crucial decision for the future needed to be made, such as choosing a partner to develop a new technology. They could also bring quantifiable knowledge compared with your competitors. But you have to be very measured in hiring consultants, as you risk depriving the company of its abilities to find solutions itself."

The success of the "Ghosn method" gave birth to a prolific body of academic literature on the Nissan recovery, with case studies by educational institutions including Harvard, Stanford and Wharton in the United States, and French business schools HEC and INSEAD. In Japan, the renaissance erased the initial sacrifices and the "Ghosn shock" was seen as a positive event. Its author enjoyed a popularity among the general public that sometimes verged on a personality cult.

"I was awarded honorary doctorates and professorships by numerous universities, including three in Japan. I was decorated by the Emperor of Japan. Until 2017, I gave lectures not only to Nissan executives but also to those from other Japanese companies." But no-one is a prophet in their own land, even if it's an adopted country, and especially if the country is France, which always tries to be different.

Return to Billancourt

"I faced a pretty bizarre situation when I returned to Renault in 2005," recalled Carlos Ghosn. "The company was doing well overall but international operations were losing a lot of money. It was undeniable that Schweitzer had initiated numerous operations, but there was no follow-up. In 2005, Dacia was faltering. Brazil was a disaster. And Moskvitch was sending nothing back from Russia. Renault was still exceedingly French, a reality hidden by the existence of the Alliance.

"The paradoxical result was that in France, I was almost being criticized for being too successful with Nissan," said Ghosn. "But there was no feeling of urgency in Billancourt, no perception of Renault's fragility, and growing resentment towards those whose annual production had increased by one million units. Renault had stalled."

Carlos Ghosn did not return to Paris alone. Some members of the "thirty commandoes" that had jettisoned into Tokyo in 1999 had already returned. Others would follow him back to Paris, notably Thierry Moulonguet and Patrick Pélata, who both became members of the Renault executive committee.

"What was fundamental about the return of Renault people from Tokyo to Billancourt was that this team had experienced growth, which is what Renault already lacked in 1997. It was a poor excuse to blame Renault's difficulties on me and a few others for having left for Japan. It was at this point that we launched the "Renault Contract 2009," whose momentum was shattered by the financial crisis from the fall of 2008. We had to digest the crisis to start an expansion phase that led to Renault recording the best results in its history."

Announced in February 2006, the plan had a global approach with three objectives—increasing annual sales by 800,000 units in three years, reaching an operating margin of 6 percent and raising the quality of the new generation of Laguna models to international standards. The following year was encouraging, but the sub-prime mortgage crisis that started in the United States in August had turned into a global storm in September 2008 when Lehman Brothers failed. Interbank markets were suddenly paralyzed and global liquidity dried up.

Devouring Capital

"Ahead of us, we saw an abyss," Carlos Ghosn said. "Automakers are big users of cash, and consumer credit activities are a significant contributor to the bottom line. Manufacturers need cash, given the considerable demands on rolling capital. Suppliers and employees have to be paid, stocks have to be financed. It's an enormous financial machine. What do you do when the banks stop lending? Liquidity is like blood—if it stops circulating, life is endangered.

"Deprived of liquidity, we were about to collapse and all the automakers were more or less in the same position—even Toyota. However much cash you had, represented only a few months of operations. We had about twenty billion dollars in cash, about two months of working capital. This money was coming in and going out all the time."

Neither Japan nor France fared badly from a strictly banking perspective. Japanese banks had their fingers burnt when the bubble economy burst at the end of the 1980s, and were less exposed to the crisis than their Western counterparts. And Japan had already been deploying for more than a decade an arsenal of monetary tools that other central banks would use to prevent a new Great Depression. Interest rates remained low, or even turned negative, as central banks began quantitative easing by buying government bonds and other assets to flood markets with liquidity.

"The complete drying up of the financial system lasted about two months before things progressively eased with the central banks coming in. In France, the problem was solved at the presidential level. I was received by Nicolas Sarkozy along with Christian Streiff, who was then the PSA chairman. It was a face-to-face meeting. Sarkozy released to each of us a four-billion-euro loan from the Treasury, which helped us keep our heads above water. The Ministry of Economy and Finance wanted to charge a very high interest rate of 9 percent, but he decided it would be 7.5 percent."

Consolidating Global Leadership with Alliance 2022

The financial crisis and the awareness that technology upheavals were extending the horizon of decision making led Carlos Ghosn to modify the structure of multi-year programs that set targets and mobilized resources.

"After the financial crisis, we adopted six-year plans for Renault and Nissan with targets for the first three years and projections for the last three years," Carlos Ghosn said. "Strategic directions were defined and priorities set. At the end of the first three years, targets were quantified again for the next three years.

"The first plan implemented at Nissan was a three-year plan like the Renault plan for 2009. But then we thought three years was too short of a horizon. We had to avoid short-term optimization at the expense of the long term. For example, you could achieve the results forecast by cutting the research budget. If I'd drained research or cut funds to develop common platforms, the current leadership would be paying the price now. But I left things in order, with a plan for 2022."

Announced in September 2017, "Alliance 2022" aims to consolidate leadership of the group, which had just risen to the top of the world podium, overtaking Toyota and Volkswagen in terms of production volumes. Sales were expected to rise from slightly more than ten million personal and utility vehicles to fourteen million units in 2022, of which nine million would be from the four common platforms used by the three companies and their subsidiaries. Under the plan, the Alliance was expected to roll out twelve new electric models and forty others, including intelligent and self-driving vehicles. Synergies, the barometer of convergence within the Alliance, would amount to ten billion euros a year by the end of the plan.

"It's an ambitious plan, that's true," Carlos Ghosn admitted. "I've always favored a risky strategy that pulls the business forward. The target of fourteen million cars a year is without external growth. The baselines reflected differences in performance. Mitsubishi was the weakest so it should have the fastest growth, followed by Renault and Nissan, which will lead to a certain rebalancing.

"Is the Alliance under tension? Always. And there are times when fatigue arises. But when people get comfortable, businesses are in danger. There were sometimes complaints that targets were too ambitious, that there was too much pressure. But I prefer that to a situation where people feel relaxed. I maintained the pressure, but made sure it didn't become counter-productive.

"And that's why I never stopped going out into the field. Some complained that they didn't see me often enough but I was checking work as I traveled and I couldn't be everywhere at the same time. I listened a lot in person, and also from the men and women in the field. I always had fairly large delegations but only got involved when things weren't going well. When the machine was running, I left the people in charge at peace. As soon as something turned bad, I'd get involved. Everyone knew that performance was key to autonomy."

Establishing Nissan's plant in Brazil was an enlightening demonstration of how Carlos Ghosn operated. Once the decision had been made, and potential pitfalls avoided, the project was entrusted to François Dossa, a French banker who had long worked in Brazil and who was poached from Société Générale in December 2011. He was joined by Atsuhiko Hayakawa, who had spent three years in Mexico and was then managing the Oppama plant, one of Nissan's biggest facilities in Japan. The team had complete freedom to do what they liked during the construction phase, from the ground-breaking to the opening of the plant two years later. "I was content with follow-up meetings from time to time," Carlos Ghosn said.

Unfortunately, it was bad timing. The plant in Resende started production in April 2014, when Brazil was entering an economic crisis fueled by external factors, notably reduced Chinese demand for its exports of primary resources, and mismanagement by the government of President Dilma Roussef. At around this same time, the "car wash scandal" erupted, which would haunt Brazil for the rest of the decade.

"Sales plunged from four million to two million vehicles, compared with a forecast for six million when the investment was decided," recalled a person who was close to the Brazilian plant at the time. "The entire economic equilibrium of the project collapsed. When we explained the situation to Carlos Ghosn in 2014, he replied: 'I don't expect you to explain to me how hard it is. I know. The business must break even within two years it's up to you.' From that day, he was constantly on the case. We turned the plant towards exports and worked intensely with Renault to reduce supply costs, and we got there. It was hard. Numbers, no feelings: 'If you want to advance in the group, you have to produce results.' He used the same language with everyone. He sets a strategy, makes decisions and has faith. And progress was assessed every year. There was never any micromanagement."

As part of his vision for Brazil in 2011, Carlos Ghosn had in sight the Olympic Games in Rio in 2016. He got personally involved, carried the Olympic torch and spent three weeks there during the competitions. For Nissan, one of the main sponsors with a 230-million-dollar investment, it was a major success. The Japanese automaker provided 4,200 official vehicles and was a big hit on social media. It used the occasion to launch the Nissan Kicks model, registering thousands of local orders. Nissan's share of the Brazilian market ultimately doubled.

"He realized it went well at the end," said the person close to the plant. "He called us on the day he was leaving and said: 'It was good, but let's not get carried away with our emotions. We'll do an assessment at the Nissan executive committee in two months based on the naked raw truth of the numbers.' A former executive committee member did not forget the meeting, which was held in a large hall at the Yokohama headquarters where Brazil manager François Dossa spoke: 'The results from Brazil were excellent. François made his presentation. When he finished, Carlos Ghosn simply said: 'We can say the strategy was good.' That's all. I know François would have hoped for a little more but he says himself that Carlos hardly lives up to the image we have of Brazilians. He was a boss, tough but fair. And when things went wrong, he never raised his voice."

Taking the Lead in Electric Car Market

On October 29, 2009, Carlos Ghosn spoke to students at a leadership conference at the Wharton School of the University of Pennsylvania. The head of the Alliance was a frequent guest at college amphitheaters where he was asked about his thoughts on management. The Nissan renaissance, the Renault recovery and the expansion of the Alliance had become case studies. At Wharton, Carlos Ghosn spoke passionately in defending what was arguably his most controversial decision—that the Alliance had decided ten years into the new century that the future of the automobile was electric and that it was starting now.

"The electric car appeared at the beginning of the twentieth century and then disappeared," Carlos Ghosn said. "It came back in the 1950s only to disappear again. It resurfaced in the 1970s and disappeared once more. But a lot of things have changed. We're laying down our cards, encouraging investment and intensifying our efforts because we believe the time has come."

Batteries are cheaper and more powerful. The appetite for cars in emerging economies means that we will soon have 1.5 billion vehicles on roads across the planet, twice the number in 2009. If the century-old monopoly of the combustion engine persists, that means higher oil prices and increased carbon dioxide emissions. Notwithstanding the constraints of the Alliance at the time, the Leaf model of Nissan and the Zoe of Renault have been offering consumers zero-emission vehicles at reasonable prices since 2010.

"The Leaf came out before the Zoe, and the technology was not the same," Carlos Ghosn recalled. "With the same team for three companies, I launched a process for different initiatives to converge towards the same technologies—with tensions, as always, but these passed."

The decision to go all-electric in 2009 gave the Alliance a considerable advance on its main rivals. Yet Leaf and Zoe sales barely exceeded a million units in ten years. Were the initial forecasts too optimistic? Yes. Speaking to students at Stanford in 2014, Carlos Ghosn admitted his frustration. "One of the reasons why the zero-emission market is not expanding as fast as I'd like is the lack of infrastructure—the charging network is being built too slowly." A lost bet? Certainly not.

In 2018, the number of electric vehicles worldwide crossed the five million barrier. That may have been only 1 percent of all automobiles, but it included an increase of two million units in twelve months. China ranked first with sales of 1.1 million, increasing the number of electric vehicles in the country to 2.3 million units—excluding tens of millions of electric motorcycles, buses and utility vehicles. Europe's sales of 385,000 units raised the number of electric vehicles to 1.2 million, slightly more than the 1.1 million in the United States, where sales grew by 361,000 units in 2018.

Change is Now

Under the most conservative scenario, annual sales of electric vehicles will reach thirty million worldwide by 2030, by which time 130 million will be on the road. In the main markets including China, electric vehicles will account for a third of overall sales. A more optimistic scenario sees global sales of forty-three million units a year, with a fleet of 250 million electric vehicles across the planet.

Why the projected change? A final awakening of public policies combined with technological advances in battery life, autonomy and recharging speed as well as belated, but massive, conversions among manufacturers, notably the Germans. Hundreds of models are in the pipeline and are expected to be at dealerships by 2024. Pioneers like the Alliance and Tesla have an advantage, but there's no guarantee. In an open world with competing industries, free lunches don't exist.

"International expansion was planned, strategized and sequenced with roles shared between two and then three businesses," Carlos

Ghosn said. "But the other driver of expansion is the electric vehicle, which I decided would be at the heart of the industry in 2009. Today, it's obvious. But at the time, ten years ago, we were alone.

"With oil prices, emission problems and global warming, I knew which way to go. What was the solution? The hybrid? Too expensive and too complicated. It was a transitional solution only and we were late with Toyota taking the lead. Wholly electric vehicles addressed my reticence towards hybrids. They were less complicated and resolved problems of scale. Electricity is produced everywhere—from fossil fuels, but also wind, the sun, biomass, sugarcane, water, the sea and uranium. That's the beauty of electric propulsion. I was also persuaded that battery development would be enormous because energy storage is going to become a key issue, especially in developing countries. It was the product of years of collective study and my personal feelings."

Diversifying Into Battery Production

The Alliance was initially so alone compared to its big rivals that it was obliged to make batteries itself for a while. In the summer of 2018, however, it sold battery factories attached to the Smyrna plant in the United States, the Sunderland plant in Britain and three plants in Japan to the Chinese group Envision.

"We made batteries quite simply because the market had no suppliers that could satisfy us. But I knew we'd have to get out of this business in the long term. I was convinced there would be plenty of Japanese, Korean and Chinese suppliers. It was a question of the investment requirements across the Alliance, estimated at around nine billion dollars a year. Why invest in batteries if others are ready to do it?

"I wanted to invest in cars, my core business, and self-driving cars are crucial for the future. The margins for batteries are fluctuating and the technology is changing very quickly. It's a skill in itself. When we sold, we got back the money we invested. To those who criticized the choice, I asked what was the alternative—what investments would have to be sacrificed to stay in the race for the best battery?

"Choosing all-electric vehicles implied positioning well upstream from the rest of the industry, for which we were criticized, of course.

But today, everyone's jumped on the bandwagon. We were also the first to position ourselves in self-driving cars. These are the two major roads to growth in the auto industry. Our choice means that we're suffering today, but we're preparing for the growth of tomorrow, even if the transition's long and painful. That's the price for becoming world's number one."

CHAPTER ELEVEN

Human Capital

"When it comes to choosing men, it's unfortunately obvious that we're all fallible," said Carlos Ghosn. "If you make an error in recruiting or selecting, you pay the price, including at the personal level as my own case shows. These choices are more complex in a multicultural environment. It's always easier to work out the personality of someone from the same culture."

Since November 19, 2018, targets of the media trial of the builder of the Renault-Nissan-Mitsubishi Alliance—orchestrated in tandem with the inquiry by public prosecutors—included Carlos Ghosn's management of people. The media complacently regurgitated the work of the Nissan communications team with a caricature of a "dictator" hitched to his mandate. He was indifferent to the question of a successor and therefore responsible for the corporate disaster after his arrest. It was the same type of media caricature that reduced his work to that of a "cost killer" after he restored growth and profitability to Nissan and Renault, elevating the two "mules" to the top ranks of the global auto industry. It was lazy journalism.

"When the time comes, I'd like a Japanese to succeed me as the head of Nissan," Carlos Ghosn told the weekly *Automotive News* in November 2013. "It's symbolic and we have numerous talented Japanese. I want Nissan to remain perceived as a Japanese brand. It can be led by a foreigner from time to time, but not permanently."

Since 1999, Carlos Ghosn had subjected Nissan to a degree of internationalization that was unprecedented for a major Japanese company. In 2013, half of the top one hundred executives were foreigners from seventeen countries. Among eight executive vice presidents were three Britons and an American. Hiroto Saikawa, the Japanese executive described by *Automotive News* as a "natural" to succeed Carlos Ghosn, was already sixty, a year older than his boss.

Why Saikawa?

"I reject criticism that I did not prepare for my succession. At Nissan, José Muñoz was the most capable of becoming chief executive. But there was the issue of political acceptance. Not putting a Japanese as head of Nissan was sensitive, as the Alliance evolved towards deeper integration under a non-Japanese. Greg Kelly, Arun Bajaj, a few others and I looked around. I never thought Saikawa was brilliant, creative or strategic. But I felt that the head of Nissan should be an operations man in a group where strategic choices would be taken at the Alliance level. We needed someone rigorous and disciplined, who knew the Alliance well."

In Japan, selecting senior executives at big companies was strongly subject to the constraints of lifetime employment and promotions based on seniority. Such advantages were reserved for about half the employees in a labor market polarized between secure jobs and more precarious positions. Thirty years of economic stagnation had embedded this dual system into the social fabric of the country.

"Lifetime employment in Japan is a reality for only some employees," Carlos Ghosn explained. "But it's offset by early retirement at around fifty-five for regular employees. These somewhat short careers are what keeps lifetime employment going. Today, lifetime employment isn't a problem in a country where the active population is shrinking every year and manpower is lacking. In addition, respect for lifetime employment is facilitated through recourse to temporary workers. Finally, we traditionally see a certain lowering of salaries as people approach the ends of their careers.

"As for promoting people based on seniority, it's not a complete constraint. At the beginning, in 1999, I was given candidates who were almost always the oldest. I realized this was wrong as I spent a lot of time visiting the company. I appointed very young people to positions of responsibility. It's true that the people at the top of Nissan today are between sixty and sixty-five. But when I started giving them responsibility, they were twenty years younger. Age counts little as a criterion at Nissan, but it's a determining factor at Japanese companies run more traditionally. This imprint has remained, as the Nissan board recently named several men who are not the oldest to its highest ranks."

In October 2019, the board of directors—handpicked by the Ministry of Economy, Trade and Industry and the Nissan Old Guard—appointed 53-year-old Makoto Uchida as chief executive and 49-year-old Ashwani Gupta as chief operating officer. Jun Seki, 58, was named vice chief operating officer, but quit Nissan a few weeks later.

"Based on seniority, Saikawa's successor should have been Yasuhiro Yamauchi," Carlos Ghosn said, referring to the Nissan representative on Renault's board who became acting chief executive after Saikawa. "I created a culture that respected age and experience but these weren't the determining factors. In short, I got around lifetime employment and did not follow promotions based on seniority but always adhered to the same principle—don't change anything unless there were questions about performance. It wasn't an issue of culture or management, it was simply efficiency."

Pragmatic Approach

"My approach has always been minimalist and pragmatic, secured by the results achieved. I'm not an ideologue at all. And for eighteen years, it was like that. Nobody can say there were ever any serious social conflicts over eighteen years.

"When I arrived at Nissan in 1999, the company's trade union—which had an awful reputation—asked to meet me. My image as a cost killer had preceded my arrival. I gave them the following speech: 'We have a common objective. You want Nissan to survive, so do I. You, because it's your company, and me, because it's my job. A failed turnaround will be foremost my responsibility but everyone will pay the price. What do you want me to do—put Nissan right?' The response: 'We won't criticize you if you bring about a recovery. But we'll be watching closely how you justify your actions.' I reiterated to them what I told the team that came from Renault—all changes needed for Nissan to recover, nothing more.

"In fact, they supported me. After three years, I gave them a raise, accepting their demands for higher salaries without bargaining—much to the dismay of Japanese employer organizations engaged in the *shunto*, the spring wage offensive. After my arrest, the Nissan trade unionists refused to join in baying for my blood, notwithstanding the urgings of the Japanese press. They didn't fall into the trap, as they didn't forget what Nissan employees were owed for work they'd accomplished over eighteen years.

"A detailed assessment of the Alliance's policies towards its employees has yet to be done. But what needs to be looked at first is how the workforce at Nissan and Renault evolved over almost twenty years. If memory serves me correctly," Ghosn said, "Nissan had about 140,000 employees when I arrived. The number hit a floor of 123,000 under the Nissan Revival Plan, but then rebounded above 140,000. What's more important is that the number of employees worldwide was 260,000 in 2017. Same goes for Renault—the group had 127,000 employees in 2005, but employed 186,000 people world-wide in 2018."

Management Without Crises

The response to persistent criticism of Carlos Ghosn's labor policies—in Japan and especially in France—was that there was never any significant labor dispute, in any of the companies concerned, over two decades.

"I never had to face a strike, even at Renault, where I was not especially popular with the trade unionists. I readily admit that I've never accepted that labor polices be conducted at the expense of business performance. You have to bring the two together, find a balance."

In 2013, in a global economic climate that was still difficult, Renault was ahead of France's law on flexicurity that sought to import practices from Nordic countries in an attempt to rescue its social "model," which was decaying. Signed by three unions after 11 rounds of talks, the Renault agreement provided for job cuts without layoffs and new hiring along with increased working hours in exchange for maintaining plants and increasing production volumes.

"When we signed the famous competition accord at Renault, there were commitments on both sides," Carlos Ghosn recalled. "It was a win-win agreement, very pragmatic. The Renault social laboratory may have been long dead, but it was still an innovative agreement."

Industrial Renewal Minister Arnaud Montebourg warmly welcomed the compromise, which was renewed in 2017. A member of the left wing of the ruling Socialist Party, he even praised

Renault's "industrial come-back" in France. Carlos Ghosn enjoyed excellent relations with the minister, who was somewhat non-conformist. Montebourg was also held in high regard among the New York diners he saved at the Balthazar Cafe in Soho in 2015.

Describing him as a "French socialist 'superman'," the *New York Daily News* reported that Montebourg "prevented a disaster" at the cafe by catching a falling mirror and "hung on long enough to prevent the patrons beneath it from being pinned."

From Billancourt to Tennessee

In despair over failing to ignite a conflict at Renault, the pro-communist CGT trade union went all the way to Nissan's plant in Canton, Mississippi. Without success—in August 2017, some 60 percent of the 3,400 workers at the plant rejected a proposal for the UAW to set up shop. The vote rejecting the autoworkers union came despite support from Senator Bernie Sanders and visits by Fabien Gâche, the central CGT delegate at Renault. UAW president Dennis Williams refused to admit defeat.

"Perhaps recognizing they couldn't win on the facts, Nissan and its anti-worker allies went negative, running ads, flyers and brochures," Williams wrote in the *Detroit Free Press*. "Unfortunately, the scare tactics worked. The election was a setback for the UAW and the cause of working Americans everywhere. But a setback does not equal a defeat."

Carlos Ghosn noted that the belief in the "right to work" in America did not necessarily mean that all workers belonged to a trade union. "Union presence in a company is not automatic. It requires the employees to vote whether or not to accept the presence of a union branch. Some American states follow this procedure. In others, the unions decide whether or not to set up a branch.

"When Asian automakers, first Japanese then the Koreans, decided to build transplants in the United States they chose states which applied the right to work—Alabama, Tennessee, North Carolina, South Carolina. It wasn't anti-unionism, but a different approach to managing labor relations in a company. Of course, local managers on the ground didn't stay neutral in cases of voting for a union presence. Neither did state authorities. It's an understatement to say that the traditional trade unions from the north, the UAW in our case, were not welcomed with open arms.

"Having said that, the UAW influence on the American auto industry is substantial. Even if they're not present in Japanese or South Korean plants, salary or social policies can't be too much out of kilter with those in unionized factories. If there was too much of a gap, it would encourage employees to vote in favor of a union presence. Plant managers know very well that what happens with UAW will influence their own personnel."

In an industry as vast and complex as the auto sector, everyone knew—or should have known—that wages were only one of the parameters that determined competitiveness and therefore the allocation of investment. "If it was only a question of salaries, Argentina would be the most competitive, which is not the case," Carlos Ghosn said. "Neither is the Indian plant. Multiple factors have to be taken into account. Robotization differs from country to country. Other factors are quality of suppliers, local taxes and the infrastructure of the country. General workforce training is very important as are rates of absenteeism, how the plant operates and rules in force. All this must be taken into account. Within the Alliance, the Chinese are at the top, followed by the Mexicans. And Chinese wages are now no longer the lowest, far from it."

Nissan Scandal

Six months after Hiroto Saikawa became chief executive, Nissan was caught up in a quality-control "scandal" involving vehicles coming off production lines. It was September 2018, and it had nothing to do with quality checks not being carried out or being done poorly. Neither did the cars coming off the Nissan lines have defects, nor were there complaints from customers. The scandal simply amounted to a few inspectors not having the certification imposed by the Kafkaesque bureaucracy of the Japanese Ministry of Transport, known for an impressive array of calamitous decisions over the years. The unforgivable sacrilege involved the use of *hankos*—personal seals, widely used in East Asia for official documents instead of signatures—that had been "borrowed" from certified inspectors. It seemed this had been going on for four decades.

"I was accused in Japan of not coming forward when Nissan was hit by the quality control affair," Carlos Ghosn said. "The division of roles with Saikawa, however, was very clear. He was in charge and he knew it. It would have been like babysitting if I got involved in such an affair. Yet I was accused of not wanting to let go of the reins and treading all over my successor's patch. What was the problem? The work was well done and there was no problem with the quality of the vehicles. But the rules hadn't been respected, so it was a mistake. The affair became public and triggered an outcry.

"Saikawa made a statement apologizing to the public, asserting that the problem had been solved. But six weeks later, a journalist investigated Nissan plants and found the situation was unchanged. A scandal—Saikawa seemed to be either a liar or a leader not being followed by his troops. The problem was never manufacturing quality but how lightly company management treated the question of public trust.

"Without the least coherence, I was accused at the same time of behaving like a dictator and no longer doing much during my final period. It wasn't personal. From the moment a chief executive takes up the position, it's up to him to manage. My work was at the level of strategy and developing synergies for the companies of the Alliance. My responsibility could no longer be implementing things at Nissan."

Renault's Changing of the Guard

In Billancourt, 12 hours by plane from Yokohama, a similar handover began. It responded to two goals—to support the strengthening of Alliance leadership and prepare for Carlos Ghosn leaving within four years at the latest.

"It was the same criticism at Renault—that I hadn't prepared for a successor. But I don't accept that Thierry Bolloré couldn't be chief executive. He was ready," said Ghosn.

"There were several paradoxes to such criticism. For a start, graduates of the Ghosn school can be found everywhere in the global auto industry, and they are not second rate. Those who left took up important positions in the industry because we had a reputation for training real professionals, learning to develop a strategic vision for our work.

"Next was that my elimination was followed by a purge of all those suspected of having been too close to me, from key members of the Nissan executive committee to the chief executive I chose for Renault," Ghosn continued. "It should be noted that no-one reproached Ashwani Gupta, who is now said to be running Nissan, for being a Baby Ghosn. I increasingly gave him more important responsibilities right up to operational chief at Mitsubishi. Go figure.

"Renault had quite capable men and women. They were resolute people who could have run the company in the near future, more or less. I won't mention their names to avoid creating problems for them."

Thierry Bolloré joined Renault in 2012. He had also worked at Michelin and more recently at Faurecia, a leading French supplier to the auto industry. In 2013, he was put in charge of competitiveness—one of the four key responsibilities in the corporate structure put together by Carlos Ghosn. In February 2018, he became chief operating officer. The arrest of Ghosn in November that year forced Renault—which stuck to its boss at the time—to set up a provisional structure with Bolloré in charge, with the title of deputy chief executive. In January 2019, when Carlos Ghosn was forced into retirement while trapped at Kosuge, the Renault board named him chief executive.

"It was me who put Thierry Bolloré on the track to succession, but the directors decided. Eight months after putting him in charge, they reversed their decision and dumped him in the circumstances we exposed earlier. He was someone who was resolute, brave, and he had a great moral sense. That's what I liked about him. He knows what's right and demonstrated that through this crisis. At the helm of a company like Renault, you can't put someone in charge who maneuvers or evades things."

Tempted to Leave

"This idea that I was clinging to my job like a clam to a rock doesn't stand up. Nobody asked me to leave as chief executive of Nissan. I took the initiative myself. In addition, I indicated I'd leave if there was no agreement on my idea of how the Alliance would evolve. In

June 2018, I was sixty-four—a very good age to leave. The Renault board had a team that worked on seeking the person who could replace me, first as head of Renault and then overseeing the Alliance. The team included Thierry Desmarest[11], when he was still there, Patrick Thomas[12] and Marc Ladreit de Lacharrière[13]. The board was able to choose from numerous names.

"But as soon as I accepted a new mandate at Renault, I knew I'd be leaving no later than sixty-eight. It was physically very hard. And I was interested in a lot of things in life from supporting start-ups to teaching. My last mandate gave us the time necessary to put the overhaul into place and prepare for my successor as head of the Alliance. I was not alone. It mainly involved the board members of Renault and Nissan."

Tavares Can't Wait

"In any case, candidates for this level of responsibility are not exactly a dime a dozen. PSA found it difficult to replace Philippe Varin when he left, and they came looking for Carlos Tavares, who had just quit Renault. Tavares had been one of the best practitioners of what they call the Ghosn method—very rigorous with implementation, very fast. On the other hand, he was less comfortable with cooperation. But it had been quite some time that he'd been flying of his own accord and he'd had time to learn. It's obvious he could have been my successor if he'd been a little bit more patient."

In 2013, "Big Carlos" was fifty-nine years old and "Little Carlos" was fifty-five. That's how the head of the Alliance and his right-hand man and brightest student were known internally. They were the same generation. One was a graduate of the École Polytechnique and the other the École Centrale Paris. They shared the Portuguese language, French culture—and a passion for cars, which the amateur

11. Desmarest, former head of oil and gas giant Total, joined the Renault board in 2008 and resigned in 2018.

12. Thomas, former head of luxury house Hermès, joined the Renault board in 2014. His current term expires in 2022.

13. Ladreit de Lacharrière, the owner of a private equity company, joined the Renault board in 2002 and retired in 2018.

Portuguese racing driver still satisfied in his spare time on racetracks and rally routes. During the summer of 2013, he reportedly told Bloomberg News: "My experience would be good for any car company ... Why not GM? I would be honored to lead a company like GM ... Anyone who is passionate about the auto industry comes to a conclusion that there is a point where you have the energy and appetite for a No.1 position." At this precise moment, GM chief executive Daniel Akerson, who was sixty-four, was on the way out, as was the 68-year-old Ford boss Alan Mulally.

"I told Tavares that his public statements put me in an impossible position," Carlos Ghosn said. "He didn't understand. He was almost comparing it with Formula 1 drivers who renegotiate their contracts at the end of each season."

In late August, Renault announced that Carlos Tavares was leaving under mutual agreement to "devote himself to personal projects." His brief period in the wilderness came to an end in January 2014, when he joined the board of PSA Peugeot Citroën, becoming chairman and chief executive of France's second-biggest automaker at the end of March. PSA was in trouble in the European market and had just taken a historic turn with the disappearance of the Peugeot family as "reference" shareholder, a role now shared between the French government and Chinese state-owned automaker Dongfeng. Even today, people close to the two men believe that Little Carlos was deliberately provoking Big Carlos with his public remarks, a way to force his hand. But the cost killer was not a killer. "I never chopped off anyone's head," Carlos Ghosn said.

According to a senior executive who oversaw one of the Alliance's major expansion programs, "the press fabricated an image of Carlos Ghosn that was the opposite of his personality ... In my opinion, he was far too nice. He put up with people around him who he understood were not up to the task when put to the test. He should have got rid of them and maybe the course of events would have been different. He's a very rigorous manager, very tough even. But when it came to people, he was always a very nice person. When I say this, people look at me like I'm insane. But it's true."

Suffering of François Michelin

"When I joined Michelin forty years ago, the globalization of the company was accelerating the demise of its paternalistic model," Carlos Ghosn said. "But the company was fretting about its social responsibilities. When it came to making humanly difficult decisions, François Michelin was not one to sleep well at night. And that affected everyone who worked with him. His suffering—and that's what it was—influenced all the staff. A lot of attention was paid to staff problems. That could not be *the* criterion for decision making, but we had to make sure that the impact on individuals was minimal."

To what extent did this experience leave its mark on Carlos Ghosn? Former Michelin employees who later joined the Alliance had similar accounts. "François Michelin didn't fire people, he sidelined them," said one who joined the French tiremaker at the same time as Carlos Ghosn. "It could be very painful, because people were falling from grace every day—shelved, not fired."

There were exceptions to every rule. At Renault, the best known was Patrick Pélata, who graduated from the École Polytechnique the same year as Carlos Ghosn. He was part of the Renault team dispatched to Tokyo in 1999 to turn Nissan around. In the wake of Carlos Ghosn, he returned to the Renault headquarters and was serving as chief operating officer when the "fake spies" scandal erupted in January 2011.

Fake Spies: A Story of Manipulation

The affair started in September 2010, with anonymous letters accusing three engineers working on Renault's electric car of sharing industrial secrets with China. A mysterious informant, known as "The Belgian," was supposed to receive several hundred thousand dollars in what turned out to be a scam mounted by Dominique Gevrey, a former soldier hired by Renault as a security officer in 2004.

"Among failures, there was obviously the case of the fake spies at Renault," Carlos Ghosn admitted. "Security came under Pélata, the chief operating officer. He made things worse by interviewing, himself, the three people designated as spies by the scammer, whose motive was financial. He wanted to get money from the company for a fake investigation. And everyone at Renault fell into the trap."

But Patrick Pélata did not have a monopoly on unfortunate initiatives. Renault's corporate communications people sent Carlos Ghosn to beat the war drums on French television channel TF1 on January 22, 2011. When it was found out what was going on, he returned in March to make amends.

"In 2010, we were just emerging from the Global Financial Crisis," Carlos Ghosn said. "On a personal note, I was at the beginning of a painful divorce that ended only in 2012. I should have been present more often. And I know Pélata's still angry with me because he thinks he was made the scapegoat. But he was still personally responsible, as he admitted at the time."

Industrial espionage was not a fantasy even if cases were an exception—because they were either not uncovered or the companies targeted preferred to stay quiet.

"We didn't come across many cases of industrial espionage in our companies," Carlos Ghosn said. "Maybe it was because the spies were particularly effective. Or maybe because there were few cases. In reality, it's more difficult to spy on a manufacturer than a supplier when the information is most often available from suppliers. Knowledge is not crucial in the auto industry, but know-how is critical. It's difficult to spy on know-how."

Difficult, but not impossible. In the 1990s, Japanese companies at the forefront of sensitive technologies began confiscating the passports of their senior engineers and technicians at the end of each week. It had been noted that some had developed a taste—a bit too pronounced—for weekends in Seoul, where South Korean rivals were located. Know-how was transmitted by humans, not documents.

"The fake spies affair deeply destabilized Renault," said Carlos Ghosn. "Public opinion was sensitive to the accusations against innocent people. I apologized publicly. But I was upset by the soap opera fueled by the press for months. Internal public opinion matters a lot in a company. Of course, we offered rehabilitation to the employees accused and financial compensation to those who didn't want to return. It was a painful period, but I have to admit it was our fault. As always in these situations, politicians believe they're obliged to find a fall guy. President Sarkozy told me: 'You're out of the question, as you're indispensable to the Alliance'."

Carlos Ghosn did not let his old student friend down. On March 4, 2011, Pélata publicly took responsibility for the crisis. He offered his resignation to the Renault board, but found a new home in Amsterdam at the joint venture with Nissan that oversaw the Alliance. In September 2012, Pélata joined Salesforce, a cloud computing company in California. After returning to France, contracts with the Dutch venture Renault-Nissan B.V. helped sustain his small consulting firm between 2015 and 2018.

But the favors were not returned. After Carlos Ghosn's arrest, Pélata's criticism of his former classmate grew, and he made a bid to return to Renault—both in private with board members and in public on BFM Business, the French business news channel. Pélata was reputed to be extremely close to Alexis Kohler—the associate of French President Emmanuel Macron who became general secretary of the Élysée Palace in 2017—and notoriously hostile to Thierry Bolloré becoming chief executive at Renault. "He came to see me to tell me that Thierry Bolloré wasn't the right fit," Carlos Ghosn said. "I replied: 'That's your opinion and I don't share it'."

Strong Management

"My regret in this affair is that I trusted and delegated too much. In fact, I changed with my role. When I arrived in Japan in 1999, I was named chief operating officer at Nissan. It was a field assignment. Then I became chief executive officer. I didn't abandon the field-work, but I left the area to my lieutenants. When I became head of the Alliance, I appointed chief executive officers at Nissan and Renault. And I was able to take a step back. So, there were different phases.

"The denunciations of dictatorial management don't hold up. You don't manage a group of such size and diversity by decree. Maybe that can work in a family-owned company operating in one country. But it wouldn't make any sense with a mix of nationalities and three different companies.

"What we found at Nissan was effectively a company divided into factions, as the analyst Nakanishi said. Japanese tend to be clannish, partly because they're traditionalists. Having major attractive projects is the only way to combat such traditionalism. Nissan's expansion was spectacular, and that convinced people to look to the future. This required a big sense of responsibility at all levels, especially at the top. That's why we needed strong management. I certainly wasn't a dictator," Ghosn said, "but I made decisions.

"Give a dog a bad name and hang him—the aim was to destroy my image," Ghosn added. "But they can't undo thirteen years of success for the Alliance, the creation of the number one in the industry worldwide from two ducks—the lame duck at Nissan and the skittish one at Renault. We got there by understanding situations, mobilizing teams and having an ambitious strategy. We were dealing with professionals, top managers and their respect for me never stopped them from taking responsibility.

"The accusation was even more absurd as I was being closely watched by the world's press, given the business model's success. Did the 250,000 employees at Nissan from bottom to top have to stand to attention before me? Did I really hide things so well from those who studied my management style, from college professors to analysts and journalists? And all those who left Nissan without denouncing the dictatorial regime they fled, and who surely still live in terror? The truth is that I listened a lot and delegated a lot—too much in some cases, no doubt. U.S. President Ronald Reagan popularized a Russian proverb: 'Trust but verify.' It's simple common sense. That's the nature of proverbs.

"You can't project careers of senior executives ten years into the future. If I think people have great potential, I give them assignments and see how they go. And depending on the results, their goals can become more and more ambitious. You have to choose people young enough to make this journey to the top. All my close colleagues went through this filter. It's more complicated with the Japanese, because there's not a culture of individual performance. Group or collective performance has to be taken into account more than anything else."

Individual Responsibility

"At the same time, responsibility for performance is individual, from the top to the bottom of the hierarchy," Ghosn said. "A company boss has to carry this responsibility on his shoulders. Deterioration, lack of earnings, have to be felt from within.

"If you blame your predecessor for a situation, you'll be surrounded by thousands of people who will always have a good excuse to explain their lack of performance. That's why, when we announced the Nissan Revival Plan in October 1999, we didn't look for excuses in the situation we inherited, even though we'd been there for six months. If our goals weren't met, we would have left.

"But when he spoke on November 19, 2018, Saikawa began a consistent discourse of blaming me for Nissan's poor results. Nissan and Renault have followed this line ever since. It's quite simply a disaster as far as management goes. It means that everyone in the chain of command behaves the same: 'It's not me, it's the other guy.' That's classic, but it's like cancer for a company. Over twenty years, I devoted a lot of time and commitment to making people accountable," said Ghosn.

"In terms of ideas, I'm obviously in the liberal camp," he continued. "My origins are Lebanese, and the Lebanese don't have a culture based on the government controlling social and economic affairs. You can only count on yourself—certainly not the government. If it's already fulfilling its own basic functions properly, that's very good. For the rest, it's private initiative that counts more than anything. I was brought up in this culture and it's a vision of the world I've passed on to my children. If you can find support, great. But don't count on it too much. God helps those who help themselves.

"I'm a liberal. I believe in work and individual initiative," said Ghosn. "Of course, governments, societies and communities exist. But they don't prevail. Yet I'm convinced that any enterprise by humans, economic but also political, can only last if they are capable of joining forces. Those who contribute must join forces. Liberalism is not individualism. Not mine, in any case. I'm an integrated liberal, a global liberal."

In a sign of deeply troubled times, not limited to France, the debate over the sex of angels has become a debate over the social purpose of a business. But it's taken a very chauvinistic turn—committees of wise men, reports to governments. All this is a mixture of opportunism and the need to respond to emergencies and the pressures of the moment, notably environmental, and timelessness, not to say dangerous abstraction.

Corporate Survival Instinct

"The first fundamental point is that all businesses are mortal, like individuals," Carlos Ghosn said. "But as it's written, you know neither the day nor the hour. What motivates the business above all is preservation, the wish to stay alive. That's what guides it. Having said that, the business doesn't have the same goal or purpose as it does when it's set up or when it's growing or reaching maturity. The purpose of a business evolves with time but always with a survival instinct.

"When you set up a business, the survival instinct is growth and income. If the business doesn't grow, the question of social purpose doesn't arise. Simple common sense. As soon as a business reaches a certain stage of development, it's sustainable growth that becomes important . . . It's a rigorous process that allows the business to be endowed with values, to define its mission, and design a strategy.

"The question of what's called in France the social purpose of the business only arises for businesses that have taken these previous steps. And for established businesses, I understand that social purpose has become a major issue. In a start-up, the daily preoccupation is to know if you'll make it to the next month—will the financing arrive, will the product find a market? The social purpose of the business doesn't even appear in the field of vision, and that's completely normal. In this sense, the debate about the social purpose of a business is meaningless.

"I'm someone who's very pragmatic," said Ghosn. "You don't manage a start-up like you manage a medium-sized company that's recently been formed, or a dinosaur like an automaker. Purposes fit into each other, like Russian dolls. First profit, then growth. Then long-term resilience, and social purpose after that. It's like a multistage rocket. As soon as a business falls into difficulty and earnings deteriorate, it must go back to the first stage. The only thing is

whether it will still be there in six months or a year. If the first stage
of the rocket doesn't work, the rest is gone."

Examples of companies whose primary vocation became second-
ary included General Motors, when it was known as a pension and
heath insurance fund that incidentally made cars, and Renault,
when it became a social laboratory after being nationalized in 1945.
Both suffered enormous losses that had to be absorbed by taxpayers.
And at the end of the road, bankruptcy.

"A business leader cannot be unaware of the company's social
responsibility," said Carlos Ghosn. "It's impossible to remain
sustainably prosperous without integrating social impacts into your
activities—for your employees, your partners and your suppliers. For
your shareholders. And even beyond.

"But if you have no growth or earnings, you're accountable. When
Mitsubishi had quality problems that jeopardized the company,
nobody cared about its social purpose. It's only after a certain time
and according to a certain state of a company that social purpose
can exist.

"Let's take the case of Nissan again. Restoring the accounts was
not the sole purpose of the turnaround. Profitability could not be
sustained. The immediate results were long-term profitability
along with the rate of growth, the product range and technological
capital. That's why I designed and implemented three-year plans,
and then six-year ones more recently. Even if things are under
control today, what matters is the engines of growth tomorrow.
When I launched the electric car in 2010, it wasn't to ensure the
company's growth in two years but in 2018. And when I decided
to enter China, it was to expand in the second decade of the
century."

Products as a Social Purpose

The debate about the social purpose of a company seemed to
ignore—as if it was taken for granted—the reason for its existence,
namely the product and what it contributed to society. The apho-
risms of François Michelin should have been passed down for
posterity like: "Being a boss is a mission, but the only real boss is the
customer." Or: "We don't make tires but objects that help transport

people who need to get around at the best possible price with the maximum security possible."

According to Carlos Ghosn, "employment is obviously an essential social contribution, but we must not forget products and technology. What has Apple's contribution been to the development of our societies? Remember how difficult it was to communicate with someone on the other side of the world twenty years ago? Today, you're linked up to the whole world and it's almost free. That obviously has to be counted as a social development—you're no longer isolated, you're connected. Moreover, consumers recognize this social responsibility. If a company launches a successful product, the public likes the company, and its boss, too. An example was Steve Jobs, who wasn't particularly nice in professional relationships, but whose public image was extraordinary as it assimilated Apple products.

"The self-driving car is also a social development, allowing people in their nineties to maintain their independence—or people with disabilities to find it. A car that costs 4,000 dollars in India is a social service. The electric car we launched in China fulfills a special purpose, bringing personal mobility to people for whom it was beyond reach. This is obviously part of a company's social purpose. And it's not a contradiction with profitability at all.

"It's not hypocrisy. The social purpose of a firm is, by its nature, linked to its economic purpose. When a disaster as big as the Tohoku earthquake occurs, your social contribution is to stand up and lead people behind you to help rebuild the country. There's no better way to show your membership in the community. And it's not meeting an obligation, because there are taxes for that. When a company has fulfilled its tax obligations, it's paid its dues and it's up to governments to make the best social use of the money."

Stakeholders Versus Shareholders

In theory, the social purpose of a joint stock company is to serve shareholders who are paid for contributing capital that determines the very existence of the company. This simple relationship had been subjected to endless controversies and polemics on the sharing of value added—roughly between capital and labor—which was in fact remarkably stable over the long term. A familiar deviation of this debate was the somewhat-dated contrast between the stockholder capitalism practiced in advanced Western economies, and the stakeholder capitalism in force in Japan.

Such contrasts were largely exaggerated, especially when they implied more "virtuous" behavior by Japanese business leaders. In reality, most company financing in Japan had long come not from cajoling shareholders but from banks at the center of a collective savings system. To the detriment of savers, the system borrowed money at low rates to lend it as cheaply as possible to the country's industrial machine and its massively indebted government. Monetary policy over twenty-five years made loans even cheaper, with low, zero or even negative interest rates.

"You can't talk about contempt for shareholders in Japan," Carlos Ghosn said. "It's more like lack of interest. Japan's still a country with a culture dominated by cash. There's no difference between putting money in the bank and hiding it under the bed, because the return is zero in either case. It doesn't really matter where you put your money as there's no or very little inflation. For Japanese business leaders, dividends are not crucial as shareholders aren't very important."

But the money deprived from shareholders did not end up in the pockets of employees, whose salaries had been frozen in an environment of persistent deflation. In a country whose dynamism had been eroded by demographic decline, the money did not go towards investment either. At the end of 2019, listed Japanese companies were sleeping on a mountain of cash exceeding five hundred trillion yen (five trillion dollars), roughly equivalent to the country's entire gross domestic product. And it had tripled since Prime Minister Shinzo Abe urged companies to stop hoarding cash in 2013. The appeal was ignored by the nomenklatura running Japanese companies, who multiply from generation to generation without being accountable to anyone.

"Old Japan is more attached to rules, rather than what they're for," Carlos Ghosn said. "The major divergence from so-called traditional sectors is that they ultimately remain prisoners of customs and rules that have lost their meaning—the reasons that justified their existence have disappeared. They're so petrified by change that they can't see the historical reasons why this or that practice doesn't exist anymore. That's fatal. And how does it show? There are very few, if any, areas of activity that have been discovered in Japan over the past twenty years. But they're still very good at following the real pioneers in a market, and doing better."

Japanese Decline

Japan is still a leading industrial power, and in a position of strength, and sometimes dominance, in areas largely ignored by the general public—in making components and advanced materials, for example, and robotics. But the list of sectors where Japanese industry is falling behind is getting longer, especially in the face of Asian competitors, and not just in traditional areas like steel and ship building.

Take NTT Docomo, which was at the forefront of text messaging and sending images by mobile phone. But since smartphones emerged, Japanese companies disappeared from the global market. This was partly because of Japan's suicidal attachment to domestic standards aimed at protecting the local market—a nice lesson on the evils of protectionism. Meanwhile, the Japanese lost the flat-screen market to Korean, and then Chinese, rivals, and the market for memories, and then semiconductors in general, to the Koreans and Taiwanese.

It's too early to assess the impact of the "second Ghosn shock" triggered by the arrest of the builder of the Renault-Nissan-Mitsubishi Alliance.

"Carlos Ghosn's arrival on the scene at Nissan not only allowed the Japanese automaker to recover, but equally changed Japanese business culture," wrote the *Asahi Shimbun* in December 2018. The newspaper, which played an active role in the smear campaign, noted the reduction in the number of suppliers and the dismantling of Nissan's network of cross-shareholdings, the adoption of English as the working language of the Alliance and its greater use at Nissan, the hiring of foreign executives and favoring promotions based on merit and performance rather than seniority. Numerous Japanese companies had followed the example, the daily said.

Carlos Ghosn's downfall, orchestrated by the Nissan Old Guard, immediately led to a great leap backwards, with the purge of dozens of senior non-Japanese executives.

"They were fired not for their incompetence, but for supposedly being close to me, because I'd appointed them," Carlos Ghosn said. Another Moscow show trial.

The sheer loss of human capital was reflected in the numbers for winners and losers in terms of market share in the United States. By May 2020, Hyundai was ranked top and Nissan was at the bottom, with sales having fallen 27.7 percent from a year earlier. By November, Hyundai had the fastest-growing market share in the American market, ahead of General Motors and Toyota, and Nissan's decline in its share of the market was the steepest. People made a difference, notably José Muñoz and the numerous former Nissan colleagues he convinced to follow him to Hyundai. At the same time, Carlos Tavares picked up people from Renault after he left for PSA Peugeot-Citroën, but with less success.

Turning Inward?

It was doubtful that other big Japanese companies with global ambitions would accompany the nationalists at the Nissan Old Guard in such a suicidal approach. Under Toyota's chief executive Akio Toyoda, the leading Japanese automaker had appointed more foreigners and women to management positions since 2013—not only abroad but also in Japan. Former Renault executive Didier Leroy became the number two executive at Toyota, where he was the right-hand man of Toyoda, the great-grandson of the company's founder.

Greater internationalization can sometimes lead to unexpected obstacles—as with Toyota's global communications director Julie Hamp, for example. In 2015, Japanese police arrested Hamp—an American who was the company's first female senior executive—for importing a painkiller regarded as a narcotic in Japan. Her arrest and imprisonment led to outbursts by commentators and politicians against Toyoda for daring to come to her defense. The incident brutally cut short her career with Toyota.

What will be the impact of vindictiveness of the totalitarian judicial system against Carlos Ghosn, who long ran one of the country's most venerated companies, on the external image of the country, and foreigners who are senior executives in Japan?

A little after November 19, 2018, the chief executive of a major U.S. insurance company wrote to a friend: "You know why we decided to pull out of the Japanese market a few years ago. It's certain we shall never set foot there again after what happened at Haneda." There were dozens of reactions like this.

In January 2020, the main leaders, experts and financiers of the global auto industry gathered at the World Economic Forum in Davos, as they did every year for a thematic breakfast of "governors" behind closed doors. Mobility was on the menu this year. About 15 percent of the people attending were Japanese, led by Akio Toyoda. The breakfast was to run from 7:30 to 9:00. Around 8:10, a participant said, one gentleman expressed surprise that nobody had mentioned the elephant in the room—Carlos Ghosn, the great absentee. "As he spoke, I watched the reactions of the Japanese," the participant said. "They looked like they wanted to disappear under the table."

The governor of a leading European central bank was the party pooper: "We have an affair that's a flagrant case of injustice that has smelled very, very, very fishy from the start."

A Honda representative counter-attacked: "In Japan itself, we don't need foreign leaders."

Another participant asked: "But if that's the case, would you protect them?"

Mobility was forgotten. Until 9:00, they only talked about Carlos Ghosn. This story had legs. And they were still running the course.

CHAPTER TWELVE

Market for Top Executives

Thierry Desmarest announced his resignation as a member of the Renault board of directors in February 2018, a few days before a board meeting crucial for the future of the French automaker and the Alliance. His mandate was supposed to run until 2020. The former chief executive of French oil and gas giant Total had been a director for ten years and his departure coincided with palpable tensions between Renault management and the French government, the company's dominant shareholder. Thierry Desmarest, who was 72, said he was leaving because of his age and personal reasons, fueling media reports of a disagreement over the selection process for Thierry Bolloré, the choice of Carlos Ghosn. But according to another board member, he was clear when he addressed his fellow Renault directors for the last time.

"French government pressure forcing us to reduce Carlos Ghosn's remuneration is unacceptable, especially given that Renault is recording the best financial results in its history," the outgoing director said. "It shows contempt for the prerogatives of the board of directors."

On February 16, Finance Minister Bruno Le Maire bragged that he had obtained a 30 percent cut in the amount received by the chairman and chief executive of Renault in 2018. "I told Mr. Ghosn very clearly that we cannot vote for a leader with such high remuneration," said the former conservative who pretended to be a "free-marketer" in the party of President Emmanuel Macron. With a commitment to "perpetuate" the Alliance between Renault, Nissan and Mitsubishi, the French government made the pay cut—actually 19 percent on the fixed part—a precondition for reappointing Carlos Ghosn.

Stingy Government

"Since 2005 at Renault, I always worked with the compensation committee under the board," Carlos Ghosn said. The committee had four members in 2018—two independent directors including Patrick Thomas, who chaired the committee, along with an employee representative, and Martin Vial, the director designated by the French government. To set the remuneration of Renault's boss, the committee used a complex formula combining a fixed component with a variable part based on the achievement of certain goals along with 'performance shares' subject to conditions. But whatever the level of my remuneration, it was always too much for the government shareholders. Starting with the financial crisis in 2009, the growing pressure didn't stop. Board members from the government always voted against the compensation committee's proposals. They were always in the minority on the board and at the annual meeting of shareholders. Except for one year."

The affair made a lot of noise. Under a new provision in 2016, the annual meeting—where the government had 27 percent of the voting shares but only 15.1 percent of Renault's capital—rejected the compensation committee's proposal for Carlos Ghosn by a very small margin. But the vote was only consultative, so the board ignored it. Despite the legality, the move prompted virtuous indignation from an army of shareholder advocates, including leftists suddenly seized by a surprising passion for business and capitalism.

The government had rejected the committee's proposal in the two previous years. But the annual meeting of Renault shareholders in 2016 was preceded by a virulent campaign against Carlos Ghosn. The figurehead was Pierre-Henri Leroy, a former banker whose investment consulting firm Proxinvest was a self-proclaimed champion of "small shareholders," a claim eagerly lapped up by the French media. Proxinvest opposed the "uncontrolled remuneration of Carlos Ghosn."

Proxinvest even took the step, which the firm admitted was unusual, of submitting no fewer than 13 questions to the shareholder meeting. This burst of activity contrasted with the resounding silence of Proxinvest after the arrest of Carlos Ghosn on November 19, 2018, and the subsequent collapse of the Renault share price leading to billions of dollars in losses incurred by the company's shareholders. The sole concern of Pierre-Henri Leroy was whether Carlos Ghosn would be receiving contractual compensation for leaving Renault while he was "detained in Japan for an indefinite period"—and if so, how much?

"It would be useful for the board of directors to clarify this gray area as soon as possible," Leroy said on January 24, 2019. Eighteen months later, he sold his 60 percent share in Proxinvest for an undisclosed sum to Alain Demarolle, a former banker who had previously held a senior position at the Ministry of Economy and Finance. So much for transparency.

"It's obvious there should be complete transparency for shareholders on the remuneration conditions for the boss and senior executives," Carlos Ghosn said. "They obviously have the right to know how the chief executive and the main people involved in corporate governance are being compensated. But I wouldn't go beyond that. These elements of remuneration are published in the company's official reports and documents. They can be broken down and justified, based on the company's performance, and compared with what other companies do, and so on. What's the overall cost of governance to shareholders? That's the only issue that's really important."

Governance: The Cost for Shareholders

"I'm in favor of transparency," said Ghosn. "It's useful for the decision making of people concerned—in other words, the company shareholders. The transparency about the assets or compensation of elected officials is a different issue. That's public money. And neither Renault nor Nissan are public bodies.

"That's why I maintain that Japan previously had the best possible system. The shareholders vote every year on the budget for the entire board of directors, which for Nissan was 2.9 billion yen or about twenty-seven million dollars. The distribution was done by the relevant board committee. And I presented to shareholders the execution of the budget which could not be higher, and was often lower, than the authorized amount. The remuneration figure wasn't broken down to individuals. From the company's turnover of 110 billion dollars, the shareholders authorized the disbursement of twenty-seven million dollars to remunerate governance. What they were interested in was the overall cost.

"It's a very healthy system as it allows for comparisons based on the company's performance and how competitors behave. It avoids what I call voyeurism, nothing to do with the health of the business, which is only the figures that are or should be important to those who decide to invest their savings. But executive remuneration has become a political issue, even in Japan. The government addressed this with a requirement that all those receiving more than 100 million yen (one million dollars) had to make individual declarations. That's where the problems started, not with the shareholders, but the press and a certain segment of public opinion."

This reform launched by the government's Financial Services Agency in 2010 reflected a vague aspiration to make the operations of listed Japanese companies comply with international norms. Such reforms were a sign of the times following the Global Financial Crisis and similar legislation passed by the U.S. Congress. But the Americans failed to address a much more crucial question in Japan.

"Of course, transparency is a good thing in itself, but the problem in Japan is not the level of remuneration," said Takeyuki Ishida at RiskMetrics Group, part of New York-based MSCI, a leading provider of research to investors. "It's that salaries are not sufficiently linked to performance."

New Capitalism

Bruno Le Maire's behavior, both before and especially after Carlos Ghosn's imprisonment in Tokyo, reflected the way executive pay could be used for political ends in France. Le Maire was a politician from the traditional right, where he frequently changed allegiances. After suffering a resounding defeat in the right-wing primaries for presidential elections in 2017, he belatedly rallied behind the candidacy of Emmanuel Macron.

Rewarded with a ministerial portfolio by the winner of the unusual election, he took over the reins of the all-powerful Ministry of Economy and Finance. Housed in a neo-Stalinist-style fortress in the Bercy neighborhood of Paris, the ministry had been practicing state intervention vaguely mixed with poorly assumed liberalism for decades. After Carlos Ghosn's arrest, Bruno Le Maire became the poster boy for a "new capitalism" that rejected high pay "for those who don't want to understand" and who hailed back to "another time, another capitalism"—and praised the fine example set by Jean-Dominique Senard, the new head of Renault.

Senard, however, succeeded Ghosn only in his capacity as chairman of the board, in principle a non-executive position that raked in more than half a million dollars a year, not exactly a handout, which he combined with a comfortable pension. Luca de Meo was hired from Volkswagen to serve as Renault chief executive from July 2020, with a remuneration package of more than 7 million dollars, of which more than 1.5 million dollars was fixed as the salary alone. That was more than the final package of Carlos Ghosn after his pay cut, and not far from what he had been getting in the past. And, it was also a lot more than the package for Thierry Bolloré, who did not get more than 4.5 million dollars. What was Bruno Le Maire going to do about this?

The nature of populism is that it denounced everything, but didn't explain anything. In most advanced economies, inflated pay packages for heads of companies may have originated in the financialization of capitalism that started in the 1980s. More seriously, however, financial capitalism fueled asset-price inflation—notably in real estate and share prices—which led to an explosion in inequalities resulting from public policies. Let's emphasize that, *public* policies.

Government Policies the Culprit

The financialization of capitalism had its roots in the mother of all decisions announced by U.S. President Richard Nixon on August 15, 1971. Nixon suspended the dollar's convertibility into gold, bringing an end to the international financial system put in place at Bretton Woods, New Hampshire, in 1944. The Bretton Woods conference—which gave birth to the World Bank and the International Monetary Fund—brought together Allied nations from World War II, which was still raging in the Pacific. Nixon's shock fulfilled the dreams of Keynesian economists of all stripes to finally break the link with gold—described by the great man himself as a "barbarous relic"—and leave the value of money to the arbitrary judgement of monetary authorities.

The second big rupture was the modernization and internationalization of financial markets amid the poorly concealed aim of facilitating public debt, which exploded in advanced economies as the post-war economic boom came to an end. With growth no longer able to support welfare-state lifestyles, budget deficits filled the gap at the expense of inflating public debt through bond markets.

The last, if not ultimate, phase involved central banks, theoretically and statutorily "independent" from governments, sinking into a monetary licentiousness that had no peacetime precedent. Since the Wall Street crash of 1987, each jolt to the economy or markets led central banks to flood financial systems with liquidity, including the Covid-19 crisis where fiscal stimulus accompanied the monetary response. Liabilities of governments, companies and financial institutions were thus transferred to the balance sheets of central banks whose extremely low, zero or negative interest rates had annihilated the cardinal economic variable—the price of money, in other words, the price of time and risk.

What the Austrian economist Ludwig von Mises called "inflationism" created bubble economies, including the bubble in compensation packages for top executives, which was neither the most important nor the most harmful. Curiously, however, it was the one that got the most attention. It was understandable, since real-estate bubbles had many beneficiaries—and collateral damage among those forced to moved out of city centers—whereas the titans of business were less numerous and easily stood out. Denouncing them as part of populist vindictiveness required less effort than trying to understand and explain the phenomenon.

Salaries Versus Rentier Income

"If it's a question of equality, everyone's situation must be made public," said Carlos Ghosn. "Not just salaried employees, but also those who benefit from private income or inheritances. Today, there's a lot of discretion around anything to do with investment incomes, and a desire for total transparency for those who receive high salaries. Let's not name names, but the big capitalists don't care because salaries represent a tiny part of their earnings compared with investment income from holding capital. Who earns what has become a social and political problem. This is not my field, but if it becomes a political or social issue, why is it limited to salaries, and only those who are in a tiny minority? Why stigmatize those who work compared to those who own?"

As is often the case, this debate took a grotesque turn in France when leftists found a new hero in John Pierpont Morgan, the New York financier who halted the stock market crisis of 1907 before the Federal Reserve even existed. He recommended that a company boss should receive no more than twenty times the lowest paid employee. But this ceiling did not apply to one of the richest men in America, whose name still graces two of the world's most powerful financial institutions—JPMorgan Chase and Morgan Stanley. Nor did it apply to Henry Ford, who believed bosses should earn at most forty times more than the lowest paid.

"Whether income or inheritance, the tool for addressing inequalities is taxation," said Carlos Ghosn. "The community should benefit from your personal enrichment—the exact opposite of prohibiting the enrichment of individuals by all means possible and imaginable. If someone earns a lot of money, it means they pay a lot of taxes. Society benefits through redistribution by governments."

When it came to finding a way to get Carlos Ghosn to relinquish his position at Renault after his arrest, the French political class turned to his tax status. On January 9, 2019, the daily newspaper *Libération* reported that he had not been a resident of France for tax purposes since 2012.

"The Renault directors were stunned," one board member said. Some were no doubt waiting for a pretext. In the fallout, Finance Minister Bruno Le Maire drew up legislation requiring French residency for the heads of all large French companies, both public and private.

Carlos Ghosn as Taxpayer

"My change in tax status in 2012 did not change my situation as a taxpayer in France," Carlos Ghosn said. "All of my income originating in France was taxed in France, even if I was a resident of the

Netherlands for tax purposes. I paid taxes in Japan on all salaries I received in Japan. And as for remuneration paid in Amsterdam, the tax was settled in the Netherlands. Nothing changed with the tax domicile, which only concerns consolidation since, in principle, there's no double taxation on the same income."

In France, a change in the wealth tax system did not impact the situation—non-residents were still taxed on certain assets, notably real estate, when the value exceeded a certain threshold. But populist magazines still maintained that Carlos Ghosn was no longer paying taxes in France as a fiscal resident of the Netherlands.

"The reason I strived to become a fiscal resident of the Netherlands was to be remunerated by Renault Nissan B.V. and position myself, first, as head of the Alliance, before being head of Renault and Nissan," Carlos Ghosn said. "When I headed Nissan, I was a fiscal resident of Japan and taxed in Japan. After I came back to Renault in 2005, I remained a fiscal resident of France until 2012. With plans to consolidate the Alliance, I chose greater neutrality in the perspective of greater convergence between different companies. Louis Schweitzer decided to domicile the Alliance in the Netherlands very early on. From 2012, we started to reinforce the staff in Amsterdam and I considered it normal to reside there as a sign of neutrality. Before 2012, it was in fact just a board comprising representatives of the two companies. After 2012, we set up a proper head office, which was destined to grow even more if the holding company project eventuated."

Populism and demagoguery went hand in hand. Bruno Le Maire's law on tax domiciliation was useless if it was a question of making people pay taxes. It was also harmful to French competitiveness, which, in a globalized economy, strived to gain talent and not just market share. In October 2019, an amendment by the Communist Party supported by the government reduced the threshold of a large company to the equivalent of 300 million dollars in turnover, down from around 1.2 billion dollars.

Competitiveness and Remuneration

"Business competitiveness, the condition for survival, is the second aspect of the debate over remuneration," said Carlos Ghosn.

"Businesses must equip themselves with competent people to survive. And competent people can't be found everywhere. Economic history is littered with the corpses of companies whose choice of bad leaders drove them to the wall. Choosing people is sensitive, as it involves personalities who are rare. And rarity comes from work, not birth. Companies buy personalities, experience and know-how.

"Talent makes a footballer unique, but so does training and experience. It's perfectly acceptable that there are huge differences in remuneration between the best in sport and the others. Why is this logic not applied to business leaders? Even the best paid among us are very far from the best-paid top athletes. Very, very far."

Indeed, French football club Paris-Saint-Germain "bought" Brazil's Neymar da Silva Santos Junior from the Barcelona football club for 222 million euros, a sum equivalent to 270 million dollars, and the world's most expensive transfer ever in 2017. In terms of salary, however, he was earning less than half of what Argentine player Lionel Messi was getting back at the Barcelona club. Messi's monthly income was around nine million dollars, above Carlos Ghosn's annual salary at Renault.

The reality was that a labor market for business leaders existed. For very large companies and very big industries, it was a global market. Like other markets, it was imperfect. But it was preferable to politicians designating company bosses as in managed economies, and the public sector in market economies. Before the collapse of its old political structure dominated by Christian-Democrats and Communists, Italy invented an expression for the appointments of managers to state-owned companies—*lottizzazione* ("parceling out").

France Ruled by a Caste System

Market deficiencies, not excesses, were the issue. In France, the positions of chief executives and board members were entrusted to the nomenklatura spawned from major elite schools and state bodies. It was a Malthusian system that lacked egalitarianism and competitiveness, sucking life out of the economy for which the country would pay a very heavy price.

In the global marketplace, however, there was demand for managers like Carlos Ghosn, and the head of the Alliance had several occasions to sell himself to the highest bidder. The difficulty was finding a formula that recognized talent, aligned the manager's interests with those of the shareholders, rewarded medium and long-term performance, and sanctioned failures. Squaring a circle, in other words. Innumerable works had been devoted to this subject, including by renowned economists such as Joseph Stiglitz, the American idol of the European left. He showed that the costs to shareholders of offering stock options to executives was not negligible, and that bonus shares weren't free of charge for everyone.

"When it came to executive compensation within the Alliance, the formula varied from one company to another," Carlos Ghosn said. "It wasn't exactly the same at Renault, Nissan or Mitsubishi. Roughly speaking, there was a fixed salary—not very high—and a variable part with portions paid upfront during the year depending on results, and later depending on medium-term performance. There was a range of tools like stock options, shares and deferred bonuses. As far as I'm concerned, I kept my shares and I'm a significant shareholder in Nissan and Renault. That could be seen as a testimony to my loyalty and faith—or stupidity as they fell dramatically after my arrest.

"At the annual meetings of shareholders at Nissan and Renault each year, I reported the level of my fixed and variable remuneration, comparing it with averages in the auto industry and other groups of equivalent size in large traditional industries. Not high-tech because that's a world apart. Not Facebook or Google, but industries like aeronautics or chemicals—so they could know where I was on the grid."

Same for All Top Executives

Contrary to what some media had been harping on about for years, such benchmarking concerned not only the chief executives of Nissan and Renault, but also hundreds of other senior executives.

"At Nissan and Renault, we used market references for senior managers, the top two hundred," said Carlos Ghosn. "I wanted to know what an industry executive was paid in a similar group—what was the average, the maximum and the minimum? Towers Perrin, a well-known American advisory company that became Towers

Watson in 2009, collected all the figures in an annual global study. The comparison was done worldwide for Renault and Nissan. The basis for comparison could not be France or Japan. We had numerous foreign executives in Japan who would have never come if we paid them like the Japanese who benefited from other advantages."

When the headquarters of Nissan was still in central Tokyo, there was an ancient building reserved for the old boys—former executives who had formally retired years, even decades earlier. They could spend their days there, sitting in lace-covered armchairs and sipping green tea served by young staff. In the evenings, chauffeur-driven cars would drive them home.

In Japan, lifetime employment was not an empty expression. As senior advisors, former executives continued to project their influence over the companies they had served since leaving college, meddling in factional intrigues and struggles. Rarely for the better, and often for worse. In 2017, a study by the Ministry of Economy, Trade and Industry found that eighty percent of companies still respected this tradition. But Nissan announced in January 2020, that it was putting an end to the system. In theory, the first victim was former chief executive Hiroto Saikawa, who continued to haunt the corridors at the Yokohama headquarters despite his dismissal, like Hitoshi Kawaguchi. But in Japan, appearances (*tatemae*) were always a long way from reality (*honne*).

The idea that Japanese business leaders were subjected to an almost monastic life was out of date. Beyond remuneration, the material advantages were not negligible—chauffeur-driven cars, lifetime membership to one or several golf clubs, generous expense accounts and so on. Retirement bonuses were mandatory and could reach considerable amounts. When Yoshihiko Miyauchi retired from financial services company Orix Corporation in 2014, he received the tidy sum of four billion yen, about forty million dollars. And in 2018, Toyota paid French number two Didier Leroy more than one billion yen, about ten million dollars.

"The rule I established was that nobody would be paid less than the international median," Carlos Ghosn said. "They should be paid at least the median level or more. I didn't want any senior executive to complain they were being badly paid. And when someone protested, I sent them to see Arun Bajaj so they could understand where they were in the hierarchy. Nobody should be able to think they're underpaid."

When Nissan's newly appointed vice chief operating officer Jun Seki announced he was resigning from the number three position in December 2019, he said he was making a financial sacrifice to join Japanese auto supplier Nidec Corporation.

"It's not about money," Seki said. "In fact, I'm going to lose, as Nissan pays us well." Passed over in favor of the new chief executive Makoto Uchida, he was seizing the chance to become number one at Nidec, the world's biggest producer of small electric motors.

Millionaires and Billionaires

The sinister irony in the "Carlos Ghosn affair" was that the builder of the Alliance was thrown into prison in November 2018, for voluntarily accepting a reduction in remuneration compared with his peers in the global auto industry.

"When the 100-million-yen rule was imposed in the middle of the financial crisis in 2009, I was well above it and thought the Japanese public would not understand that I could have an annual salary of eighteen or nineteen million dollars, even if it was in line with the global industry average," Carlos Ghosn said. "Some bosses received more, at Fiat or BMW, but others less, especially the Japanese.

"I decided to cap my salary at one billion yen, voluntarily. I wasn't particularly happy. There was a certain frustration, that's true. Some people in my immediate entourage noted that I was being underpaid compared with my peers and were worried that I'd leave, including Greg Kelly, who has since said it so publicly. They looked at different possibilities, none of which worked. They couldn't find anything that was satisfactory and legal. Violating or circumventing regulations was obviously not a question. The conclusion was that the eventual solution would be put in place after I retired—I could continue to work as a senior advisor, a practice that's more or less widespread in Japan. They said Nissan would continue to need me and that I would be paid accordingly.

"That's what was proposed. It wasn't official; I signed no document and the company made no commitment. The question of fearing the French government reaction never arose. If that had been the case, I'd have simply left. I wouldn't have had too much trouble finding a place to go in 2010. If I'd accepted the offer to take charge of running General Motors, I'd have made a lot more money without causing any controversy. It was a concession to the political and social climate in France and Japan at the time. It's an issue that wouldn't arise in the United States."

After the shock of November 19, 2018, an investment banker took out his calculator to compare the financial profile Carlos Ghosn would have achieved by agreeing to become the head of General Motors in 2010. Taken into account were the annual salary of around twenty million dollars earned by GM chief executive Mary Barra, and the GM share price after the recovery—it soared from around 1 dollar in May 2009, to $37.90 in November 2018. The banker estimated Carlos Ghosn would have been sitting on a personal fortune of around 400 million dollars by the end of 2018. Bloomberg Billionaires Index estimated his actual net worth at 120 million dollars, not enough to join the club of the 500 biggest fortunes in France, where rankings were dominated by families and heirs.

These amounts might seem enormous, but were modest compared with the fortunes built from investment income at the heart of the capitalist system. According to *Institutional Investor*, the combined earnings of the twenty-five best-paid hedge fund managers in 2019 were 20.2 billion dollars with eight of them each taking home more than 1 billion dollars. Many were "quants," quantitative analysts, who used computer algorithms to automatically milk the cows that the hormone-fueled markets furnished by central banks had become.

Algorithms were also at the origin of colossal fortunes made by companies with entrenched monopoly positions in Silicon Valley under the bovine watch of unarmed or passive anti-trust authorities. At least the global auto industry was still competitive. Operating margins were modest—about six percent was a good average for generalist manufacturers—but products enjoyed remarkable price stability over a long period, despite constant and major technological improvements.

"I imposed a limit on myself, but felt frustrated," Carlos Ghosn said. "I didn't know I was going to pay a much higher price. It can't be said enough times—I was thrown in prison for thinking about something that never happened. The prosecution accuses me of thoughts or intentions—but without beginning to start to carry out the act. It's not even a crime of intention, it's a crime of prospecting.

"The sole alleged evidence—if we can understand the tortuous approach of the prosecution—is emails sent between those who worked on different hypotheses, none of which took the slightest shape. The prosecutors tried for months to back this accusation up, but they were incapable. And a fair trial would have no trouble proving it. But they succeeded in making me look guilty, as it's difficult to imagine I was thrown in jail for a sum of money I never received, and that the company never transferred or promised. In fact, Nissan never set aside the nine billion yen (ninety million dollars) allegedly involved until several months after my arrest."

The Tenant

That's why prosecutors had to urgently fabricate new charges that were less fragile, and why the character assassination started feeding the media with details of the "lifestyle" of the head of the Alliance. Apartments, private jets and the Palace of Versailles were more photogenic and spoke more to the man on the street than Japanese financial information or commercial transactions in the Gulf.

"Let's remember that these apartments belonged to the company," Carlos Ghosn said. "In some cases, I was renting them—Nissan bought the property and I was the tenant. When I returned to Renault in 2005, we still owned the house in the suburbs of Paris we bought just before learning that we were going to Tokyo in the spring of 1999.

"But it was quite far from Billancourt, and I thought an apartment in Paris would make life easier. Nissan bought the apartment in Paris, which turned out to be an excellent investment. So, I paid rent from 2005 until I changed my residency to Amsterdam in 2012.

"When I moved my principal residency to Holland, I became a tenant in Amsterdam. But the use of company accommodation was directly related to my professional life. The rule I agreed to with Nissan was that I would pay for my primary residence, first Paris and then Amsterdam. In Tokyo, I was a tenant since arriving in 1999, and it was Nissan that insisted I keep an official residence in Japan after 2005 for appearances—they didn't want me to look like I was coming from time to time, so it was always in the name of balancing the two companies.

"Then came Brazil and Lebanon. The apartment in Rio was bought well before the house in Beirut. Every time I went to Rio, people would raise their eyebrows because of the lack of security that reigned—and still reigns—in the city. When I went to a hotel, security measures were taken with bodyguards and parts of the buildings blocked off. It cost a lot of money without providing optimal security. Greg Kelly and other directors estimated it would be better to buy an apartment where I could stay when I was in Rio, but also work and entertain in a secure discreet environment. I went there an average of four times a year, mainly for business reasons."

Business Practices in Rio

The business year started in Brazil with a news conference by Carlos Ghosn in January. This outlined the strategy for Nissan and Renault in Latin America over the 12 months ahead.

"In Rio, January 4 or 5 was like August in Paris, but there was always a crowd of reporters who came," said a former Alliance executive who worked in the region. After Carlos Ghosn's arrest, such details were not reported by the media being fed by the Nissan Old Guard. Carlos Ghosn also visited Brazil for the Rio Carnival in February and the Formula 1 Grand Prix, the last of the season, in late October or early November.

"Taking into account his business schedule and family time, he never had a social life as generally understood in Paris or New York," the former executive said. "Dinners in town bored him, but he had to return invitations." The Carnival and Grand Prix were occasions to thank customers with invitations to these two events. Unlike in France, where major companies rented VIP boxes for customers at football matches and the French Open, Nissan and Renault disclosed selected customer names from the guest lists to the media in Brazil. "He came a fourth time in July so he had the entire year covered," the executive said.

"Given his personal history, his links to the country whose language he spoke and his personal relations with presidents and state governors, how could Nissan or Renault have sent anyone else? What was shocking about investing in a country which everybody thought represented one of the engines of future economic growth, along with the other BRICS? Even more so as he was rolling up his sleeves. He'd be at work the day after he arrived, leading meetings, seeing authorities and making plant visits. We'd set up crazy schedules for him, including so-called social responsibility contacts with civil society. He never said no. But he never let up the pressure. Everyone knew his schedule was set 18 months or two years in advance. It would be enough to get back to his schedule at the time to confirm that the BRICS were a priority."

Beirut as a Hub

The accusers would retort that Lebanon was not a growth area. Devastated by years of confessional regimes built on the ruins of civil war, the former Switzerland of the Middle East was in a hostile regional environment alongside Israel, Syria and Turkey. And, it was sinking into an unprecedented crisis with no foreseeable outcome. But it was still, until recently, a financial hub and holiday destination for wealthy people in the region, including the Gulf.

"Beirut came later," Carlos Ghosn said. "We had a base in Dubai, but it was a lot easier to get from Europe to Lebanon—a three-hour flight. Our distributors and other partners in the region came to see me in Beirut, and they were very happy to go there. But there were worries about the situation in Lebanon and some board members at Renault echoed these concerns. On the ground, I was constantly accompanied by security personnel." Like the apartment in Rio, the house in the Achrafieh neighborhood of Beirut was used for living, working and entertaining, and had a professional and secure computer network.

"Given my links with Lebanon and Brazil, Greg Kelly and Hiroto Saikawa included in their proposals that I could keep using the residences in Rio and Beirut after I left my position as chief executive of Nissan, provided I was still working for the company. And then I was to have the possibility of buying them at prices which would have had to have been neutral for the company's finances.

"These properties were owned by Nissan, which took back those in Paris and Rio. Nissan wasn't able to take the Beirut house back for the simple reason that it violated all the legal rules in Lebanon, and the Lebanese judge considered it to be my home. In a completely illegal manner, representatives of Nissan broke into this house, and the judge ordered them out and my home returned."

Nissan initiated searches in France, Brazil and Lebanon with a Japanese warrant, but no local warrants. In Paris, they tried to enter the apartment but could not find the key. In Lebanon, the representatives of Nissan brutalized the guard and broke the lock.

"I would have liked them to have violated my home in Paris, as they would have had serious problems under French law," said Ghosn. "Brazilian judicial authorities condemned them and there's a lawsuit underway in Lebanon.

"The Japanese prosecutors acted by proxy except in Tokyo, where they had a warrant. Employees of the American law firm Latham & Watkins and Nissan staff violated my home. Latham & Watkins were well established in Chicago, but in this case they acted like thugs."

Hari Nada's Strange Visit

Like the arrest at Haneda on November 19, 2018, the raid on residences made available to Carlos Ghosn were part of a long-planned operation whose linchpin was Hari Nada in collusion with the Tokyo Public Prosecutors' Office.

A month before the arrest, Hari Nada made a whirlwind visit to Rio on October 23, with the exclusive aim of meeting Carlos Ghosn's personal assistant Vania Rufino, who was employed by Nissan's subsidiary in Brazil.

"He asked me to prepare all the documents related to the Copacabana apartment, which I found strange," she recalled. "He'd been the one responsible not only for acquiring this residence, but also the furnishings and equipment. He already had the documentation." The meeting with Mrs. Rufino took place in the offices of the law firm Gouvêia Vieira and began with another strange request from Hari Nada, who had known the personal assistant for years. He wanted to record their conversation.

"I need to remember precisely every word you say," Hari Nada said. Mrs. Rufino said he then placed his mobile telephone on the desk.

"Does Mr. Ghosn know about your visit and this interview?" she asked.

"Not yet," he replied. She asked Hari Nada to alert the head of the Alliance immediately. In a message to Carlos Ghosn, Hari Nada said he was in Rio to meet with his Brazilian assistant but that she was "not comfortable" with the meeting. Mrs. Rufino did not agree.

All questions were in the single direction of finding evidence to incriminate Carlos Ghosn for misusing company assets. These ranged from bills for maintaining the apartment, which were sent to Hari Nada himself, to the use of a credit card linked to a bank account for managing the residence (there was no credit card), and the use of the apartment by third parties outside of Carlos Ghosn's family (which never happened). After an interrogation lasting several hours, Hari Nada left Brazil.

At six o'clock in the morning in Rio on November 19, 2018 (six in the evening in Tokyo), Vania Rufino received an email from Christina Murray telling her to go immediately to the Nissan office with her phone and laptop. In vain, she tried to contact Carlos Ghosn, who had already been arrested at Haneda. She found out what had happened from Carlos Ghosn's sister, Claudine, and went to the Nissan headquarters for Latin America.

Locked in a room and prohibited from speaking to colleagues, Mrs. Rufino was interrogated for three hours by Salvador Dahan, the regional head of risk, governance, compliance and internal audit. Without being implicated in the slightest, she received a letter advising that she had been suspended without pay for thirty days. Salvador Dahan accompanied her to the apartment to take possession of the keys and documents found there.

"They later asked me to go to Japan to be questioned by the prosecutors," Mrs. Rufino recalled. "I refused and got fired."

Growing Paranoia

After the interview with Hari Nada on October 23, Vania Rufino informed Carlos Ghosn of the strange incident and told him how she did not understand what was going on. He told her not to worry. In hindsight, the warning signs of what was being hatched in Yokohama were easy to see. There had also been other signs, long before. At the beginning of July, Hari Nada had arrived at Schiphol airport for a monthly meeting of the Alliance at its head office in Amsterdam. He was supposed to be sharing a car with another Nissan executive who arrived around the same time. The two knew each other well, had worked together on numerous projects, and had cordial relations.

"I sensed a very clear change in his behavior towards me," the executive later recalled. "He got into the front with the driver and not in the back with me, avoiding looking at me in the eyes, even though we were very close. During my face-to-face meeting with Carlos the next day, I described his attitude. I added that Saikawa had been acting strangely, saying that he wanted to Japanize the company, that he'd be a much better chief executive than him and so on. He replied: 'You're being completely paranoid like Mouna Sepehri. This sort of behavior's not surprising when there's a change in management.' He didn't want to take the alert seriously, like several others."

With all due respect to Andy Grove—the Intel founder whose memoirs were entitled *Only the Paranoid Survive*—Carlos Ghosn was absolutely not paranoid. His management style, which should be clear by now, was rational and pragmatic, based on figures, situations and the strength of projects. Secondly, nothing is built on mistrust, which is as toxic for a company as it is for a country—as illustrated in *La Société de Défiance: comment le modèle français s'auto-détruit* ("Society of Mistrust: How the French Model is on Auto-Destruct"), a book by economists Yann Algan and Pierre Cahuc, which describes a disintegrating France. There were few clues about what was about to happen, given the extraordinary magnitude of what was being cooked up by Nissan in Yokohama and the public prosecutors in Tokyo. Besides, Carlos Ghosn's management had always been accompanied by careful legal scrutiny, as required by the complexity and chronic instability of the laws and rules that frame the lives of large companies operating in multiple markets, cultures and socio-political environments.

Legacy of a Bankrupt French Government

In the avalanche of fabricated allegations against Ghosn, the builder of the Alliance, the ridiculous would far outweigh the rest. The ridiculous, if not pathetic, was obviously Versailles. But nothing was surprising in a nation that French writer François-René de Chateaubriand described as being "governed by envy." The sum of fifty-thousand euros, about sixty-thousand dollars, was all it took for some media to enthusiastically lower themselves into the smear campaign initiated by the Nissan Old Guard. With the festivities at Versailles, the media that had looked at the unique industrial venture of the Alliance through a key hole would be able to get an eyeful.

The bankrupt French government—which had not recorded a budget surplus since 1974—did not have the means to maintain the heritage the country had inherited from a thousand years of history. After World War I, the palace of the Sun King at Versailles was saved by American millionaires led by John D. Rockefeller, the oil king. Catherine Pégard, who chaired the public body that took care of the palace, offered to forego the fifty-thousand euros regular price tag as a commercial gesture from an important sponsor to use the Grand Trianon for a private dinner for the birthday of Carlos Ghosn's wife, Carole. For other expenses, Carlos Ghosn used his own money.

"For Versailles, I'd decided that Renault would make a donation of one million euros to finance the restoration of the Salon de la Paix," Carlos Ghosn said. "Nobody criticized me, although a shareholder could legitimately ask why the company should subsidize the Palace of Versailles. But as soon as profits are made and dividends paid, it should be nobody's business. The donation was made with a clear purpose—Versailles is one of the most visited sites in France. And the millions of tourists who passed through the Salon de la Paix every year would know that the Alliance had made the restoration possible. It was very good for the images of the companies.

What's been said or written in this context is part of the smear campaign triggered by my arrest."

As for the fifteenth anniversary of the Alliance in March 2014, that we've already discussed in these pages, the judges will decide its nature, an exercise to be watched with interest. Suffice to say, that Amsterdam-based Renault Nissan B.V. financed the celebration in the palace's Galerie des Batailles. Dozens of people were employed for the evening, including musicians who benefited from a ruinous unemployment scheme for intermittent workers in the entertainment industry.

"There are always critics when a private company leaves its strictly defined areas of activity to invest in a cultural activity, for example," Carlos Ghosn said. "I'm accused of misusing company funds by making a donation to Saint Joseph University in Lebanon. It's the same for the American School in Paris, which I also assisted. But I did it after my son completed his schooling. When they asked us, I made sure many academic institutions were helped, especially in France, where public funding is parsimonious. Not only the Polytechnique and the Paris School of Mines but also HEC, INSEAD and so on. If the company wasn't making money, it would have been at the expense of shareholders. But that was never the case."

Five for One

Judges would also have to decide whether private jets, of which Carlos Ghosn was not the sole user, involved business or private trips.

"Today there are five people employed in functions that I used to perform for the Alliance and its different components," said Carlos Ghosn. "Five—chairman of the boards of three companies and two positions as chief executive. How would that have been possible without this mode of transport? How?"

CHAPTER THIRTEEN

Tomorrow

The twentieth century was the century of the motor vehicle. The economic, social and cultural influence of this object of mass production was immeasurable for the lives of people who had access to it (not all, far from it). It was more influential than railways and at least as much as electric power. And infinitely more than air transport, whose popularization was recent and relative at the same time. A civilization built itself around automobiles. But evoking French writer Paul Valéry, some think this civilization is doomed to die, and that humanity would be no more worse off if it disappeared.

On a planet where the efficiency of energy spending is becoming a question of human survival, the toll of the automobile is mixed. It's a disaster for short or very short journeys which account for a big majority of trips in urban and peri-urban areas where most of the world's population now lives. Making and using cars weighing one or two tons, usually occupied by a single person, to drive a few miles to and from work is a luxury. It's become an aberration.

Cars are under siege in the cities of advanced economies. Pedestrian zones are expanding dramatically and velocipedes are making a comeback. In Copenhagen, the pioneering capital of Denmark, a third of all trips are by bicycle, and a half in the city centre. The democratic nature of car use is being undermined by fees such as the congestion charge Singapore has applied for decades. Half the households in Paris have given up owning a car amid economic, physical and regulatory constraints, along with environmental and health concerns.

Faced with such issues, the industry's response has not been commensurate to what's at stake. The worst example has been "dieselgate," in which Germany's Volkswagen was found to have falsified pollution tests on diesel-powered vehicles in the United States and Europe, triggering investigations that were extended to other companies. Although the diesel engine had made significant progress in terms of cleanliness and efficiency, it is now doomed—not a single diesel vehicle will be running in Paris by 2025, five years ahead of a ban on gasoline engines.

Carlos Ghosn began preparing for the demise of the internal combustion engine in 2010 with his "adapt or die" approach, making the transition from pumps to plugs, as computer systems and connectivity advanced. It was not the beginning of the end, but a new beginning.

Fundamental Needs

"You've always got to come back to the fundamental needs of human beings," said Carlos Ghosn. "They haven't changed since we appeared on this planet and won't change. What has changed is the means of satisfying needs—for food, clothing, health care, shelter, communications and transport. With all the technologies, the car of today responds to many basic needs, notably autonomy in getting around. I decide where and when I want to go without relying on public transport or a third party. With communications added, the car's becoming a space for communicating by telephone, internet, videoconferencing and emergency calls. And like at home, you're sheltered. The car's become an essential part of human life.

"I'm not a techno-optimist or a theologian when it comes to science. But I see that technological advances can solve multiple problems. It's through scientific advances that we've largely solved the problem of world hunger. It's through technology that we've curbed or eliminated some of the major pandemics that have affected human beings from the dawn of time. Scientific and technological progress has allowed us to not only increase life expectancy but also made those final years better through traveling, reading and listening, rather than how they used to be, which was often painful. We're told that children born today have a life expectancy of one hundred years. In three generations, it's gone from sixty to seventy years to one hundred years, whereas it was thirty years for hundreds of thousands of years. The difference is knowledge."

The anti-car movement fashionable in certain political circles in advanced economies has found itself in the wrong era. Accounting for a declining share of the world's population and wealth, Western countries can no longer impose their social and economic paradigms on the rest of the planet.

"Demand for transport will increase phenomenally, regardless of how the world population evolves as it continues to grow, and then stabilizes," Carlos Ghosn said. "Moreover, most companies working on using artificial intelligence—which ultimately consists of making objects intelligent so they produce better services to their human users—are interested in cars, and are even making it a priority."

Soaring Vehicle Demand

"The automobile has, until now, been a fairly inert object—depending on its driver, kind of a slave. It will become a partner whose role is to make your life easier. In terms of the number of miles traveled per capita each year, global transport will grow impressively in the coming decades—tripling, or even quadrupling. This was the discussion I had with Nvidia boss Jensen Huang, who explained that one reason they're working a lot on integrated systems for autonomous cars is that they share this conviction about demand for transport." Based in California, the graphic-processing technology leader has been investing in artificial intelligence and working on autonomous vehicles with companies such as Daimler, Toyota, Volkswagen, Audi and Volvo.

"This technological revolution will extend to all forms of transport—individual, collective, across platforms and so on," said Carlos Ghosn. "The changes accompanying this soaring demand will be diversified. In the least developed countries, demand will be traditional and focus on individual vehicles to satisfy professional or family needs. In India, Africa and Latin America, rates of car ownership remain low, even extremely low." Compared with more than 80 percent of households with cars in the United States, and 50 percent in Europe and Japan, fewer than 5 percent of Indian households have cars, even fewer still in Pakistan, and hardly more in Africa.

"These countries won't suddenly go from the near absence of private cars to domination by Uber-style platforms," Carlos Ghosn said. "The process won't be comparable to telecoms in developing countries which leapfrogged to mobile phones and then smartphones without developing traditional fixed-line networks.

"But even if younger generations don't feel the need for individual cars in big metropolitan areas like Paris, the global auto market will continue to grow because slower demand there, will be accompanied by a boom in emerging and developing countries. Over the next ten years, there's no doubt that all modes of transport offerings will continue to expand to meet this demand for personal cars, hubs, taxis, carpooling or free-service cars.

"Having said that, infrastructure demand in all emerging and developing countries is enormous, and they have to invest massively to meet the demand. China's auto sales—personal cars and light-utility vehicles—are approaching thirty million units a year, compared with barely five million in India. That would have been impossible without the massive development of road infrastructure. The Chinese put priority on infrastructure and that's what supported the growth of the market.

"When we were negotiating with Dongfeng at the beginning of the century," Ghosn continued, "China already had a freeway network, but few cars were using it—like the housing complexes that were almost deserted. But the cars came, and so did the residents. And China's still investing massively. In countries like Brazil and India, the lack of infrastructure is obvious. They devoted a lot less money and chose other socio-economic priorities. The comparison of results favors China, without question."

Avoiding a Sudden Break

"We need to manage a natural and progressive evolution and avoid a sudden break that would have disastrous impacts," said Ghosn, "especially in terms of auto industry jobs in the broad sense, both upstream and downstream. First, greenhouse gas emissions from cars are declining, and this will accelerate with electrification. Second, car use needs to be rationalized to combat congestion—carpooling, hubs and so on. And taxation is there to regulate demand when it's very strong and puts enormous costs on infrastructure. Look at Hong Kong, Singapore and now the big Chinese cities where there are regulatory tools that are targeted, intelligent and modern. If it's considered that using personal cars has a very high social cost, you have to make them pay. By taxing car purchases, the freedom to choose is maintained, and the use of public space is taxed. You tax choice as a function of social utility."

The problem is that fiscal tools are always tricky to handle in democratic countries—as seen by the collective inability of the European Union, and the individual inability of member states, to put in place an economically efficient and socially acceptable carbon tax. That's why tax paradigm shifts and technological revolutions have to be jointly considered and carried out.

"Solving our problems doesn't mean returning to a world of pastures and horse-drawn vehicles," said Carlos Ghosn. "We have a problem, global warming, and the answer is primarily with technology. The electric car is one response to massive emissions caused by fossil fuels. Moving to zero-emission vehicles is now inevitable. The revolution's begun, and will advance through overlapping technological stages. First was the light hybrid, a minor advance in terms of consumption, then new-generation hybrids followed by wholly rechargeable electric vehicles. Internal combustion engines will gradually be replaced by electric and then hydrogen engines. The transition will take well over a decade, but the jury is already out. Because of the intrinsic advantages of electric engines, increased production volumes will trigger falls in price.

"There's no obvious obstacle to the shift to electric vehicles. The problem of battery recycling is being resolved. For example, with the Leaf—the first affordable electric car—batteries that can no longer power the vehicles still have other suitable uses and Nissan has developed recycling solutions. At this stage, the battery is the only efficient way to store electricity.

"Every technological revolution faces skepticism. It'll take time but the industry—even those who still have doubts—will be obliged to climb on board. All the big industries that invested in internal combustion engines will progressively switch to become suppliers of electric engine components, entire electric engines, batteries and fuel cells. And I'm all the less worried as the complete transition on the global level will be slow, a generation at least."

LG Chem, a subsidiary of the South Korean electronics giant, was an excellent example of the transition. The petrochemicals company won a contract to supply batteries for the Tesla Model 3 manufactured at a new plant in Shanghai. In record time, it became the world's largest battery supplier at the expense of massive investment in an activity that will soon overtake its traditional business.

"What counts a lot is the life cycle of a vehicle," Carlos Ghosn said. "In advanced economies, the life of a vehicle is about twelve years—in the United States, for example. In developing economies, it's more like twice that. Since nobody can reasonably believe the electric engine is not the future of the automobile, economic agents are starting to integrate this into their decisions to renew fleets of cars. We're facing a self-fulfilling prophecy."

Autonomy for All

But if one revolution is not enough, the industry will have to be able to manage a second—autonomous vehicles. Driverless vehicles are not the result of environmental constraints, but of new possibilities offered by spectacular advances in artificial intelligence which involves collecting and processing data at scales and speeds out of reach until the end of the twentieth century.

"Autonomy's a bit like the electric car," said Carlos Ghosn. "The road to the autonomous car starts with driving-assistance functions that take care of drivers in dangerous situations. People will get used to intelligent cars, with the end result of this intelligence being the driverless car. The question is how long this evolution will take." Views differed greatly, from a few years to one or even two decades.

"The car will cease being a simple object to becoming a partner that helps, advises on your itinerary, brakes for you, takes complete control of the vehicle in certain circumstances, and wakes you up when the time comes. These vehicles won't be reserved for the very wealthy. They're still very expensive today, but prices will plunge as soon as we enter the era of mass production. Different autonomy functions are currently reserved for high-end models. Autonomy is sold as such. But costs and prices will go down, which will stimulate demand. And then you enter the virtuous circle of mass commercialization."

The impacts will be major on an industry where human failure is behind 90 percent of road accidents—from alcohol impairment and drowsiness, to various distractions and speeding. Automakers have sought to counter this with real but limited success in active and passive security features which have made cars increasingly heavier and higher (in the case of SUVs), with greater volume and complexity. With annual road deaths worldwide estimated at 1.3 million people, autonomy responds to a road safety imperative that is constantly stressed.

Electric self-driving cars will be smaller and consume less in terms of natural resources and energy. They will also be a lot easier to make and maintain. It remains to be seen whether the emotional and even passionate attachment to cars seen in twentieth century literature and film will survive the revolution.

According to Carlos Ghosn, "this emotional attachment will change, but won't disappear. As autonomy develops, the car is going to become a personal mobile space equipped with all the tools for work, leisure and connectivity, allowing you to do more than drive during a journey. Instead of being a mythical object of desire, it will be the place where I can listen to my favorite music, read emails and look at my photos—a refuge to work, have fun and rest."

Key Role for Manufacturing

The technological revolution will lead to a social evolution in the rapport between ownership and the car itself, a consumer durable that represents the second biggest item in household investment after buying a home. The relationship between the manufacturer and the customer will also evolve, with the latter becoming less of a simple individual than in the past.

"For example, a global platform like Uber will need fleets of electric and self-driving vehicles," Carlos Ghosn said. "They're not going to become a manufacturer, so they'll have contracts with one or two automakers to provide 100,000 or 200,000 vehicles a year worldwide with whatever specifications. But buying the cars is out of the question. To the manufacturers, they'll say: 'You produce them and take care of them and we'll pay you with a percentage of our revenues.'

"Within the Alliance, we did some calculations based on different hypotheses and quite a few unknowns. What would be the profitability of this new formula compared with the traditional system of selling fleets to car rental companies? It turned out that remuneration as a percentage of turnover's a lot more profitable than traditional sales. You have to look for ways that lead to new horizons of profitability. The battle for sharing value added isn't between manufacturers and suppliers. It's played out in the manufacturer being paid for by the new uses of the car."

But automakers are not expected to transform themselves into service companies like IBM did in the information technology sector. The automaker "without factories" is not expected either— unlike the smoke and mirrors that dressed up the disappearance of the French telecommunications industry, one of the world's most advanced thirty years ago (it still has plants, but they're located in Asia).

"Auto manufacturing has huge challenges in terms of safety, environmental protection and controlling industrial processes," Carlos Ghosn said. "A car is not a computer or a telephone. The industry's based on know-how that's not obvious. I don't see automakers becoming consultants or application managers. If Uber talks with manufacturers, it's because they know that building automobiles is not an easy job. This complexity gives automakers upstream and downstream negotiating leverage. What's at stake in negotiations is the manufacturer's renumeration under the framework of agreements with companies highly specialized in new uses. The case of Uber is not hypothetical—negotiations with the Alliance were launched and it was Uber that decided the specifications and determined the number of self-driving cars and their level of autonomy.

"The completely autonomous car doesn't exist today but it will be crucial in the future as driver salaries are a very significant part of transport costs. The first to succeed in reducing or eliminating these costs will have an enormous competitive advantage," said Ghosn.

Socially Delicate Transition

Automakers will still have to manage a delicate transition. Less complicated to make and easier to maintain, electric and self-driving vehicles will always require more engineers at research centers. But they will need less manpower at factories, without counting the downstream impact on the semi-artisanal maintenance sector.

"The evolutions will be slow," Carlos Ghosn predicted. "The impact on jobs will be felt over five to ten years, even longer. Adaption can be through regulating new hires, reducing or increasing temporary jobs and diversifying activities. I don't believe we need to think in terms of a crisis. A well-managed company will be able to meet these changes without dramas. I wasn't worried about the Alliance—I even saw these upheavals coming faster than they occurred. Slower transitions are easier to manage. Companies will have the time to anticipate and prepare for change, and train staff for new tasks.

"A big automaker today employs tens of thousands of engineers. There's a pressing need to hire specialists in artificial intelligence, autonomy and so on. At the same time, there are engineers whose knowledge is gradually becoming obsolete. Training is a primary means of resolving this shortcoming. With such training efforts, managing staff and creating parallel activities, I don't foresee a social crisis in the auto sector. I think evolutions will take place at such a pace to allow time for the necessary adaptations to be made.

"To be honest, this is already the daily bread of manufacturers. In Europe, automakers and their suppliers have to manage the death of the diesel engine, which represents more than half the market in many countries and went from being a favorite to a pariah in just a few months. Changes in opinion are important because they influence political decision makers. Diesel's been cursed, and the business is folding. It's better to look ahead."

In 2002, the Portuguese publication *Revista* ran a graphic illustrating concentration in the auto industry in 1964, 1980 and 2002. What was notable was the number of brands that had disappeared, been absorbed or were only a shadow of their former selves—especially Italian and British brands. Also notable was the absence of new entrants. The concentration was in the hands of a dozen major automakers and had been partly reconfigured. Chrysler was acquired by Daimler and then Fiat, Volvo belonged to Chinese automaker Geely, and the premium brands of Ford—Jaguar and Range Rover—had been acquired by Indian conglomerate Tata. But the overall landscape had hardly changed. In January 2021, the shareholders of Fiat-Chrysler and PSA Peugeot-Citroën agreed to a merger under a new company name, Stellantis. Will future changes bring about a new world order?

"I don't think this technological revolution will necessarily lead to greater concentration in the industry which is already highly concentrated," Carlos Ghosn said. "The Alliance, Toyota and Volkswagen were the three leaders in 2018, with about a third of the global market, which was about ninety million units a year. If you took 80 percent as a reference, the number of players would be very limited."

Investment Surge

"For those who want to stay in the race, it's taken for granted that investment is growing as a share of turnover in the auto industry. That's why allocating investment is one of the crucial decisions of a business leader, because the long-term survival of the business is at stake. All manufacturers face growing rates of investment in technologies, defining what their cars will become, which is what customers are already demanding or will be soon," said Ghosn.

Such financial constraints were obviously behind the merger of Fiat-Chrysler and PSA Peugeot-Citroën. A more discreet, but no less significant, convergence was being seen in the Toyota-led technological coalition among Japanese automakers, with the notable exceptions of Honda and Alliance members Nissan and Mitsubishi. There was also unprecedented cooperation between Volkswagen and Ford.

"Sharing technologies and cooperation is quite common, and has been going on for ages, to avoid being weighed down by the investment required while remaining competitive in different markets," Carlos Ghosn said. "And such agreements will multiply among automakers— between automakers and suppliers, as well as between automakers and the high-technology, artificial intelligence and service sectors."

For these reasons, the threshold for entering the auto industry is still extraordinarily high. As a traditional industry more than a century old, with colossal fixed assets, it must reinvent itself. But the industry is not comparable to an entirely new business starting from a clean slate. Moreover, in new sectors, the failure of competition policies has allowed companies like Google, Apple, Facebook, Amazon and Microsoft to become quasi-monopolies.

"If this was a very profitable industry, and margins were very high, there would be new entrants en masse. But if you look at the track record of new entrants, it's not very impressive," Carlos Ghosn said. "For the time being, existing companies have the advantages over new entrants like Tesla or some of the Chinese automakers. All the big automakers know the future is electric and self-driving vehicles. Given the complexity of the auto industry and the relatively weak profitability, the current manufacturers are in a better position."

2020: Year of Tesla?

While 2020 was a year dominated by a global pandemic, it was also Tesla's year. The company's share price soared in the wake of four profitable quarters that reversed years of losses following the Model S launch in 2013. Fueled by liquidity provided by central banks and a spectacular rebound in stock prices after some initial turbulence caused by Covid-19, the Tesla share price soared eight-fold in 2020. Ten years after it was listed, the California-based electric carmaker's value exceeded the market capitalization of Toyota, which had long been world leader. In 2019, Tesla produced 367,500 vehicles, compared with ten million at Toyota.

"I'm not at all skeptical about Tesla," said Carlos Ghosn. "I explained to my teams in the Alliance that they were our allies—Tesla in the high-end segment with us in other segments with the Leaf and Zoe models. From the beginning, we were fighting together for electric vehicles and familiarizing the public with this new mode of transport. But investors classified Tesla as a high-tech start-up rather than an auto industry player, and financial markets gave them preferential treatment. Elon Musk played it very well and so much the better for him. But we weren't measured by the same yardstick. They've gone through, and are still going through, a lot of problems, but they're still there and they're still fighting. But Tesla is still an exception whose long-term viability has yet to be seen."

It was revealing that the first victims of Tesla's arrival in China—the world's largest automobile market, which also accounted for half its electric vehicles in 2019—were not the traditional automakers, but Chinese newcomers. The launch of the Model 3 dealt a blow to companies like Byton, Bordrin and Jiangsu Saleen, which were already distressed by the pandemic and reduced government assistance. But the Chinese newcomers were not the only companies to shelve their auto ambitions. So did Dyson, a British design company known for revolutionary vacuum cleaners.

"The beauty of the market is that nobody can predict with certainty what's going to happen," said Carlos Ghosn. "There'll be winners and losers. But as soon as the order's given, resources are mobilized and investments are made, the combat begins."

War on Two Fronts

"We're going to see two battles. The first is traditional competition, which will continue. That involves price, quality, reliability, equipment, enrichment, design, brand attractiveness and so on," said Ghosn. "These are the elements or values that weigh on customer choice—independent from technological advances integrated into products as one goes along. Traditional management challenges include quality, costs, distribution, marketing and after-sales service. None of this will disappear, and that is what makes automakers ordinary in today's battle.

"But everyone knows that another battle's begun over technology. Functions and services offered by technology will be at the heart of competition. What are we talking about? Cars that are cleaner and cleaner, and smarter and smarter, through autonomy but also connectivity. It's clear what's at stake for consumers. They want cleaner and cleaner cars that are completely connected and autonomous, with electric engines and electrical vehicle components taken into account, along with artificial intelligence on board. Operating accounts don't reflect this second battle, or, if they do, it's reflected negatively, as we're talking about very heavy investments with no immediate return."

"You have to look twice at these players on the battlefield—at their ability to stay competitive in traditional operations and their ability to enter the future. There's a big contrast."

Winners and Losers

"Toyota is very strong in today's market. But it's way behind in wholly-electric engines and it's going backwards," said Ghosn. "It's not up to speed with self-driving connected cars. They're very good at traditional cars, and average when it comes to the future.

"Let's take a group like Volkswagen, which is very good now and increasingly heading—aggressively even—into the future. They've decided to go all out with electric and self-driving cars, even if you have to distinguish between corporate announcements and the reality on the ground. Next come the other German carmakers, Daimler and BMW. They're obviously performing very well with traditional products and are now advancing very rapidly into electric and self-driving cars. They control their market segments and are preparing themselves well for the future, the shock of which will be a test of Tesla's resilience.

"Tesla today has about 0.5 percent of the global market. Despite the pandemic, they came very close to achieving their sales target of 500,000 in 2020. How do you compare that with ten million by Volkswagen or Toyota? Tesla is anti-conformist, a challenger, a disrupter, as people say today. But Elon Musk still has to show he's got a winning formula for the medium and long term. Until now, he's practically the only one in the high-end segment. But things will change when Mercedes, Audi and BMW enter the market.

"What about the Hyundai-Kia tie-up? For the time being, their workforce doesn't have enough talent, which is why they recruited José Muñoz and an army of executives from the Alliance. As for technologies of the future, I'm not sure. They're betting heavily on hydrogen, but that's a technology way in the future and we have to get there first."

China remains the great unknown. "There's no doubt that the Chinese government is massively supporting the country's companies," Carlos Ghosn said. "But China's market is very open, if you consider the domestic market share of Chinese automakers compared with Nissan, Volkswagen, Toyota, GM and so on. Of the three great economic powers of Northeast Asia—China, Japan and South Korea—the most open market is the Chinese market. Try to get into the Japanese market, outside the high-end segment, or the South Korean market. Good luck.

"The Chinese government already anticipates a change in evolution, which will see the disappearance of the obligatory character of joint ventures equally owned by two partners, as was Nissan's case with Dongfeng Motor. It was a necessary phase to allow a young industry to grow, but they seem to be admitting that they have to open the door to regular competition."

As the world's largest automobile market and its biggest market for electric vehicles, China will be the decisive battlefield. For French automakers, the future does not augur well with the collapse of the Chinese operations of PSA Peugeot-Citroën, and Renault's almost complete withdrawal from the market.

Mistrust and Suspicion Inside Alliance

The future of the Alliance is not near clear. The coup plotters at Nissan, and the appeasement lobby at Renault, dragged it into an existential crisis at a critical moment for the world automobile industry. The Alliance was never a marriage of love, but it was a solid betrothal of reason. It now resembles a forced union for the sake of the children—rarely a recipe for happiness.

With the return of political interference, the Alliance lost control of its destiny. It suffered from a hemorrhaging of top executives. It lost the confidence of financial markets, which viewed it with distrust at a time when automakers were having to raise vast amounts of capital to stay the course. In 2019, when the shares of Nissan and Renault were hit by intense short selling, the Japanese company lost half its value and its French partner lost two thirds. What Carlos Ghosn described as the "stay-at-home" strategy for the Alliance, has consisted of letting the wind out of its sails— shutting down plants, cutting jobs, reducing investment, abandoning markets and blaming the former chairman for past and future difficulties.

At the Nissan headquarters in Yokohama, a board member said, the new chief executive Makoto Uchida suffered from a triple handicap of legitimacy—he did not study at the elite University of Tokyo, he joined Nissan relatively late and was therefore detached from those who grew up in the company, and his professional background was with Nissho Iwai, a major trading house but not among the top ranked in Japan. When Luca de Meo took over the reins at Renault on July 1, 2020, the company's strategy had already been set under the leadership of Jean-Dominique Senard, who was not expected to resign himself to the role of non-executive board member. That was bizarre, as demonstrated by Luca de Meo's comment at his first attendance of Renault's executive committee when he strongly criticized the "leader-follower" approach adopted by the Alliance. "Nobody wants to be a follower," the Italian said, according to one witness. It made sense.

"I'm very skeptical about the Alliance," Carlos Ghosn said. "This skepticism is based on observation. I was always aware of the weaknesses of these companies when I ran them, and I'm afraid these shortcomings will now come back. A weakness I found at Renault was a tendency to make nice speeches with fancy phrases, but to lack rigor in carrying things out. As for Nissan, it's a complicated company due to constant clashes between different factions, as you often have in Japanese companies."

EPILOGUE

At 4:37 p.m. on December 12, 1969, a bomb devastated the Piazza Fontana branch of the Banca Nazionale dell'Agricoltura in Milan, the capital of Lombardy and the economic heart of Italy. From the rubble, sixteen corpses and eighty-eight wounded were removed. Italy was entering the "Lead Years" and getting the first taste of the strategy of tension that culminated in an attack on the Bologna railway station on August 2, 1980, which left eighty dead and more than two hundred wounded.

Despite initial efforts by the Italian police to implicate anarchists, the Piazza Fontana and other bombings led to extreme-right splinter groups. The way they were used by the Italian secret services, with occult-like practices like the P2 Lodge, is still the subject of research and speculation. The Italian extreme left was caught up in its own murderous activities at the time, but had a different modus operandi by targeting individuals and not anonymous crowds.

The far-right group behind the Piazza Fontana bombing in 1969 was the neo-fascist Ordine Nuovo. Delfo Zorzi, one of its members directly implicated in the bombing, found refuge in Japan. Welcomed and protected by the most right-wing circles of conservative power, he obtained Japanese citizenship and made a fortune in the fashion trade with Italy under his adopted name of Roi Hagen. For decades, Japan refused Italian requests to extradite the Italian citizen, who was not accused of financial wrongdoing, but an attack that left more than one hundred casualties.

Italian diplomats argued in vain that Japanese law did not provide for granting citizenship to a person being investigated for a crime in his or her country of origin. In 2005, the Italian Supreme Court of Cassation acquitted Zorzi. But the country's highest appellate court ruled nevertheless that Ordine Nuovo was responsible for the

Piazza Fontana attack, a contradictory ruling that triggered aston-
ishment and indignation across Italy.

Great Escape

Like many countries, Japan generally opposes the extradition of its
own citizens. But it does not accept Lebanon doing the same by
refusing to deliver Carlos Ghosn to Japan's non-democratic judicial
system, which still practices the death penalty. Moreover, the system
is considered so inconsistent with basic rights and general principles
of law that only two countries have extradition treaties with Japan—
the United States and South Korea. France has extradition treaties
with about fifty countries.

But the Takata scandal proved that an extradition treaty carried
little weight in the face of Japan's desire to protect its own people,
especially when they came from the world of business. In 2017, the
Japanese airbag maker agreed to pay a criminal fine of one billion
dollars in the U.S., not only for delivering defective equipment that
killed twenty-four people and injured hundreds, but also for a deliberate strategy of concealment.

The Takata airbag scandal led to the biggest recall in the history
of the automobile industry, with manufacturers having to recall
tens of millions of vehicles. But as *Automotive News* noted: "Three
of its executives were accused of crimes in the United States but
they stayed in Japan and never faced American justice." Warrants
for their arrest are still active. The Detroit-based newspaper
recalled that U.S. anti-trust authorities had convicted forty-six
original equipment manufacturers and thirty-two of their executives for anti-competitive practices as of 2018. Most were Japanese,
and around three billion dollars in fines had been issued. More
than twenty Japanese executives implicated in fraudulent transactions never appeared before American judges and are considered
fugitives.

But, without the slightest shame, the Japanese political-judicial
machine was demanding American citizens Michael and Peter
Taylor be extradited to Japan for helping Carlos Ghosn to escape
from its claws. With cut-and-paste files sent by Tokyo, American
prosecutors won their case and the Taylors were incarcerated. And,

U.S. judges obstinately turned a blind eye to evidence and testimonies, including those of Carlos Ghosn, regarding the way convicts were being treated in Japan, rejecting several appeals against extradition. The defense lawyers for the former Green Beret and his son cited the Takata scandal as an example of how Japan was unilaterally using its extradition treaty with the United States.

Michael and Peter Taylor were duly extradited from America to Japan in March 2021 and detained upon arrival at the same prison in Tokyo where Carlos Ghosn had been incarcerated for 130 days. On June 14, they went on trial at the Tokyo District Court, pleading guilty to helping the former chairman of the Alliance escape from house arrest 18 months earlier. Two weeks later, the father and son were back in court, apologizing for the "difficulties" and "trouble" they had caused, bowing before three judges. As the Associated Press reported, "showing remorse for wrongdoing is considered crucial for defendants hoping for judicial leniency" in Japan.

Japan's political-judicial machine will stop at nothing to wash away the stain of national humiliation inflicted on it by the Great Escape of the former head of the Renault-Nissan-Mitsubishi Alliance on December 29, 2019. And with irrepressible procedural vindictiveness against Carlos Ghosn, the machine will pursue his wife Carole and even his children.

Financial Blackmail?

In late May 2020, *Arab News* reported that Japan was making Carlos Ghosn's extradition from Lebanon a condition for assistance to the country from the International Monetary Fund (IMF). The Riyadh-based newspaper said Sakher El Hachem, the legal representative of Nissan in Lebanon, was the source of the information. But he later denied the report and said he had never made such a statement. *Arab News* responded by uploading a recording to its website: "Japan is a large contributor to the IMF," Hachem said clearly in the recording. "If Japan puts a veto on the IMF, the IMF is not willing to lend any money unless it hands over Carlos Ghosn."

In an Arabic incomprehensible to the man on the street, Takeshi Okubo, the Japanese ambassador to Lebanon, delivered a kind of diplomatic denial to Al Arabiya, the Saudi-owned television channel in Dubai. After the incident, Hachem was still Nissan's legal representative in Lebanon, which was suffering from a combined economic, social and health crisis, exacerbated by a devastating explosion at Beirut port on August 4, 2020, which killed at least 200 people, wounding thousands and displacing around 300,000.

Should difficult negotiations between Lebanon and the IMF succeed, the assistance program would be subject to a vote by the fund's Executive Board in Washington. It is doubtful that Japan's strange approach to IMF conditionality could prevail, since the United States has an effective veto as the largest shareholder. Washington has, in the past, used political motivations in decisions by multilateral institutions. Unless mistaken, such motivations have never included a personal vendetta.

Welcome to Lebanon

"Bonjour, Monsieur Ghosn," said the border police officer who readily recognized one of the world's most famous corporate leaders. "We haven't seen you for a long time. Welcome to Lebanon." It was six in the morning and Carlos Ghosn was returning after thirteen months of forced absence. News of his escape—which would soon be broadcast across the planet—was not yet public.

Since his arrest on November 19, 2018, Ghosn had been fighting for his life. As he arrived at Beirut-Rafic Hariri International Airport, he knew he had just won the decisive battle. He had regained his freedom. And with it, freedom of speech.

The international media immediately dubbed the exfiltration from Tokyo as the "Great Escape," and almost all the technical aspects are known. The initial account reported by the *Wall Street Journal* was followed by others, such as the reports by the American prosecutors who got the Taylors incarcerated at the request of Japanese authorities and targeted leaks by the Tokyo Public Prosecutors' Office. As for details of the escape, the main person involved decided to remain silent until mid-2021 to protect those who took the risk of helping him.

As news of his arrival spread, the Japanese media erupted in an upheaval of denunciations of the "feeble" and "cowardly" fugitive. In fact, the risk could not have been higher, as failure would have meant returning to prison in Japan, presumably for years.

"I was perfectly aware of the risk of failure," said Carlos Ghosn. "There were several critical stages when the operation could have failed. I decided to go because I was already living in hell. The conditions were obviously less painful after I was released on bail, but I'd been cut off from everything that had been my life until November 19, 2018. The status quo was not an option. There's a very good saying in English: 'When you're going through hell, keep going'."

A Clear Choice

"The danger was effectively falling down even further. But I didn't care as the status quo was unbearable. On the other hand, I'd be brought back to life if the operation succeeded. Compared with the status quo, there was such a gap in the prospects of success or failure that the choice was clear. At worst, the discomfort of prison and even less hope for the future would be added to the hellish situation. But on the other side, the rewards were infinitely greater than the risks—escaping the grip of the Japanese prosecutors, regaining my freedom and family, and the possibility of finally being able to defend myself publicly. Even with a low chance of success, it was worth a try.

"I approached this situation as I've always done in my professional life," said Ghosn. "As soon as the option opened, the planning, organization and final decision had to be done very quickly. That was the condition for success, as well as strict confidentiality. If I was able to raise the possibility of fleeing with Carole—which was not possible, as our exchanges were either prohibited or monitored—would she have encouraged me or dissuaded me? I think the fear of losing a loved one for many years would have probably prevented her from saying yes. I decided to mention it to nobody, as I knew there'd be no consent. I was doomed to keep the decision to myself.

"In addition, it shouldn't be forgotten that I was subjected to constant surveillance, and I didn't know how extensive it was since the surveillance carried out by Nissan by a well-named shadowy outlet—Japan Secret Service—was completely illegal. Could I be sure that I could spot all the people following me? Were there long-distance listening devices when I was in the street, in addition to telephone surveillance? I had to limit my exchanges to a bare minimum, the people directly involved with the operation. The greater number of people implicated, the greater the risk of leaks and failure."

Contrary to media reports, the exfiltration did not require long months of preparation—even if Japanese authorities had every reason to save face by allowing credit to be given to the idea of a very costly and complex operation. Anyone who has lived in Japan knows the high degree of preparation for natural disasters that leaves the country largely helpless in the face of the unexpected.

Flight Triggered by Japanese Judges

"Decisions and measures followed one another from the beginning of December, leading to the launch of the operation on December 29," Carlos Ghosn said. "I made the decision at the end of November when the judge in charge of bail refused—for the eighth time—to allow a meeting with my wife over Christmas. There was no procedural justification. It was sadism. Secondly, the other judge, the presiding judge, reversed his earlier decision, under pressure from the prosecutors, and announced that the trial on the second charge would not start until the end of the first trial. I understood that the affair would take five years—even before any eventual conviction—and that I didn't want anything more to do with Japan. Those two judges pushed me to leave."

In an interview with the Japanese edition of *GQ* magazine in early December, Takafumi Horie, the maverick businessman who had, himself, been imprisoned at the Tokyo Detention House, predicted that Carlos Ghosn would not be freed for about fifteen years. By then, he'd be eighty.

At the end of December, the pace of life slows in Japan as the New Year holidays approach, the most important on the annual calendar. Christmas is no more than a commercial event and not a holiday, the only Japanese celebrating being the country's tiny Christian minority.

On December 29, as he left the charmless and poorly furnished house in Azabu-Nagasakacho, not far from Roppongi, Carlos Ghosn's image was, for the last time, captured on the automatic surveillance camera.

"During the voyage on the bullet train, there were dozens of people in the carriage. But I was wearing a hat, mask and glasses. People would have had to be really good to recognize me in that outfit."

Mad Hope

"When I finally found myself on the airport tarmac, I started to believe it would succeed. Without seeing where I was, I felt the air was different and I could hear the plane's engines. I'd spent my life in airports and it must have been fourteen months since I'd taken a plane. It must have been half a century since I'd not flown for so long. The noise of the plane was the sound of hope. And I was seized by a mad hope. But I wasn't yet out of the woods. We'd cleared many obstacles, but still faced risky situations. The moment I felt a huge weight being lifted from my shoulders was when the plane landed in Beirut. I told myself: 'Finally, I've won'."

At Harvard University, the Carlos Ghosn case went from the business school, which devoted cases studies to the Nissan renaissance, to the law school. One lecturer asked students to put themselves in his shoes and ask the question: "If you were him, what would have been your motives to leave? What would have been your motives to stay?"

Carlos Ghosn lent himself to the exercise. In the "leave" column were eighteen motives, which have all been explained in detail in this book. In the "stay" column was only one real motive—to confront the Japanese judicial system in court before witnesses under the eyes of the international media.

"In any other jurisdiction, there would always be doubt," Carlos Ghosn said. "Tokyo was the only place where we could have exposed the truth without question, confused the accusers and informants, denounced the violations of the basic principles of the rights of the defense under the Japanese criminal code, and exposed the submission of judges to the dictates of prosecutors. In short, to make it a trial of this iniquitous system of hostage justice for the whole world to see. This is a trial to which the numerous Japanese victims of this system have the right. Even in the opinion of my lawyers, the difficulty was that the judges would not have been neutral, and the proceedings would have taken at least five years—with all the inhumane privations and humiliation that would have gone with it."

On Trial: Greg Kelly—or Japan?

The Japanese judicial system will undergo this examination with the trial of Greg Kelly. The American lawyer, freed on bail on December 25, 2018, after thirty-seven days in detention, waited for almost two years to respond to the charge fabricated against him. He was in a precarious condition with his wife, Dee, who was forced to study Japanese to stay in Japan. If she failed a single test, her student visa would be revoked. They lived as recluses in a small apartment in Tokyo, forgotten by the Trump administration, as Carlos Ghosn had been by authorities in France.

Kelly's lawyer, Yoichi Kitamura, carried a heavy weight on his shoulders. So did members of the Japanese legal community who were fighting the hostage justice system by demanding that the country's judiciary finally abandon the feudal epoch for the democratic modern era.

But the stakes are so high in the political game for Japanese officials and the Nissan Old Guard, that Greg Kelly and his family have every reason to fear a denial of justice.

The Japanese justice system still refused to separate the cases of Carlos Ghosn and Greg Kelly from that of Nissan. So Kelly will find himself in the paradoxical situation of being co-defendant with his former employer, which acted in complete collusion with the Tokyo Public Prosecutors' Office to lure him into a trap. For Nissan, there was little at stake—it was strictly financial, as the prosecutors had decided not to bother with Hiroto Saikawa and other Japanese executives implicated in the misappropriation of funds for which the two foreigners had been accused.

The United States Securities Exchange Commission was invited to involve itself in the affair by virtue of the prerogatives of extraterritoriality. Without admitting any guilt, Carlos Ghosn agreed to pay a one-million-dollar fine, and Greg Kelly agreed to a fine of 100,000 dollars to avoid spending years, and blowing much more money, to take part in a bad American remake of proceedings artificially transferred from Japan. Nissan had to pay a fifteen million dollar fine, but that was a drop in the bucket compared with the costs of mounting the "Carlos Ghosn operation," and the ocean of losses the Japanese automaker had suffered since 2019.

Targeting the Family

Carlos Ghosn's lawyers, who tried to get Interpol to cancel the "Red Notice" that prevented him from traveling freely outside Lebanon, relied on the three principles of the international police organization protecting all citizens from abusive pursuits. One, and as amply shown in these pages, the judicial proceedings against Carlos Ghosn and Greg Kelly were politically motivated. Moreover, the Japanese justice system's violation of human rights were obvious for all to see, except for those who did not want to look. Nothing Carlos Ghosn was accused of justified the penal costs of the affair, which amounted to internal company procedures, even in the opinion of Prime Minister Shinzo Abe.

For the architects, the executors, the accomplices and the propagandists involved in the arrest in November 2018, it was crucial for Carlos Ghosn to shut up. For almost fourteen months of detention in Japan, in his cell at Kosuge or under house arrest, he had been gagged by confinement or intimidation. It was impossible to gag him now, but that would not prevent them from trying.

"Each time I spoke to the media, they retaliated with a low blow, targeting my wife and children," Carlos Ghosn said. "When the news conference in Beirut on January 8, 2020, was announced, the Japanese prosecutors had the nerve to call it unilateral communication, although they'd reduced me to silence for fourteen months. The next day, they launched an international warrant to arrest Carole. The warrant was for alleged perjury eight months earlier, when she voluntarily returned to Tokyo to address—before a judge—questions from prosecutors. She had not been targeted at the time.

"The prosecutors from the special team told me: 'If you don't confess, we'll extend our investigation across the entire world. Trust us, we'll find other charges.

"And we'll implicate those close to you'." It was a common practice in Japan, where the "suffering" and "shame" of the families of accused are used as pressure to extract confessions. Vychinsky would have been proud of his students.

The records of the prosecution's interrogation of Carlos Ghosn were, in principle, available to media who made the request. No request had received a positive response as of July 2020.

Code of Silence

The Nissan Old Guard and the Tokyo Public Prosecutors' Office had invested considerable resources on this communications war. It was therefore necessary to impose a code of silence on Nissan and Renault employees who could contradict the official version of the affair. We saw the level to which Hari Nada and his cronies valued the collaboration of José Muñoz to the inquiry incriminating Carlos Ghosn. In Yokohama and Billancourt, most of the collaborators who had been purged or resigned had to sign confidentiality agreements. Most victims of the witch hunt are distressed and want to turn the page.

But with time, the word will get out and the documents will speak, including the six thousand emails that the Japanese judges allowed Nissan to keep out of the proceedings, despite the protests of Carlos Ghosn's defense team—if they have not been destroyed. On June 15, 2020, Bloomberg published a report on emails sent by Hari Nada to his colleagues at Nissan in 2018. In the middle of the year, he urges Hitoshi Kawaguchi to "neutralize" Carlos Ghosn's initiatives "before it's too late."

A day before the head of the Alliance was arrested, Hari Nada told Saikawa that the operation, which he planned at the request of the prosecutors, be "supported by media campaign for insurance of destroying CG reputation hard enough." The response of the Nissan Old Guard is to describe the emails as forged . . . As for his "friend" Greg Kelly, who prosecutors were preparing to arrest as soon as he put his foot on Japanese soil, Nada wrote to Saikawa shortly before November 19: "If he doesn't come, he'll never come back. I'm scheduling a plane to get him."

In this Shakespearian drama, there are obviously dark areas to explore, interests to elucidate and personal relationships to comprehend. And how did Greg Kelly trust Hari Nada? Former executives at Nissan North America in Nashville said nobody trusted him. "He had a reputation as a backstabber," said one. How had this not reached the ears of Greg Kelly, who joined Nissan in Nashville and worked there for twenty years?

Not Going Too Far

Books, films, documentaries, television series . . . this saga will play out in the months and years ahead. One thing is certain—Japan's image will not improve. A global automotive empire, the dream of Lee Iacocca and Jürgen Schrempp, given flesh and blood by Carlos Ghosn, would have deserved a better epilogue. The plotters behind November 19, 2018, have decided otherwise. Like Dr. Frankenstein, they have given birth to a creature they no longer control and which has started to destroy them. It's even more tragic for the three companies and the 450,000 they employ.

"The real problem with the leadership in Japanese organizations, and in particular government agencies, is that they don't know when to stop," said investment banker Kenneth Courtis, who has known the country and its culture for forty years. "They have a problem understanding and then accepting that they have gone too far. After the Battle of Midway in June 1942—six months after Pearl Harbor—the Pacific War was effectively over for Japan. Three years and millions of deaths later, with Tokyo reduced to ashes and Hiroshima and Nagasaki vaporized, and much of East Asia devastated, the Imperial government finally accepted reality and the Emperor called on the people to bear the unbearable, the surrender and occupation of the country." History, again and again.

Index